LOST
AT SEA
Found at Fukushima

LOST
AT SEA
Found at Fukushima

THE STORY OF A JAPANESE POW

ANDY MILLAR

Pen & Sword
MILITARY

First published in 2012 by Big Sky Publishing Pty Ltd
PO Box 303, Newport, NSW 2106, Australia

Reprinted in this format in 2017 by
Pen & Sword MILITARY
An imprint of
Pen & Sword Books Ltd
47 Church Street, Barnsley
South Yorkshire
S70 2AS

ISBN 978 1 47387 806 8

A CIP catalogue record for this book is
available from the British Library

Printed and bound in Malta
By Gutenberg Press Ltd, Gudja Road, Tarxien GXQ 2902

Pen & Sword Books Ltd incorporates the Imprints of Pen & Sword Aviation,
Pen & Sword Family History, Pen & Sword Maritime, Pen & Sword Military,
Pen & Sword Discovery, Pen & Sword Politics, Pen & Sword Atlas,
Pen & Sword Archaeology, Wharncliffe Local History, Leo Cooper,
Wharncliffe True Crime, Wharncliffe Transport, Pen & Sword Select,
Pen & Sword Military Classics, The Praetorian Press, Claymore Press,
Remember When, Seaforth Publishing and Frontline Publishing

For a complete list of Pen & Sword titles please contact
PEN & SWORD BOOKS LIMITED
47 Church Street, Barnsley, South Yorkshire, S70 2AS, England
E-mail: enquiries@pen-and-sword.co.uk
Website: www.pen-and-sword.co.uk

CONTENTS

PREFACE

KERI KERI – NEW ZEALAND

9 December 2003

It was overcast with a light drizzle, as it often is at funerals. The family, together with fifty or so friends and acquaintances, had gathered in New Zealand's far north, at the little missionary church at Waimate North, to celebrate the life of my father, David Millar. Three months earlier we had gathered in the same place to say goodbye to my mother, Muriel: they had been married sixty-seven years.

At ninety-two and suffering from cancer, my father quietly went about putting his affairs in order following Muriel's death, then died in his sleep on 4 December 2003, holding his daughter's hand.

Sitting quietly in the little church I began to reflect on who our father really was. We had been an odd family in many ways and never very close. My elder brother Don and I had little recollection of the man who always seemed to be away at sea when I was little and 'visited' us only irregularly. I remembered him as being very strict and more than a little frightening. I was 10 years old when he retired from the sea and came to live with us on a permanent basis. I was never quite comfortable in his presence, nor was I, in either an academic or sporting sense, able to live up to what I imagined were his expectations. The arrival of our sister, Margaret, when I was 15 years old, transferred the focus from us boys – much to our relief.

Don and I knew that Dad had been in the Merchant Navy and had been a POW in Japan, but he was a very private man and never spoke of these things until very late in life.

After the funeral, in a wardrobe in the retirement home he had shared with my mother during the last years of their lives, I found a cardboard carton, a relic of some bygone move, stencilled: EMPIRE FORWARDING COMPANY LIMITED – REMOVALISTS

Full of documents – dates, places, ships' names, photographs, papers, letters and even a poem in my father's handwriting – I began to realise that the carton was saying: *My name is David Millar and this was my war.*

The story inside this unassuming cardboard box was remarkable. My father had kept it hidden from us for nearly sixty years; all we'd heard until then had been hints, comments and asides and what seemed, to us boys, to be a totally unreasonable, and little understood, attitude towards wasted food.

Using my father's material, my memories of the limited conversations I'd had with him about the War, interviews with the few remaining people scattered across the world who were there and remember those days, and public records, I have put together this story.

All of the significant events, times, dates, places, ships and people in the story are true, although I have taken one small liberty. As it is not possible to know precisely what was said, or the detail of some of the events, I have used my own experiences from forty years' service with the Royal New Zealand and Royal Australian Navies to reconstruct military and technical dialogue, and to add detail that I believe very closely follows what was actually said and done. With this qualification, what follows is true; this is what really happened.

Some of the technical and military terms used may need explaining. To assist in this regard, I have gathered them together in a Glossary at the back of this book.

This, then, is the story of David Millar's War.

David Millar 1937.

PART I

CAPTURE

November 1941– April 1942

DEN HELDER – NETHERLANDS

1530 hours, Friday 28 November 1941

'*Leinen los!*'

Oberleutnant zur See Karl Mueller, Commanding Officer of *Schnellboot S-52,* gave the order to cast off.

The last lines tethering the E-Boat to the pier at the Squadron's base, near the entrance to the Waddenzee, splashed into the water and were quickly recovered by the small party of sailors on the dock. The little ship backed away into the main shipping channel and her sister ships, *S-51* and *S-64,* took up their positions in line astern. They were stationed approximately half a cable's length (90 metres) apart for the passage through the shoals out into the North Sea.

As they passed the outer channel marker, Mueller, who was the senior Commanding Officer of the three, glanced astern to ensure that *S-51* and *S-64* were keeping station. He grunted with satisfaction. *S-52* rose and twisted gently in the light northerly swell. Mueller reached out and eased the main throttles forward. The response from the three powerful Daimler-Benz diesels was virtually instantaneous. The little ship surged forward, alive and eager, throwing up a cockscomb of boiling white water in her wake.

The three E-Boats were part of the 4th *Schnellboot* Squadron, under the command of *Kapitänleutnant* Baetge of the German *Kriegsmarine* (Navy). Their mission was to lay mines northwest of Cromer off the English Norfolk Coast, then attack British shipping in that area as the opportunity presented.

An almost stationary, intense, low pressure system over Iceland created a stiff south-westerly breeze, whipping up whitecaps that slapped against the boat's hull. At the pre-sailing briefing, the Squadron Met. Officer had advised that an associated frontal system was crossing the Irish Sea and would bring deteriorating weather, with the wind veering to the west and freshening to Gale Force 8. This would almost certainly bring squalls and driving rain to the E-Boats' planned operations area within 24 hours. Visibility during the day was expected to be 10 miles, dropping to 2 miles or less in heavy rain. Already, the towering foul-weather cumulus was building to the west; a warning of the worsening conditions to come.

Mueller was grateful for his heavy fisherman's sweater, thick flannel trousers and warm socks, thrust deep into his seaman's leather boots, but he still needed the warmth of his reefer jacket and his black fisherman's knitted bonnet, to keep out the biting cold of the late November afternoon.

S-52 and her sister ships belonged to the early series of E-Boat. They first entered *Kriegsmarine* service in 1935. At 80 tons and 32 metres in length, they had a maximum speed of 35 knots in a light to moderate sea. Powerfully armed for their size, the boats each carried four 533-mm torpedoes, their primary offensive armament, a 20-mm anti-aircraft gun mounted aft and two heavy machine guns. Each boat was also capable of carrying up to ten mines.

Muriel Millar 1937.

The reliability of the torpedoes was Mueller's greatest concern. They were the recently introduced G7-e electric torpedoes that had a designed range of 5000 metres at 30 knots. They could be fitted with either magnetic or contact pistols but the magnetic variants had proved so unreliable that Mueller had insisted the Armament Depot provide him only with weapons designed to explode on impact. Even so, these torpedoes had an annoying tendency to run up to 2 metres below the set depth and would often pass directly under the target without detonating.

As the grey afternoon light merged into the gathering dusk, there was one last but essential task to be completed before settling down for the passage westward to the English coast. Mueller reached for the klaxon and pressed it twice, firmly, at the same time switching on the boat's tannoy broadcast system.

'Hands to action stations! Hands to action stations!'

There was a clatter of feet over the wooden deck as officers and men raced to man their battle stations. Guns were cleared away and readied for firing. The torpedo tubes were manned and all electrical circuits checked and tested. Hatches clanged shut and were fully clipped to achieve maximum watertight integrity throughout the boat. The Chief Coxswain, having taken over the helm, glanced at Mueller and, after receiving a nod of approval, eased the throttles forward to *Höchstgrenze* (maximum). *S-52* leapt forward like a greyhound leaving the starting gate, her powerful diesels whining as they reached their maximum operating R.P.M. Mueller clicked the stopwatch he held in his right hand as his Executive Officer reached the conning position from the main deck in two quick strides, saluting smartly.

'Boat closed up and ready for action, *Herr Kapitän*,' he reported. 'Permission to proof fire all guns?'

Mueller glanced at the stop watch. 'One minute twelve seconds. Not bad,' he replied, 'but we will have to do better if we're to survive this war. Carry on and proof fire the weapons.'

The staccato *rat-tat-tat* of automatic gunfire proved all guns were functioning correctly, and the ready-use lockers near each gun were checked to ensure there was sufficient ammunition close at hand for the operations ahead. With checks completed, *S-52* and her consorts reduced speed, prior to settling into their normal state of readiness for wartime patrol operations. Mueller ordered the two outboard engines shut down. Alone, the third engine maintained a cruising speed of 12 knots, which conserved fuel and minimised their wake. At this speed it would take the E-Boats 12 hours to reach their operating area, where the shoal waters of Outer Dowsing and the Haisborough Sands would force enemy coastal shipping into the restricted waterway known as 'The Wold', a favourite E-Boat hunting ground. Earlier in the day a Junkers high-level reconnaissance aircraft had reported that a British north-bound convoy appeared to be forming in the proximity of Southend, but the aircraft had been driven off by a patrolling Hurricane before further intelligence could be obtained.

Mueller ordered course to take the boats north of the Brown Ridge shoals and bring them to the Norfolk coast in the vicinity of Lowestoft before first light. Hopefully, they would have time to lay their mines and still be in position to intercept the British convoy, should it exist, some time on the 30th. A British defensive minefield, approximately 10 miles wide and 10 miles off the coast, stretched in an unbroken line from the Straits of Dover to the Orkneys in the north. It did not present a problem for the shallow drafted E-Boats; they would pass safely over the British moored mines.

Mueller took a final all-round look through his night-vision binoculars, before going below to eat and rest, leaving instructions to be called immediately should any contact be sighted or anything untoward occur.

ENGLISH COAST OFF HARWICH

2330 hours, Saturday 29 November 1941

David Millar, First Mate of the tramp steamer *Empire Newcomen*, was cold. Despite the heavy duffle-coat buttoned to the neck, his thick seaman's clothing and rubber half-wellingtons, after three and a half hours as officer-of-the-watch on the open bridge, the biting wind was having an effect. He was looking forward to the warmth of his bunk, in his cabin three decks below. He sipped gingerly at the steaming mug of Ki which he cradled in his woollen gloved hands, and grunted as the scalding chocolate singed his throat and stomach. He checked the deck-watch in the dim lighting that illuminated the chart table and noted with satisfaction that the watch-on-deck would soon be calling his relief. The Third Mate normally kept the midnight to 0400 watch. Just time for David to fix the ship's position and carry out the final zig for the watch. The next turn was scheduled to occur in 12 minutes.

David was a fine looking man, 5 ft 10 inches in his socks and weighing 154 lbs. He had a fair complexion and kindly blue-green eyes highlighted by dark brows.

His fine dark hair was generally parted in the middle and brushed flat-back in the fashion of the time. At thirty, he was strong and totally confident, although two years of war in the North Atlantic had left its mark; he had an air of sadness that was impossible to hide.

David had been born in the family home in King Edward Street, Alexandria, Scotland on 24 October 1911. At the time his father, also David, was foreman in the finishing department of the Argyle Motor Company at their Alexandria Works. David's father married Margaret Ferguson in 1907. They had three children: Flora, the eldest, was born in 1909, David in 1911 and Fergus in 1917. Following World War I, the family moved to St Andrews, where David's father took a position with Messrs Wm Johnston, motor hirers.

David's parents were staunch Scottish Presbyterians and his father was an elder in the local parish church. Although David never openly rebelled against them, the atmosphere at home was often difficult and the strict discipline and moral values that their beliefs imposed upon David were instrumental in his determination to leave the family home as soon as he was able, and pursue a life at sea.

David was educated at Madras College, St Andrews, where he displayed no particular aptitudes other than a certain skill in mathematics. From there, on 21 June 1928, with the very lukewarm support of his parents, he was indentured as an apprentice in the British Merchant Navy with Watts, Watts & Company Limited. His passion for a life at sea was not born of any wish to serve his country as much as a burning desire to travel, and to be free of restrictive parental discipline.

David completed his apprenticeship in June 1932 'to the entire satisfaction of this Company' and served across the world in a number of the company's ships until the outbreak of World War II.

In 1936 David joined the *Star of Alexandria* in Barry, South Wales, where he met and married Beatrice Muriel Roscoe. Their eldest son, Donald, was born later that same year, and their second son, Andrew, arrived on 30 August 1939, four days before the outbreak of the war with Germany.

David was philosophical about Britain's entry to the war. He saw it neither as an adventure nor an opportunity, but simply as a job to be done – and felt a desire to play his part to the extent he was able. He was aware of the dangers and accepted that each time he put to sea there was a good chance he would not return but he was able to push such thoughts to the back of his mind – most of the time.

Before joining the *Empire Newcomen* on 28 November David served on a number of the Company's ships plying the North Atlantic to Halifax, Nova Scotia, and participating in Arctic convoys to Murmansk and Archangel, high within Russia's Arctic Circle. He was acquainted with appalling weather and the horrors of war at sea as, time and again, he witnessed the destruction of ships and men at the hands of Germany's submarine wolf packs and Luftwaffe dive bombers, as they desperately tried to strangle the supply lifeline provided by Britain's merchant marine.

The fact that David was on board the *Empire Newcomen* was something of an accident. He had been looking forward to completing the examinations for Master Mariner, and had already passed the written portions of the examination but had failed the orals due to illness. He needed a further three months at sea before re-presenting himself to the Board for another attempt. As a pre-requisite, he had been attending an advanced seamanship course at the Marine School attached to the Cardiff Technical College, when he received an urgent call from the local shipping office in Barry, requiring him to replace *Empire Newcomen's* regular First Mate who had been taken ill. David arrived in London from South Wales by train on the evening of 28 November and signed on at the Company's offices in Dock Street, before going on to join the ship, at anchor off Southend, that same evening.

On the *Empire Newcomen's* bridge with David was the helmsman, two lookouts, who were relieved every 30 minutes to maintain concentration, and an Officer Apprentice whose job was to understudy David and act as an additional lookout, bridge messenger and general factotum.

Despite the cold, the wind was moderate, but freshening. The sea was choppy but the gentle movement of the ship was not uncomfortable. The Norfolk Coast, a little under 10 miles to windward on the port beam, gave a degree of protection from the prevailing south-westerly. *The Third Officer won't be so lucky,* David reflected, as he made a mental note to brief his relief on the latest Fleet Weather Message for the Humber area, clipped to the board hanging beside the chart table:

> 'Wind veering to the west, increasing to Gale Force 8 throughout 30 November. Overcast with intermittent rain and heavy squalls, becoming continuous during the forenoon, clearing slowly later in the day as the front moves further east. Visibility 8 to 10 miles, reducing to less than a mile in heavy rain.'

Currently, visibility was good, so David had no difficulty maintaining his station, 5 cables (1000 yards) from the next ship in the column, which loomed ahead as an even darker mass against an already dark horizon. He took comfort in the fact that he did not need to rely on her dimmed, shaded stern light to keep his proper station but this could, and would, change very quickly as the weather worsened. The increasing build-up of cauliflower-shaped, foul-weather cumulus and the rapidly dropping barometer warned of the approaching storm.

Andy Millar (author) 2002.

Empire Newcomen, under charter to the Admiralty through the Ministry of War Transport, was the last ship in the starboard column of the two-column twelve-ship, convoy designated FN 17. Formed under special wartime regulations for the Naval Control of Shipping, and under the control of the Admiralty Department of Trade, FN 17 was the 17th northbound, East Coast convoy in the current series. The convoy had formed off Sheerness earlier in the day and was scheduled to disperse off Methil, on the Firth of Forth, on the morning of 2nd December, just under 36 hours away. Tactical command of the convoy was exercised, through the convoy Commodore in the lead ship of the starboard column, by the senior naval escort officer on a 'Hunt Class' destroyer escort. Two Motor Anti-submarine Boats (M.A/S.B.s) and three Seaward Defence Motor Launches (S.D.M.L.s) provided meagre anti-submarine protection. Lightly armed and with a maximum speed of 12 knots in good weather, these latter struggled to provide protection to the extended columns of merchant ships. Two 'balloon ships', converted from Grimsby trawlers, and a covering flight of two Hurricanes from R.A.F. Colchester, provided some protection from the Luftwaffe's Stuka dive bombers. Finally, a Rescue Tug trailed astern to pick up survivors from any enemy action, completing FN 17's escort force.

At five minutes before midnight, the Third Officer's still sleepy face emerged above the ladder leading to *Empire Newcomen's* bridge. It took a few minutes for his eyes to adjust to the darkness but he could already make out the shadowy figures and the muffled conversations as the helmsman and bridge lookouts changed over the watch.

After exchanging greetings, David went through the formalities of handing over the ship to his relief: 'course is 330 with the next change a zig to starboard to 015 in 17 minutes. The zig-zag plan with all course changes is in the folder on the chart table. Speed to maintain station on the ship ahead is 9 knots and we seem to hold that pretty well at 94 shaft revolutions, with occasional adjustments. We're in our proper station but you should keep an eye on the Rescue Tug astern of us; she seems to be having trouble keeping proper distance and she's come bloody close a couple of times.

'Our last fix puts us on our planned track with Landguard Point bearing 258 degrees at 8 miles. The latest met. report is on the clipboard. We're expecting nasty weather in the next few hours; the glass is dropping like crazy. Hopefully the weather will keep Jerry away – certainly it should keep the Luftwaffe on the ground for a few hours. The Captain's night orders are in the book. He wants to be called if we have trouble keeping station due to the weather, if there is any activity by the enemy or if anything else unusual occurs.

'If there are no questions I'll leave you to it.'

'Seems pretty straightforward,' the Third Mate responded; then formally, 'I have the ship.'

With a cheery wave, David disappeared down the bridge accommodation ladder, all thought now focused on the prospect of a warm bunk and six hours' uninterrupted sleep, before breakfast and taking over the watch again from the Second Mate at 0800 the following morning.

NORTH SEA OFF THE ENGLISH COAST

0815 hours, Sunday 30 November 1941

Mueller wiped the lenses of his binoculars with a damp cloth for what seemed the hundredth time and once more made the effort to peer directly into the freezing rain, driving almost horizontally into his face and stinging his cheeks like needles.

The mine-laying operations off Cromer had gone well with only one minor scare when a patrolling RAF reconnaissance aircraft from Coastal Command had briefly broken through the overcast, but the E-Boats were almost impossible to spot against the churning grey sea and the moment passed without discovery. Their primary mission complete, *Schnellboot* Squadron 4 was now free to hunt and attack the British convoy, reported to be in the vicinity.

As forecast, the wind had veered to the west about two hours earlier and increased to Force 8, a full gale, with winds gusting to 40 knots. The waves were short and steep with the crests breaking into spindrift that was blowing in streaks along the direction of the wind. It was only the proximity of the Norfolk Coast, some 12 miles to the west, that gave some slight protection from the weather and the building force of the angry sea. Although twilight had occurred some 40 minutes earlier, the darkened sky and driving rain had barely improved the visibility from the blackness of night, although there was some slight, noticeable lightening of the horizon to the south-east.

S-52 and the other two E-Boats, one now on either beam to increase the search front, had been at action stations for 40 minutes. Cruising at 8 knots they were handling the conditions well but it was impossible for anyone on deck to remain either warm or dry.

Every nerve and fibre in Mueller's body strained to gather, absorb and evaluate each scrap of information his adrenaline-pumped senses provided to his racing brain. Twice now, he had been aware of a slightly darker mass against the grey background. Every instinct told him the enemy was near and about him, but he could see nothing. Uncertainty was gnawing at his brain.

If only this damned rain would ease and the visibility lift for even a few minutes, I could sort the bloody situation out, he mused.

He was secure in the knowledge however that, despite the difficulties, the weather was on his side. The small size and silhouette of the E Boats, together with the element of surprise, swung the tactical advantage very much in his favour.

The break came some 10 minutes later with a suddenness that was quite startling. For a few minutes, the rain eased, visibility improved, and there they were, three, no four, fat, lumbering merchant ships: grey masses against a slightly lighter background, in column, doggedly ploughing on through the rising seas. Mueller estimated the range of the nearest ship as 5000 metres: too far for his unreliable torpedoes. He resisted the temptation to shorten the range by increasing speed, fearing that the E-boats' wakes would alert the enemy and, instead, opted to set a converging course that should bring the nearest ship within optimum torpedo range in about 20 minutes.

Mueller was certain that Meyer on *S-51* and Wilcke on *S-64* would have spotted the British convoy, but, in the prevailing conditions, a coordinated attack was not practical. Using his shaded aldis lamp, Mueller flashed the pre-arranged signal to each of his consorts: 'AAA'– meaning 'enemy in sight; act independently to carry out attack.'

As each E-Boat manoeuvred to obtain the optimum position to release its torpedoes, the weather again closed in and visual contact was lost: with each other and the enemy. Mueller's mind was racing. *Where are the bloody escorts?* The minutes ticked by – seven, eight, nine – still nothing.

Then, from the starboard lookout 'Ship close on the port bow, range 600 metres closing fast!'

Mueller silently swore: *damn, damn, damn! The bloody convoy has zigged towards me.* His boat was in danger of being run down. The British lookouts could not possibly miss seeing the E-Boat almost directly ahead. The hunter was in danger of becoming the prey.

'Stand by one and two tubes! Set gyro angle zero! Set torpedo depth 3 metres!' Mueller barked as he reached forward and engaged the captain's permission-to-fire switch. 'Standby, steady, steady; fire one! Steady, fire two! Come *hard* left! Full ahead all engines!' Mueller rapped out his orders in a continuous stream.

The little ship bucked and reared as the torpedoes left the tubes; she leapt forward, reeling under the effect of full helm and the sudden surge in power.

S-52 was able to avoid the approaching ship, but it came so close that Mueller could clearly see the stark white faces of those on the bridge, as they raced past on opposite courses.

Angry that he had lost the initiative, Mueller had little confidence that his torpedoes, fired in haste, would be effective, but still he had two left.

A blinding flash in the middle distance, closely followed by a dull *crump,* caused a surge of elation but Mueller soon realised that it was too far away to credit either of his torpedoes with a hit. One of the merchantmen had either blundered into the recently laid minefield or *S-51* and *S-64* were having a greater measure of success than Mueller himself.

Mueller's luck changed. Next in line and 1000 metres astern of his earlier target was the *Empire Newcomen*. Mueller had hardly recovered from that first abortive encounter when the new target presented itself. *S-52* was 75 degrees on the *Newcomen's* starboard bow, range 800 metres, track-angle an almost perfect 95 degrees.

'Stand by three and four tubes! Set gyro angle zero! Set torpedo depth 3 metres! Steady, steady, fire 3! Steady, fire 4!' The little ship shuddered again as the torpedoes leapt from the tubes.

A shower of spray close aboard on the port side, followed by the sound of heavy gunfire caught Mueller by surprise. He knew instinctively what it was and a quick glance over his shoulder confirmed his worst fear. A British destroyer, bone in its teeth, was racing through the columns of merchant ships towards him. The range could be little more than 6,000 metres and each barrel of the destroyer's quick-firing twin 4-inch guns could pump out shells at a rate of 16 per minute. One round hitting *S-52* would turn the little boat to matchwood, but again the odds were in Mueller's favour. A weaving E-boat at a speed of 30 knots was an almost impossible target. Still, with no primary weapons remaining, Mueller saw little to be gained by hanging about.

'Let's get the hell out of here!' he yelled at nobody in particular, 'Steer course 110 degrees.'

The manoeuvre would put the maximum distance between him and the convoy in the shortest time. Mueller glanced at the stopwatch clutched in his left hand. At a closing speed of 36 knots it would take his two torpedoes 40 seconds to reach their target. 25 seconds had already passed. If they were to hit, he would know one way or the other in the next 15 seconds.

SS EMPIRE NEWCOMEN – NORTH SEA

0850 hours, Sunday 30 November 1941

Back on the bridge after eight hours below decks, David was settling down to the routine of the forenoon watch. Six hours, undisturbed sleep and a good

English cooked breakfast, now seldom enjoyed by the civilian population ashore, had done wonders for his morale. A steaming mug of tea added to his sense of wellbeing.

Although he had been aware of the forecast, David was mildly surprised by how quickly the weather had deteriorated since he had left the bridge at midnight. The movement of the ship had changed dramatically and he needed to brace himself against the compass binnacle to maintain balance. The driving rain reduced visibility to less than a mile, as predicted in the previous day's Fleet Weather Broadcast, but the comforting outline of the next ship in the column was still visible ahead, enabling *Newcomen* to keep station without difficulty.

'How long 'til the next zig?' David asked the apprentice-on-watch, one of whose duties was to keep track of the convoy's course changes.

'Seven minutes,' came the reply. 'It'll be a change to port to a new course of 355.'

David grunted his acknowledgement and was about to turn his attention to fixing the ship's position when a violent eruption in the middle distance caught his attention and brought him, in three quick strides, to the port side flying-bridge. He raised his binoculars and rapidly scanned the horizon. Even before he spotted the billowing column of smoke, he knew what was happening. Convoy FN 17 was under attack and some poor bugger had just copped it. After two years' wartime service on North Atlantic and, most recently, Arctic convoys to Murmansk, David was hardened to the horrors of loss of ships and life at sea: he had seen this same scene repeated many times. Without such hardening, it would have been emotionally impossible to survive. There was nothing he could do for those on the stricken merchantman. Standing Admiralty instructions required that merchant ships in convoy maintain their station without slowing or stopping to pick up survivors from stricken vessels; that task was left to the rescue vessel, normally trailing astern of the main convoy. Hard as it was, it was the only way to ensure the greatest good for the greatest number and avoid putting more ships in harm's way.

David's sole aim now was to focus on the immediate danger in order to maximise the chances of survival for his own ship and its people. He called on the voice-pipe connecting the bridge to the Captain's day cabin: 'Officer-of-the-watch to Captain. The convoy is under attack. *Sir*, I need you on the bridge, *now!*'

Almost simultaneously from the starboard lookout: 'E-Boat. Bearing green seven five. Range one thousand yards. Closing fast!'

David's brain switched to automatic. He had rehearsed this situation in his mind many times and knew exactly what to do. He judged that, at this close range, the E-Boat had already launched its torpedoes – there was nothing he could do to alter that. Further, the lumbering, somewhat ancient *Newcomen* was far too slow and cumbersome to avoid the onrushing weapons – but he had to try.

'Hard-a-starboard!' he yelled at the helmsman, while simultaneously reaching for the engine room telegraph and, in one movement, ringing down 'Full Astern'.

Clang, clang from the telegraph repeater acknowledged that the watch below had received the order. Valves spun and machinery screamed as steam from the boilers attempted to stop, then reverse, the massive pistons driving the ship's single propeller.

Next, David grabbed the handset for the ship's broadcast system and spat out the orders: 'Hands to Emergency Stations. Hands to Emergency Stations. Close all hatches and watertight doors. The ship is under torpedo attack!'

Only now did he have time to scan the ocean for the tell-tale bubbles that he hoped would reveal the tracks of the onrushing torpedoes but, unknown to David, the G7e electric torpedoes, newly introduced into the *Kriegsmarine*, produced no such trail. In any event, it was all too little, too late.

David turned to acknowledge the arrival of the Captain, still struggling to pull on his duffle coat, when the deck beneath his feet seemed to lift, then a pause for maybe half a second before the shock wave hit, jarring every bone in his body. In a strangely detached way, in what seemed like slow motion, David watched the ship's funnel and the deck adjacent to No. 3 Hatch lift and erupt in a brilliant flash of light and flame. His mind seemed to float; *how pretty it looks,* he thought – then blackness.

It was the stabbing cold that brought David back to consciousness. With every breath, daggers of pain pierced his chest. His eyes, mouth and lungs were choked with black oil and the pain in his head and neck was blinding. He had no feeling below the waist and it was only his lifejacket, thrown on in haste when the attack commenced, that kept his head above the freezing sea. There was no sign of the ship, its crew or the convoy and David had no idea how long he'd been in the water or how he got there. His mind began to wander as he drifted in and out of consciousness. Momentarily, the pain seemed to lift. His body was telling him to sleep but a portion of his brain willed him to stay awake. A noise? He tried to turn his head but couldn't – he didn't care. A face swam before him: an extended arm, voices, *Why don't they let me sleep?* then the blessed relief of blackness once more.

CROMER AND DISTRICT HOSPITAL, UK

Monday 1 December 1941

David knew he was dead because he could see the angel quite clearly, all in white, hands reaching out, gently repeating his name. Everything was clean and white and beautiful. His young wife, Muriel, was there. *Is she dead too? Who's minding the children? God, it hurts. How can that be if I'm dead?*

He remembered the ship: *I can't stay dead – I should be on watch!* He tried to rise but the pressure of a hand on his shoulder prevented him.

'Call the Captain. I must talk to the Captain.' The voice came out as a barely audible croak, then, as he struggled; 'Why won't you let me get up? I need to take care of the ship.'

There was a short, sharp stab in his left arm, then oblivion.

~

The official report of the Cromer Royal Lifeboat Institute recorded that the lifeboat had been called out at 0914 on Sunday 30 November 1941, in response to a telephone call from the Admiralty in Whitehall. A northbound convoy off the Norfolk Coast was under attack and several ships were believed to have been sunk. The lifeboat's task was to search the area and recover survivors.

The weather was appalling. The Cromer lifeboat spent four hours criss-crossing the area and picked up fourteen survivors and six bodies. David was the last to be rescued.

Subsequent analysis showed that the attack on FN 17 by the 4th *Schnellboote* Squadron had accounted for three British ships: *Oblt.z.S* Meyer in *S-51* accounted for the SS *Cormarsh* of 2848 tons; *Oblt.z.S* Wilke in *S-64* was credited with sinking the 699 ton tanker *Asperity*; and Mueller, the *Empire Newcomen.*

Of the combined crews in the three vessels, comprising a total of seventy-four officers and men, twenty were lost. In addition to the Cromer lifeboat, a number were plucked from the freezing sea by the Rescue Tug and several others by the convoy's escort vessels. Of the twenty-two survivors from *Newcomen's* crew of thirty-two, David was the only deck officer.

⌒〜

On his second day in hospital David awoke hungry. 'Hello Muriel. What are you doing here?' he chipped casually to his young wife sitting close by. 'You couldn't rustle up a couple of eggs could you?'

At 11.25 a.m. on Monday 1 December, Muriel had been busy at her sewing machine in a small factory in Barry, producing uniforms for the men and women of Britain's Armed Forces, when she learned of the loss of David's ship and his remarkable survival. She had quickly arranged time off and made her way to Cromer, arriving that same evening.

The relief when David spoke was overwhelming. Amid tears of joy Muriel replied, 'I'll see what I can do, but don't you know there's a war on?'

⌒〜

A smartly turned out Lieutenant Commander, from the Admiralty's Department of Trade, debriefed David at the hospital on 3 December. It was essential to know what had happened, what went right, and what could be improved. As the only surviving officer, David's information was invaluable.

He was kept in hospital for six days. Shock and hypothermia were the main problems, with some superficial lacerations and bruising. Rest and relaxation were the remedies. He was sent on 28 days' survivors' leave.

BARRY – SOUTH WALES

December 1941

There was very little to occupy David's time. Muriel was back at work, Donald was at school and, at two, Andrew was too young to be interesting. Some evenings David and Muriel would walk to the Colcot Arms at the end of the road and enjoy a meal of cod and chips and a pint of ale. Muriel generally had a gin and lemon.

However, at fourpence a pint, it was hard for David to go past the local Welsh ale. At weekends they spent as much time as possible together; sometimes wandering through the woods at Wenvoe or along the pebbly Knap Beach, reflecting on the war and what might become of them and their young family. Perhaps they should evacuate the children to Canada as many others had done?

Muriel was adamant. She and the children would stay in Barry. Her logic was faultless: a trans-Atlantic crossing was too dangerous and the Luftwaffe's nightly bombing raids were only targeting the Barry Docks. The house was more than 3 miles from the docks so they would be extraordinarily unlucky if a stray German bomb hit them. Besides, weren't the children tucked away safely each night in the cupboard under the stairs? The matter was settled.

Times were hard and rationing was strictly enforced. The children received one egg each per week, which Muriel made into an egg custard. Bread was generally available and there was enough milk for the children, but butter was non-existent. Some weeks it was possible to buy a few sausages or a small piece of ground beef or perhaps a piece of pork. Donald had a hot midday meal at school, each weekday, together with a Government issue of half a pint of milk. This helped enormously.

Pre-war imports of food, oil and raw materials from Britain's Dominions and Colonies were in the order of 65 million tons per year. Doenitz and his U-Boats and Goering with his Luftwaffe had reduced the food and resources lifeline to a barely sustainable 45 million tons annually. In 1942 alone, Britain lost over 1500 merchant ships – a rate that British Shipyards could not replace.

Life was hard, but not impossible. The Battle of Britain had been won and the danger of invasion, temporarily at least, had been averted. The campaign in North Africa was underway but going very badly for the British. In the middle of 1941, Hitler had invaded Russia.

On 8 December, the world awoke to the news that the Japanese had attacked Pearl Harbor and America had formally entered the war, although moral and material support had been forthcoming for some time. Formal entry by the US was good news. From that time David knew, with absolute certainty, that with the industrial might of America behind them, ultimate victory was assured. A careful optimism became apparent in the shops, on the buses and wherever people gathered.

Although Christmas in Britain, 1941, was lacking the lights and glamour of bygone years, the festive spirit could not be suppressed and whatever the state of the war, it was still Christmas for the children. A few gifts for the little ones were possible – painted lead soldiers for Donald, especially the Germans, were very popular and were received with squeals of delight as was a little wooden dog on wheels for Andrew. Christmas dinner was difficult but there was enough to eat for everyone and Nanna Roscoe's Christmas plum pudding, with its silver thruppences hidden away inside, was a great favourite.

The letter from David's shipping company arrived, much as expected, on 4 January 1942.

'Dear Mr Millar

You are directed to join the Company's vessel, SS *Willesden*, which will be lying at South Shields, on 12 January. A rail voucher from Barry is enclosed and we shall be glad if you will report, with your gear, to the Company's agent in that port, on the appointed date, to sign Articles as Second Mate. You should take with you your Pool Form, Merchant Navy Identity Card and Certificate of Competency.

We have advised the ship's master, Captain R W Griffiths, that you are coming through.

We enclose a cheque for twelve pounds two shillings and nine pence, representing shore pay and subsistence allowance until 11 January. You should sign Articles on 12 January.

Yours etc

For Watts, Watts & Co. Ltd.'

The last few days of David's leave passed too quickly. With Andrew perched on her hip and clutching Donald's hand, Muriel struggled to hold back tears as the little group gathered at Barry's main line station. A whistle and a hiss of steam, a wave, another tear, people in uniform, people pressing. 'There he is; wave, quickly now; he's gone. Oh God, bring him back safely.'

Neither Muriel nor David could know that it would be four years before they saw each other again.

SOUTH SHIELDS

Sunday 11 January 1942

David took a taxi he could ill-afford from the station. It was the only sensible way to transport his large tin seaman's chest which contained his complete, brand-new sea-going kit. The weather was still awful; heavy overcast with cold drizzle – but what else could be expected for the time of year? It was barely daylight when they reached the docks and the port was busy so it took the driver some time to find David's ship. The crew was expecting him and one of the young apprentices, Jimmy Harland, quickly organised a couple of seamen to help David aboard with his baggage.

There was nothing to commend *Willesden* or set her apart from a thousand other British tramps that plied the oceans to maintain the country's supply of food and raw materials. Built by Workman Clarke & Co Ltd of Belfast and delivered in 1925, she was a coal burner and had a single screw. The ship was painted in the company colours: grey hull and pink boot-topping with a black funnel emblazoned with the company's House Flag, a blue 'W' on a white surround. The bridge and upper-works were white. The paint was old and flaking and she was showing her age.

Lloyd's Register of Shipping recorded her as 4563 Gross Registered Tons. She was 416 feet overall with a 54-foot beam and a deep draft of 25 feet. Her maximum speed, with a clean bottom, was 10 knots and her total complement was forty-seven officers and men. A team of dedicated engineers kept her going – most of the time.

David was shown below by young Harland and was pleased to note that he had been allocated his own cabin in the amidships section of the ship, abaft and slightly below the bridge and handy to the officers' saloon. After he had stowed his gear, Jimmy took David on a tour of the ship and introduced him to the First Mate, J (James) Gardiner, and several of the other officers who were on board for the evening. Captain Griffiths was not expected until just before the scheduled sailing time the following afternoon. David had served under Griffiths previously, on the *Marcrest*. They had been on several Atlantic convoys together and one to Murmansk in the twelve-month period from July 1940, so neither of them was a stranger to the North Atlantic in winter during wartime, nor under any illusion of the dangers that lay ahead. Griffiths was a senior captain who would certainly have been looking forward to retirement if it were not for the war. He was a competent seaman and a staunch Welsh Methodist. However, the stress of command in wartime had taken a toll on his health and, without knowing quite why, David had a gut feeling that in a crisis, Griffiths's ability to think quickly and act decisively might no longer stand the test.

Due to wartime requirements, details of the intended voyage were classified and not generally known. However, the ship was fully coaled, but in ballast, and David was experienced enough to know that this almost certainly meant a destination in North America. Had it been Russia, or the Mediterranean, the other two most likely destinations, the ship would have been fully laden with war materials.

As part of the program for the defensive arming of merchant ships, the Ministry of War Transport had provided *Willesden* with a 4-inch Naval gun, of World War I vintage, fitted on the poop deck, and a Lewis AA, heavy machine gun on either side of the bridge. The 4-inch was very limited in range and capability, but it did provide a small degree of comfort – at least the ship was not totally defenceless.

The guns' crews were made up of a mixture of Royal Navy and Royal Marine Reserve gunners, backed by members of the *Willesden's* crew. As Second Mate, David had overall responsibility for the maintenance and operation of the guns. Under him, the Third Mate was the Quarters Officer for the Lewis guns on the bridge.

David completed the formalities of signing on and *Willesden* sailed on the afternoon tide of 12 January, Captain Griffiths having arrived on board some two hours earlier. The ship joined the East Coast convoy system for the passage north to Methil then around the top of Scotland via the Pentland Firth and The Minch, to Loch Ewe where they met and integrated with convoy ONS 57. ONS 57 was designated a slow convoy, outward bound from Liverpool for Halifax and New York. Barring accidents and the enemy willing, they were scheduled to arrive in New York in twenty-one days.

THE GIRONDE – FRANCE

Wednesday 14 January 1942

Käpitan zur See Günther Gumprich, Commanding Officer of *Schiff 10*, the German armed merchant raider otherwise known as the *Thor*, drew his duffle coat closely about him against the bitter cold, as his ship cleared the shelter of Pointe de Grave and butted into the south-westerly gale raging across the Bay of Biscay.

From a strategic viewpoint, it had always been the intention of the German Naval Staff, the *Seekriegleitung* (or *SKL* as it was known) to send out a wave of armed merchant raiders to prey on the merchant ships that provided Britain with food and raw materials. As a vital spin-off of this strategy, the raiders would also commit the Royal Navy to hunting them down, using a disproportionate number of warships, desperately needed elsewhere.

The *Thor* was the first of the German raiders to undertake a second war patrol and, after refitting in Kiel, had left that port on 30 November 1941, ironically the same day that *Empire Newcomen* had met her fate in the North Sea off Cromer. The weather had been appalling but it successfully covered *Thor's* movements down the European Coast, through the English Channel and into the Bay of Biscay where she had eventually been forced to take shelter in the Gironde. Gumprich's orders were to take *Thor* into the South Atlantic, to search out and capture or destroy Allied merchant shipping bound to or from Cape Town, as well as to attack, and preferably capture, Allied whaling fleets known to be operating in the Southern Ocean.

Whale oil was valued as a lubricant which maintains its viscosity characteristics better than any mineral oil. It was therefore ideal for automotive transmission fluids, and as an aircraft engine oil, due to its low freezing point. Sperm whale oil was also used for the manufacture of margarine. For all these reasons, whale oil was of inestimable value during wartime.

SS Willesden circa 1940.

At 3144 Gross Registered Tons, *Thor* was the smallest of Germany's armed merchant raiders. Built by the Deutsche Werft Yard in Hamburg she entered service in 1938 as a banana boat, the *Santa Cruz,* before being converted to a commerce raider at the outbreak of war. The ship had a cruising range of 40,000 nautical miles at 10 knots and a maximum speed of 18 knots. She was the first of the German raiders to be fitted with a search radar, albeit of a primitive and rather unreliable nature. The ship's main armament comprised six 15-cm naval guns, concealed behind hinged metal screens. She was also fitted with a variety of anti-aircraft weapons and four torpedo tubes. The ship carried an 'Arado', twin-seat, reconnaissance floatplane that could be lowered or recovered by derrick. *Thor's* crew strength totalled 349 officers and men of the *Kriegsmarine*.

Again, bad weather in the Bay of Biscay helped *Thor* avoid the attention of the British patrols but she had been forced to seek shelter off the north coast of Spain to repair damage sustained in the storm, before venturing out into the Atlantic for the passage south to her patrol area.

SINGAPORE

Wednesday 14 January 1942

John Guy was a very worried man. As he peddled his bicycle the half mile from the Dockyard Offices in the Sembawang Shipyard to his allocated married quarter, within Britain's largest and most extensive overseas naval base, he reflected on the outcome of the hastily called special briefing he had just attended.

The Japanese were now in Johore, less than 50 miles over the causeway into Malaya, and were pressing south towards Singapore from Muar and Sengarrarang. At their present rate of advance, they could be on the outskirts of Singapore in fourteen days. The battleships *Prince of Wales* and *Repulse* had been destroyed and Singapore was virtually defenceless. As a senior civilian engineer in the dockyard, John had responsibility for the demolition of any facilities that might prove useful to the Japanese occupying forces. This included the massive KG V dry-dock, capable of accommodating the largest battleships or aircraft carriers. This meant he would need to stay to the end, but his immediate concern was for the evacuation and safety of his wife, Helen, and his six-year-old stepson, Howard.

Thirty-two years old, tall, slim, and with dark hair and flashing hazel eyes, Helen was very attractive by any standard, but there was a sadness about her face that reflected the grief and hardship of times past. Her first husband and Howard's father, Wilfred Gunstone, had died of cancer in 1938 while on a posting to Singapore. Helen and Howard had stayed on in the colony and in 1940 she was remarried to John Guy.

When he arrived at their bungalow John told Helen the grim news. 'Pack a suitcase and be ready to evacuate at a moment's notice,' he told her. 'There are ships leaving for Australia with women and children every few days and I want

Howard Gunstone age 5.

you and Howard to be on the next available vessel. The Japs are getting close and I need to know that you're both safe.'

Helen agreed. John's position in the dockyard gave him influence and he arranged for Helen and Howard to take passage on a small steamer scheduled to depart for Australia on 16 January, just two days' time. The ship would take a thousand women and children evacuees and John was determined that Helen and Howard would be on it; beyond that date he could not guarantee their safety. Over the following forty-eight hours the situation deteriorated further. On the morning of the 16th John packed Helen and Howard, with their two small suitcases, into the family's Austin 10 for the 12-mile journey down the Thomson Road to Singapore City and Keppel Harbour, where the ship was making final preparations for departure.

The confusion and press of people at the dockside was alarming but, with the proper papers and authorisations, John was able to get his family safely on board. A quick hug, 'Good luck,' and, 'See you in Sydney,' and they were gone, Helen and Howard to find their living quarters on board and John back to the dockyard to do what he could to create problems for the advancing Japanese.

The ship cleared the Singapore Roads (anchorage) in the late afternoon, decks packed with women and children. The harassed crew was still struggling to find sleeping accommodation for the passengers, on a vessel designed to carry less than a quarter of those crowded on board.

As they entered the Singapore Strait the roar of a fast approaching aircraft caused panic amongst the exposed passengers, desperate to seek shelter where there was none. A single Japanese Zero fighter screamed low over the ship, cannons blazing. Helen and Howard became separated. One of the crew, standing next to Howard, collapsed in a bloody mess as a 20-mm cannon shell ripped through his chest, spraying Howard with warm blood. Miraculously, the aircraft made only one pass and did not return, perhaps going to attack some other luckless vessel or called to a higher priority mission. Even so, six of the passengers lay dead, two of them children, and many more were wounded. Howard was lucky. He was hit in the ankle with a piece of shrapnel but the wound was not serious. Approaching darkness provided a welcome blanket of safety and by morning the little ship was making good progress to the south-east for the Java Sea and Australia.

There was no further incident. On 20 January they cleared the Lombok Strait into the Indian Ocean and on 8 February they arrived safely in Sydney, to be met by anxious family and friends.

NORTH SHIELDS – UK

Monday 26 January 1942

Alfie Round, known to his Geordie mates as 'Roondie', was getting restless. At nineteen and born into a poor, working-class, North Shields family, Alfie had endured a difficult childhood but he had an instinct for survival and a great passion for a life at sea. As long as he could remember, he had watched the comings and goings of ships on the River Tyne, certain in the knowledge that one day he would join them. Indeed, the previous week, Alfie had stood on the bank of the great river, watching but unknowing, as the tramp steamer *Willesden* made her way to the open sea. The sea was in Alfie's blood and dreams of exotic places and far-off destinations were forever in his mind.

Alfie had realised his dream twelve months earlier when he signed on to the Motor Vessel *Athol Princess* as an Ordinary Seaman. As the ship's agent was having problems finding a crew he had no difficulty getting a berth, despite his lack of experience. *Athol Princess* was an oil tanker and in his innocence and enthusiasm Alfie did not realise that an oil tanker in wartime was no place to be. However, the Patron Saint of sailors[1] was clearly watching over Alfie, because twelve months, several ships and three Atlantic crossings later he was safely back in North Shields, blooded by the reality and horror of war and the battle of the Atlantic with its U-boat menace. As a consequence of his experience, he was already wise beyond his years. On 10 January he had been paid off in Sunderland from the *Josewyn* and now, a little over two weeks later, he was ready to get back to sea.

On this Monday morning, Alfie was making his way home when he bumped into a neighbour, 'Ginger' Robson, three years older than Alfie and also a merchant seaman. The two often spent time together, swapping stories of their experiences.

'Hello Roondie,' said Ginger with a cheery wave as they met. 'I heard they're calling for hands for the *Kirkpool* and I'm away to sign on.'

'I need a berth too,' Alfie responded, 'I'll come with you,' and together they headed for the shipping office.

The Shipping Superintendent went through the list of ships and vacancies, calling men forward to sign: 'Steam Ship *Clan MacPhee*. One fireman wanted,' he called, and a young man from the group of seamen gathered to find work raised his hand and stepped forward, then 'Steam Ship *Kirkpool*. Two Able Seamen wanted.'

Alfie and Ginger raised their hands and stepped forward. Alfie watched as Ginger signed on, then it was his turn. Alfie was still only an Ordinary Seaman and signed as such but, because of his experience, he attracted an Able Seaman's pay.

SS *Kirkpool*, under the command of Captain Kennington, was owned by the Pool Shipping Company Ltd. She was built in Sunderland by Sir James Laing and Sons Ltd. Launched in 1922, *Kirkpool* was 4842 Gross Registered Tons, and a coal burner with a maximum speed of 9.5 knots.

The following morning the two friends joined the ship with their sea kits. Three days later the ship moved to the coaling wharf at Dunstan on the southern side of the Tyne and on the following morning, which dawned cold, bleak and overcast with a light drizzle, they parted company with the two tugs that had assisted them from their berth, dropped the harbour pilot and headed for the open sea.

---

1   Saint Elmo, although sometimes also said to be Saint Nicholas

NORTH ATLANTIC

Monday 2 February 1942

Convoy ONS 57 was now five days out from New York. It had crossed the mid-Atlantic air-sea gap (the area where convoys were out of range of air support from either side of the Atlantic) relatively unscathed. Although it had received the attention of Admiral Doenitz's U-Boats for three days, the convoy escaped with the loss of only one merchant ship. There were two reasons for this: firstly, in September 1941, Hitler had personally ordered Doenitz to send every available U-Boat to the Mediterranean to support Rommel's campaign in North Africa, leaving few submarines for the wolf pack war in the North Atlantic and, more significantly, the savage winter weather in the North Atlantic made U-Boat operations difficult.

For the officers and men of the *Willesden,* the foul weather was a blessing. For David, life melded into a seemingly unending routine of being on watch, sleeping, eating then back on watch. The thirty-six ships of ONS 57 were organised into four rows of nine columns each and *Willesden* was the third ship in the first column. While on watch, David's primary tasks were to keep station on the next ship ahead, to carry out zig-zags in accordance with the convoy commodore's orders and to keep a sharp watch for U-Boats operating on the surface within the convoy limits.

SS Kirkpool circa 1940.

Nerves were on edge and false alarms were frequent. On 28 January one of the escorting destroyers raced through the convoy and, without warning, dropped a pattern of depth charges less than fifty yards from *Willesden's* starboard beam. On the *Willesden*, the effect was devastating. It seemed that the entire ship lifted bodily and was being struck with a giant hammer. It was hard to believe that the ship's half-inch steel plates could survive such a beating. *Pity help the poor bastards in any submarine nearby,* David mused, but there was no further sign of a U-Boat and the destroyer soon raced off busily in another direction.

The most spectacular attacks were at night when the escorting destroyers and corvettes fired star shells to illuminate the U-Boats operating on the surface within the convoy columns. Night turned instantly to day. The merchant ships added to the confusion by opening fire with their 4-inch guns at any fleeting shadow, with shells ricocheting alarmingly off the water with a greater likelihood of hitting another ship than an attacking enemy submarine.

On the third day of the attacks the ship ahead of *Willesden* was torpedoed. A little later, *Willesden* passed a man in the water, clinging to a hatch cover. There was nothing they could do except shout encouragement and pass an urgent message to the rescue ship at the rear of the convoy. They never found out if he was rescued. Such was the way of war.

By 31 January the convoy was under cover of the Royal Canadian Air Force operating out of Halifax, Nova Scotia, and the period of greatest danger was over. On 7 February, *Willesden* arrived safely in New York.

SINGAPORE

Sunday 15 February 1942

All forms of reliable communication had broken down and it was impossible to know what was happening anywhere but in the immediate vicinity. Despite the destruction of the Causeway linking Singapore to Malaya by the retreating British forces, the Japanese Imperial Army had crossed the Johore Straits on the night of 8-9 February and was now pressing on the outskirts of Singapore City. It was total chaos in what remained of Britain's remotest and most 'secure' outpost.

On the previous day, with the help of a locally recruited Indian, Malay and Chinese labour force, John Guy had detonated charges that had destroyed the lock gates of the KG V dry-dock in the Sembawang Shipyard. Cranes, workshops and other key facilities were also destroyed to make life as difficult as possible for the advancing Japanese.

Nothing else could be done. John shook hands with all of those who had served him so loyally: from now on, each was on his own. All possible shipping had been cleared from Singapore Roads over the previous days, taking with it everyone who was not essential to the final defence.

John figured his best chance of survival was to make his way to Keppel Harbour on the southern side of the island. He had plenty of 'Straits' dollars[2] and a vague plan that he might be able to buy a passage to somewhere, anywhere, provided it got him out of the chaos that was Singapore. The roads were blocked with retreating troops and every imaginable form of military and civilian transport.

Explosions were occurring all about him but it was impossible to tell whether they were from shelling by the advancing Japanese or from the British and Australian Sappers demolishing the last of the installations and infrastructure. Japanese Zeros roared overhead, headed for the docks, to bomb and strafe the mass of people still attempting to flee by sea. Travel by car was impossible. John managed to get as far as Newton Circus on his dockyard bicycle before the press of people became such that even the bicycle had to be abandoned. On foot, he pushed on, down Clemenceau Avenue, past the Goodwood and Cockpit Hotels, avoiding the mass of humanity on Orchard Road, preferring to take the more direct route via River Valley Road. He pushed his way through the mass of people in Raffles Place, passing that great bastion of the English establishment, Robinsons Department Store, hurriedly being boarded up as looters helped themselves to anything small enough to be carried off. John eventually arrived at Collier Quay, then made his way south to Telok Ayer Basin, arriving late in the afternoon. This was it – any further progress was impossible.

The chaos on the waterfront was worse than in the city. Almost on the verge of despair, John spotted a man pushing through the crowd towards him, waving and shouting frantically. It was his loyal Sikh Overseer from the Dockyard.

'Mr Guy sahib,' he yelled, 'we found an abandoned Kumpit drifting in the harbour. Some of our dockyard workers are minding it but it's in pretty bad shape and has no fuel.'

'If that's all there is,' yelled John with a sense of relief, 'we'll take it and make do somehow.'

---

2   The currency in use throughout Singapore and Malaya at this time. Originally used in Singapore, Penang and Malacca which were known as 'The Straits Settlements', the 'Straits' being the Singapore and Malacca Straits.

Together they pushed through the mass of people to the concrete dock where the little wooden trading vessel lay. Half a dozen of John's loyal Chinese workers were frantically trying to hold back the press of people desperate to flee the stricken city.

John was aware that the Headquarters of the Singapore Royal Naval Reserve was nearby and that they kept a supply of diesel fuel to operate their small boats – it was certainly worth investigating. They were in luck. The headquarters was abandoned so they smashed the lock off the fuel storage shed and found a dozen 44-gallon drums of diesel. There was sufficient fuel to fill the Kumpit's ample tank and space on board for an additional four drums. In the meantime two of John's Chinese workers had been able to buy, scrounge or steal water and enough food to last several days. They would need to obtain further supplies as and when they could.

By 1900 all was ready. John figured their best chance was to head north, up the Malacca Straits and make for Rangoon or Colombo. The chaos in Singapore and the onset of darkness would give them their best chance of slipping through the Japanese patrols undetected.

The passage was relatively without incident. They travelled mostly by night, lying up in the mangrove swamps along the Sumatra Coast by day. The all-conquering Japanese had more immediate and important tasks to attend to than to bother about the tiny motorised Kumpit and its 'native' crew, making its way slowly up the Straits.

John was not sure whether or not the Japanese had occupied Rangoon so, once in the vicinity of the Nicobar Islands, they turned west for Ceylon, crossing the Andaman Sea and the Bay of Bengal. They arrived safely in Trincomalee on 2 April 1942.

SS KIRKPOOL – ATLANTIC OCEAN

Tuesday 17 February 1942

At midday, *Kirkpool* and Convoy ONS 61 parted company. They were in the North Atlantic, roughly 300 miles NE of the Azores. The convoy turned westward, bound for Halifax, and *Kirkpool* continued on to the south, proceeding independently for Lourenco Marques in Mozambique where she was to pick up cargo for the UK. The passage so far had been without incident. After leaving North Shields the ship had made its way northwards around the top of Scotland before pausing a few days in Oban to take on more cargo. They joined ONS 61 on 12 February. The weather improved daily as they steamed south and the war seemed very far away. Alfie and his mates were looking forward to the prospect of shore leave in Cape Town and, for the moment, life seemed pretty good.

NEW YORK'S BUSH TERMINAL

1630 hours, Monday 2 March 1942

Willesden was delayed in New York due to main engine problems, and for four days the engineers had worked tirelessly to get the ship repaired and ready for sea.

David stood on the port bridge wing, foot resting on the rail, watching the stevedores working the dockside cranes as the last of the main cargo was swung into the ship's No. 2 Hold. When the work was completed, oregon hatchboards were lowered into place and the heavy canvas covers, secured to the hatch combings with hardwood wedges, were spread, giving a completely weatherproof covering. With the hatches secured, the final task was to load the deck cargo: 450 drums of diesel oil and aviation fuel, on pallets, with nine drums to a pallet. These were stowed in the ship's two well-decks and secured with wire rope to ringbolts in the deck. It was well after midnight before the work was finished. The ship was scheduled to sail on the morning tide.

Willesden was loaded with war supplies desperately needed by the 8th Army in North Africa, aircraft and tank spare parts, ammunition, heavy machinery, tents, food and clothing, in addition to the deck cargo of fuel. The Mediterranean was considered too dangerous for shipping, except for the most heavily defended convoys, so *Willesden* was routed to Alexandria via St Lucia in the West Indies, where she was to take on coal, then Cape Town and the East Coast of Africa.

Earlier that afternoon, the Royal Navy's liaison officer (RNLO) on the staff of the Senior British Naval Representative, New York, a smartly dressed Lieutenant Commander sporting a well-trimmed King George V beard, had briefed Captain Griffiths and *Willesden's* officers on the coming voyage.

'As *Willesden* is under charter to the Admiralty,' he explained, 'you'll be operating under Navy procedures. There are no escorts available so you'll be proceeding independently.

'U-Boats are known to be operating off the coast between New York and St Lucia,' he continued, 'but once you're out into the South Atlantic the threat should ease. However, German armed raiders, disguised as merchant ships, are known to be operating in that area, but your chance of running into one is fairly small.'

Griffiths interjected, 'What support are we likely to get if we're attacked?'

'Not a lot, I'm afraid,' the RNLO responded. 'The Americans may be able to give you some support if you run into trouble before you reach the West Indies, and there's a British cruiser squadron operating in the South Atlantic, but your best defence is to remain undetected. For that reason it's vital that you maintain radio silence; unless, of course, you make contact with the enemy,' he said. 'In the event you *are* detected you should transmit, and keep transmitting as long as possible, one of three enemy contact reports: "SSS" if you are being been attacked by an enemy submarine, "QQQ" if it's a disguised enemy merchant ship and "RRR" for an enemy surface warship.

'No need to write them down,' he said, 'the details are in your sealed orders.' Then, 'If possible, your alarm report should be followed by the ship's position and name and any other details, such as identity, course or speed of the attacking ship or submarine, should be added if known and if the situation allows. With any luck, one of our cruisers will pick up your signals and come to your assistance.'

Willesden's First Mate chipped in, 'What tactics would a surface raider be likely to use?'

'Their main aim,' the RNLO explained, 'will be to prevent you sending off any wireless messages, while standing off sufficiently far to shell you into surrender with their big guns. They'll try to remain outside the range of your 4-inch deck gun. Also, they may work in cooperation with a seaplane that they often use for reconnaissance,' he added. The briefing continued, 'Any changes to your orders will be sent via the Admiralty broadcasts to merchant shipping for the area you happen to be in at the time. You should also maintain a listening watch on both the Fleet and International distress frequencies for any ships in trouble; but you're not to respond to these messages or go to anyone's assistance. That task is the responsibility of the Navy or, if appropriate, the US Coastguard.'

The RNLO went on, 'Finally, the weather for the next few days is expected to be relatively benign. There's a stationary high over the continent and it's some months yet before the hurricane season starts. However, sometimes, east of the Bahamas, quite violent storms can spring up without notice. These are generally very local and of short duration. In any event, you'll be updated on conditions by weather messages, broadcast twelve-hourly from the Fleet Weather Centre at Fort Lauderdale.

'Are there any further questions?' he asked.

There were none.

The officer handed Captain Griffiths a heavily sealed buff envelope. 'Everything I've told you is in these orders. Have a safe passage and good luck.' He shook hands with Captain Griffiths and was gone.

At 0730 on 2 March, assisted by a single tug, *Willesden* backed away from her berth at No. 9 Pier and began the journey to the mouth of New York's Hudson River. The ship stopped briefly a little way to the east of Staten Island to drop the pilot. Once clear of the coast, she turned to the south-east. Barring accidents, she would make St Lucia, at the southern end of the Leeward Islands, in about seven days.

SS WILLESDEN – CARIBBEAN SEA

1000 hours, Saturday 7 March 1942

It was two hours into the forenoon watch and *Willesden* had just passed through the Mona Passage, separating the Dominican Republic from Puerto Rico. The helmsman was holding a course just to the south of east, to take the ship across the western Caribbean and bring her to St Lucia, where they were to take on bunker coal, on the afternoon of 9 March.

So far, the passage had been without incident. However, on several occasions *Willesden's* wireless operators had picked up 'SSS' messages on the international distress frequency, indicating enemy submarines were active in the area. In accordance with her orders, no action had been taken. Indeed, there was very little that the crew could have done, but it made them conscious of ever-present danger.

The weather had grown steadily warmer and more settled as the ship made her way south and David was now very comfortable on the bridge in his tropical white shorts and shirt and brown leather sandals. The wind was light, but freshening, and the ship rose and dipped in a not unpleasant motion as she butted into the moderate, easterly swell. But David was far from happy. For the third time within the hour he checked the barometer, fixed at the rear of the bridge, and tapped it lightly with his index finger. The pressure was dropping quickly. He recalled the weather briefing given by the RNLO prior to sailing from New York. He also had experienced, on earlier voyages, local storms called 'Northers' that occurred throughout Central America and the West Indies, particularly at this time of year. David suspected that such a storm was approaching. He checked the Admiralty Weather Manual, which was always kept on the bridge:

> 'In terms of wind force,' he read, 'the Norther sometimes attains a severity which renders it dangerous, not only to ships in the open sea, but also to those in some of the continental harbours and the harbours of some West Indian Islands, and as far south as Panama. While they might be quite severe in their intensity, the duration of these storms is seldom more than six to eight hours.'

The anti-cyclone (high pressure system) over North America had moved south and was intensifying. David no longer had any doubt that a very uncomfortable night lay ahead. He decided to call the Captain.

'Sir, I think we're in for a bit of a blow. I suggest we secure the ship for heavy weather,' David reported, when Griffiths arrived on the bridge.

The Captain studied the chart and the latest weather messages before checking the barometer for himself. 'I agree,' he said, 'no point in taking chances.'

David sent for the ship's Bosun, the senior non-certificated sailor on board, and explained what he wanted done. 'Looks like we've got a storm coming up "Swain",' he said, 'go through the ship and secure everything for heavy weather. You know what needs to be done, but pay particular attention to the deck cargo and make doubly sure it's well secured,' he ordered, 'and get the men to stow away, or lash down, anything that might move,' then, as an afterthought, 'and don't forget to warn the galley.'

The Bosun was an experienced and capable seaman and David knew that the job would be done well, without interference or further direction.

Shortly after the Bosun had left the bridge, there was a shrill whistle from the engine room voice-pipe. David removed the stopper and leant over the speaking tube. 'Bridge here,' he called, 'what's the problem?' The engine room seldom called the bridge unless there was a problem.

'Chief Engineer here,' came the response, 'one of our big-end bearings is badly overheating. We'll have to shut the engine down right away or she'll seize up.'

'How long will it take to fix, Chief?' David asked.

'Could be as much as twenty-four hours,' the Chief Engineer replied, 'maybe less if there are no problems.'

David glanced at the Captain, who had overheard the exchange. Griffiths looked concerned and rather agitated but nodded to David who immediately rang down 'Stop' on the engine-room telegraph.

'Just what we need with a storm brewing,' Griffiths muttered, then to David, 'Get Chief and the Mate up here right away.'

By the time the officers reached the bridge the ship had lost steerage way and was lying almost beam on to the freshening wind, wallowing in the swell. The four officers considered the problems presented by this new setback: firstly, without the power of the engine, the ship would lay beam to the wind, as she was now, and drift down to leeward at something in the order of 1–2 knots. When the storm hit, the ship would roll violently. If the wind rose to anything above Force 8, and that was almost certain, she would be in danger of broaching or capsizing. Jettisoning the deck cargo would help, but only marginally, and would not necessarily avert disaster. Secondly, Puerto Rico and the islands of the Mona Strait were still visible and less than 20 miles distant. If the ship didn't capsize in the storm there was a possibility that the wind would drive her onto the rocks. Finally, they could break radio silence and summon assistance. There was almost certain to be other ships in the vicinity but they would be under the same orders as *Willesden* regarding the provision of assistance to ships in trouble. *Willesden* would have to rely on the US Navy or Coastguard responding to their call for help. If they did break radio silence, the transmissions would likely be intercepted by patrolling U-Boats. This would have a high probability of not only bringing destruction on the *Willesden*, but also on any vessel that might come to her assistance.

They discussed the issues between them before Griffiths said, 'What's our best option?' in a voice that lacked the certainty of command.

'We could keep the ship's head into the wind and cut down our drift by using some of the deck cargo to make a sea-anchor,' David volunteered, 'and we could use the bridge awning to create a makeshift mizzen sail. That would also help keep her head-to-wind.'

'That might work,' the First Mate responded, 'it's certainly worth a try, and if we stream some oil bags from the bow, it'll stop the waves breaking over us.'

'OK,' said Griffiths, 'let's do it,' and he turned to leave the bridge to return to his cabin. He paused briefly at the top of the ladder, and turned towards the Chief Engineer, 'I want that bearing replaced in record time Chief,' he said. – 'I doubt we can keep the old girl afloat for twenty-four hours.'

As the watch-on-deck were still busy securing the ship for the coming storm it was necessary to call all hands. The Mate instructed the senior Petty Officers on what had to be done and the men quickly set to work.

They lashed together two pallets of diesel drums from the deck cargo, then lowered them over *Willesden's* bow, attached to the ship with twenty fathoms (120 ft) of 3-inch manila rope. As the drums were almost neutrally buoyant, they floated low in the water. Unaffected by the conditions therefore, they tended to pull the bow up into the wind. To make the mizzen sail, the bridge awning was taken down and lashed between the mizzen mast and the No. 4 Hold derrick, near the ship's stern, where it had the same effect as a wind vane or the feathers on an arrow.

It was late afternoon and well into the dog watches before the work was complete. The First Mate, with the Bosun and the Chippy (the ship's carpenter), undertook a final inspection and reported to Griffiths that they were satisfied everything possible had been done. Already, the effects of their improvisations were apparent and the ship was holding a heading within thirty degrees of the wind's direction. More importantly, the dangerous and sickening rolling motion of the ship, as she had laid beam to the wind and sea, was dramatically reduced. It now remained to see if their hasty preparations would withstand the coming storm.

The engineers made good progress with the repairs but replacing a big-end bearing at sea was not a task to be hurried. The rest of the officers and crew could do nothing more but wait, hoping that a skulking submarine would not add to their troubles.

A little after 0200 the storm hit. Despite the preparations, those on the bridge were surprised by the suddenness and intensity with which it struck. Rolling foul-weather cumulus blacked out the stars, and torrential rain was driven into their faces by the force of the wind. Thunder was almost continuous. Visibility was less than 100 yards and even then, only when the brilliant flashes of forked lightning illuminated the boiling sea, momentarily flashing an unearthly blue light over the forward part of the ship. The pounding, tumbling waves, driven by the fury of the wind, hammered at the ship as if to tear her apart. The superstructure and rigging howled in protest.

All those not on watch, or working on the engines, mustered in the officers' saloon, two decks below the bridge, life jackets on, ready to abandon ship should the need arise. Wet, cold and miserable they huddled together in little groups for comfort and support.

At 0620 as the eastern sky paled, giving notice of the coming dawn, the head and shoulders of the Chief Engineer, white-overalled and grimy-faced, appeared on the ladder leading to the bridge. 'The job's done,' he announced, with a huge grin, 'but I can only let you have slow speed 'til the new bearing is bedded in.'

'We'll take anything you can give Chief,' David responded, also breaking into a wide grin, as he rang down 'Slow Ahead' on the telegraph, 'and be bloody thankful for that.'

Almost immediately, the sickening movement of the ship steadied as she slowly gathered way, allowing the rudder to take effect. The worst was over. Shortly before 0900, the storm blew itself out, almost as suddenly as it had begun. An inspection attested to its fury. The starboard lifeboat was damaged, several pallets of deck cargo had been torn loose and swept away, the steel railing stanchions in the forward well-deck on the starboard side were bent almost horizontal and paint had been torn from the hull and upper-works. But the ship was still afloat and they were all alive. All-in-all they had fared extremely well and there was no damage that couldn't be repaired with the resources available on board.

Strangely, Captain Griffiths had closeted himself in his cabin since giving the orders to rig the sea-anchor and mizzen sail the previous day and had left responsibility for the running of the ship to the First Mate, who had shared the watchkeeping duties with David throughout the night. Communication with Griffiths had been by the bridge voice-pipe. The only response to reports had been grunts, or a mumbled, 'Very good.' David remained concerned for the Captain's wellbeing, but said nothing.

The south coast of Puerto Rico was again visible on the northern horizon, enabling the officer-of-the-watch to fix the ship's position. They had been driven some 16 miles to the east during the storm but remained clear of reefs.

By early afternoon the makeshift mizzen sail had been unrigged and the ship's routine was back to normal; the sea-anchor had been cut adrift earlier, as soon as power had become available to the engines. The new bearing was bedding in well and the ship was maintaining a speed of 8 knots. Barring further accidents they should make St Lucia late on the evening of 10 March.

The following day at 1055 local time, *Willesden's* Second Wireless Officer sat huddled over his set, tuning it to Admiralty's 1600 GMT broadcast for merchant shipping, from Bermuda. Precisely on the hour, the wireless burst into life. The operator's pencil raced across the signal pad, recording the message as it came streaming in:

'CT GBMS 7 GBMS 7 GBMS 7 DE VRT VRT VRT BT

From Captain-in-Charge Bermuda

To All British merchant shipping in Area 7

IMMEDIATE   091548z

CD001A

XV7WD WDK9E3 QKL129 …'

followed by further groups of six-figure letters and numbers; then the ending sign, 'BT-AR.'

The Wireless Officer removed his earphones and reached for the safe. He sorted through a number of keycards until he found the one marked CD001A, to match the indicator group on the coded message. The date and time of the message gave him the start point on the keycard. He then quickly began transposing the code into plain language. Ten minutes later the task was complete. He read the message through quickly then tore it off the pad and headed for the Captain's cabin. He knocked and waited for the call to enter. There was no response, so he entered anyway. Captain Griffiths was huddled over his desk, fully dressed, with his head resting on his crossed arms, apparently asleep. The Wireless Officer coughed loudly and Griffiths stirred, rose, and turned towards him before reaching out to take the proffered message. He read:

'AN UNIDENTIFIED U-BOAT OPERATING IN THE CARIBBEAN AREA ENTERED CASTRIES HARBOUR, ST LUCIA, DURING THE NIGHT OF 8 MARCH. THE SUBMARINE SLIPPED THROUGH THE DEFENCE LINES AND AT 2252, TORPEDOED TWO BRITISH SHIPS, THE *LADY NELSON* AND *UMTATA* MOORED AT THE NORTHERN BUNKERING WHARF.

2. BUNKERING FACILITIES AT ST LUCIA ARE CONSEQUENTLY UNAVAILABLE UNTIL FURTHER NOTICE. VESSELS SCHEDULED TO BUNKER AT ST LUCIA ARE TO PROCEED DIRECTLY TO ST THOMAS WHERE ALTERNATIVE ARRANGEMENTS ARE IN PLACE.

3. THE U-BOAT IS LIKELY TO BE STILL IN THE VICINITY AND ALL SHIPPING IN THE AREA SHOULD THEREFORE MAINTAIN THE UTMOST VIGILANCE.

MESSAGE ENDS.'

Captain Griffiths placed the message on his desk with a trembling hand, hit by the realisation that, had it not been for the storm and the engine failure, *Willesden* too might be lying at the bottom of Castries Harbour.

'My compliments to the watch officer,' he said, 'and I would be pleased if he would set course for St Thomas.'

David worked on the chart for several minutes before altering course to the NE. He stepped the distance off with the dividers and calculated a new ETA at Charlotte Amalie Harbour of 2215 that evening. They arrived without further incident, berthed at the bunkering wharf and began taking on coal the following morning, 10 March.

~

There was little opportunity for exercise at sea so David, who was not involved in the bunkering task, took the opportunity to go ashore and explore the town. *Willesden's* Third Officer, Alex Runcie, accompanied him. The day was warm and sunny with a pleasant cooling breeze. The busy streets of Charlotte Amalie were abuzz with the chatter of barter, and full of colour, as the population went about their daily business, oblivious to the war or its effects. The markets were abundant with fresh fruit, fish and vegetables that those in beleaguered wartime Britain might only dream of. Here, a smiling Creole offered the pair fresh mangoes at five BWI cents each and there, another, offering pineapples, coconuts and bananas at equally cheap prices. A steel band in bright, colourful shirts beat out a happy calypso rhythm on home-made, cut-down 44-gallon drums, adding to the carnival atmosphere.

On returning to the ship David was delighted to find that mail from home had arrived on board during his absence. How it had been diverted from St Lucia they were never to discover but whatever the means they were extremely grateful.

There were two letters from Muriel, bright and cheery and full of news about the children. They contained little about the war except to say that, although rationing was very strict, they were managing very well and there was always food on the table, especially for the children. Muriel was still working full-time with her sewing. Donald was doing well at school and two-and-a-half-year-old

Andrew was at home in the care of Muriel's mother. They were planning to take a short holiday in Scotland, staying with David's parents in St Andrews, when the weather improved, probably in June or July.

SS WILLESDEN – CARIBBEAN SEA

Thursday 12 March 1942

Fully bunkered and provisioned, *Willesden* sailed from St Thomas on the morning tide. Once clear of the harbour, course was set to take the ship south of Grenada and out into the South Atlantic.

Concern over the submarine attack on shipping in St Lucia harbour was playing on Captain Griffiths' mind so, while still in the shelter of the Leeward Islands, he decided to exercise the ship's company in 'Abandoning Ship'.

There was something of a holiday atmosphere as the officers and crew donned their life jackets and tumbled into two of the lifeboats. The Captain, Third Officer Runcie and the ship's cook were the only three to remain on board: the Captain to observe the exercise, the Third Officer to conduct flag exercises between the ship and the lifeboats and the cook to prepare the midday meal. The exercise was successfully completed to peals of laughter when the bowman in the No. 2 lifeboat 'accidentally' fell overboard and spent several minutes splashing around in the warm tropical ocean to the accompaniment of much comment and gratuitous advice from his shipmates. However, Captain Griffiths was not amused by the cavalier attitude and made that point very clear to the Third Mate, whom he irrationally saw as the cause of the incident, before departing the navigating bridge for the security of his cabin.

While waiting for the lifeboats to return Runcie decided to check the mechanisms of the two Lewis guns, for which he had responsibility, fitted on either side of the bridge. The subsequent inquiry, headed by the First Mate, was unable to determine exactly what happened next but somehow one of the guns jammed and, while trying to clear the fault, it accidentally discharged. At the time, the gun was pointing downwards and three rounds penetrated the wooden deck and missed Captain Griffiths, now in his cabin directly below, by a matter of inches.

Griffiths was furious and immediately associated the accidental discharge of the gun with his recent rebuke of the Third Officer, whom he now accused of attempted murder. Such was his rage that he threatened to clap the luckless officer in irons for the remainder of the voyage. The whole episode would have been laughable had it not been so serious, and sanity was only restored with the return of the lifeboats and the Third Officer being removed from the scene. From then, Griffiths became even more remote and withdrawn, choosing to remain secluded in his cabin most of the time.

GERMAN RAIDER THOR – SOUTH ATLANTIC

Friday 13 March 1942

It was still early morning and Gumprich sat hunched in the Captain's chair on the starboard side of *Thor's* bridge, reflecting on his ill luck. Three weeks in the Southern Ocean and he had failed to find even a trace of the whaling fleet, despite the constant use of the Arado floatplane and the ship's radar to extend his area of search. On 25 February the wireless office had picked up some short-wave transmissions, indicating whaling activity in the vicinity but, despite an extensive search, nothing was found. Gumprich decided to head north to a scheduled rendezvous with the supply vessel *Regensburg*.

Thor's captain was a practical man but still mildly susceptible to a seaman's superstitions, born of many years' experience at sea, and the significance of the day's date was not lost on him. *Nothing good can come from such a day*, he mused. They were in the vicinity of Cape Town and, lost in thought, Gumprich was brought suddenly back to the present by a report from the lookout, stationed up *Thor's* foremast. 'Officer-of-the-watch – upper foremast lookout – ship's mast bearing green three five, estimated Range 22 thousand metres!'

The ship kept an efficient lookout with two men stationed on each mast. The uppermost lookout on the foremast was positioned in a revolving chair which provided him with an uninterrupted view across the full arc of the horizon. From here, on a clear day, it was possible to see the smoke from coal-burning vessels at distances up to 50 kilometres. Below him, a second lookout was stationed in the crow's nest. The two on the mainmast were stationed in the top.

On the lookout's report, those on the bridge raised their binoculars and swept the horizon in the direction indicated. However, it was several minutes before the black, pencil mast of a rapidly approaching ship was visible from *Thor's* deck. *Where? Where? Yes, there it is. My god, it's a bloody warship!* Gumprich's brain was racing; then to the Officer-of-the-watch, 'Sound off Action Stations!'

It was soon apparent to Gumprich that he was looking at the topmast of a British cruiser. There was nothing showing on *Thor's* radar but this was no surprise because, even in the best conditions, the set was notoriously unreliable. He estimated the range to be 20 thousand metres, and closing rapidly. He daren't alter course or speed for fear of arousing suspicion.

The crew raced to their action stations, feet clattering over steel decks, making ready to clear the screens to bring *Thor's* big guns into action, should the need arise. As the British vessel came hull up Gumprich identified her as a light cruiser, probably of the older 'D' Class. With six 6-inch guns and a top speed of 29 knots the cruiser could remain outside the range of *Thor's* guns and pound her to bits. However, although outgunned and having a lesser speed than the British warship, Gumprich was aware that *Thor* could beat her in battle, given the element of surprise and a little luck. However, his best chance was to bluff.

KMS Thor in the South Atlantic - 1940.

Thor was disguised as a British merchant ship and for Gumprich it was a question of holding his nerve. It was late in the afternoon and the two ships were on converging courses. Gumprich was very much aware that his primary mission was to destroy enemy merchant shipping and not engage more powerful warships, so he would avoid the uneven contest with the cruiser if at all possible.

An aldis light flashed from the cruiser. 'What ship? Where bound?'

Gumprich had been expecting the challenge and had the answer ready, but delayed sending it to give the impression of relaxed casualness, without the efficiency normally associated with a warship.

'This is the British freighter *Levernbank,*' blinked back across the water, 'Out of Cape Town, bound for Liverpool via Freetown.'

Gumprich had picked the ship's name some weeks earlier from Lloyd's Register, and had painted and disguised *Thor* accordingly. He was hopeful that the disguise would pass all but the most critical inspection. He was also banking on the assumption that the British Captain would be reluctant to break radio silence to check his credentials. The two ships were now only 8000 metres apart, still too far for Gumprich to be sure of a hit with his first salvos. 7000 metres, 6500; still closing. Each minute seemed like an eternity. Just as Gumprich was about to take the chance and open fire there was a puff of black smoke from the cruiser's after funnel indicating a sudden demand for increased power from her six Admiralty-pattern boilers. The British ship heeled gracefully to port as her helm was put hard over and she turned away under increased speed, aldis light blinking a final message: 'God speed,' from the cruiser, to which Gumprich cheekily replied, 'Good hunting,' hoping that his good wishes would not be self-fulfilling.

SS WILLESDEN – SOUTH ATLANTIC

Tuesday 24 March 1942

'The Meridian passage of the sun, or Merpass as it is commonly called, is navigationally, the most significant astronomical event of the day.' It was almost midday, and David, with the ship's four apprentices, was on *Willesden's* navigating bridge to observe the ship's noon position. As well as his other duties, David had responsibility for instructing the young officers in navigation. He went on, 'Merpass is the moment in time when the apparent sun crosses our meridian of longitude. At that moment, it's at its maximum altitude and, in our situation, bears due north. The importance of this is that the position line obtained from measuring the sun's altitude at this moment enables us to directly calculate the ship's latitude. From that, we can determine the ship's noon position, then calculate the distance run over the previous twenty-four hours.'

David was an excellent teacher and mathematician and took great pleasure in passing his knowledge on to his eager young students. He looked forward to these daily sessions and took pride in observing his pupils' rapid progress.

Since passing through the inter-tropical convergence zone several days earlier, the weather had improved and sea was calm. They were near the equator in the vicinity of St Paul's Rocks, and well south of the area where U-boats might expect to be operating. The previous day, the wireless office had picked up a partial message on the international distress frequency from a Greek freighter but the signal strength was poor and the message was abruptly terminated before a bearing on the transmission could be obtained.

Captain Griffiths now spent most of the time in his cabin. Since the incident with the Lewis gun he had chosen to eat alone and was seldom seen. However, life on board was settled and largely routine with little to disrupt the smooth running of the ship. Thoughts were turning towards Cape Town, and the possibility of spending some time relaxing ashore.

Meanwhile, David continued with the lesson.

GERMAN RAIDER THOR – SOUTH ATLANTIC

Saturday 28 March 1942

At last, Captain Gumprich had reason to feel satisfied. *Thor* was some 600 miles SW of St Helena and the ship's motor launch had just returned from the abandoned British tramp SS *Wellpark,* where *Thor's* engineers had placed demolition charges to scuttle the ship. There was a satisfying *crump* as the charges detonated, breaking the back of the British vessel and sending her quickly to the bottom. *Wellpark's* crew was recovered from the ship's lifeboats before *Thor* resumed her passage northwards in search of further victims.

Gumprich reflected on his change of fortune. On the 23rd they had their first success since leaving Germany when they intercepted and sank the 3942 ton Greek steamer *Pagasitikos*. She had been stopped by gunfire then, after the crew had abandoned ship, quickly dispatched with a single torpedo. On the 24th they had rendezvoused with the supply ship *Regensburg* and were able to transfer prisoners from the *Pagasitikos,* as well as replenish stocks of stores, fuel and ammunition. On 26 March, shortly before noon, they sighted the masts of another vessel and Gumprich altered course to give chase, but *Thor* had insufficient speed to overhaul the ship, and now on the 28th, there was this latest successful action against the *Wellpark*. Fresh food was again plentiful, morale was high and prospects for the immediate future were good.

Four days passed. The weather remained fine but the ocean suddenly seemed empty of Allied shipping. Then, on 1 April, they again struck lucky. *Thor's* Arado was launched at daybreak, as was the practice when the weather was suitable, and was carrying out a box search some 100 miles to the east of *Thor's* position. The aircraft carried a crew of two: *Leutnant* Meyer-Ahrens the pilot, whose primary task was to fly the plane and operate the two fixed 7.9-mm machine guns, and an observer, who was responsible for navigation, operation of the winch and bomb aimer, as well as being an additional lookout.

Just after 0800 the observer reported smoke on the eastern horizon and Meyer-Ahrens turned the Arado to investigate. His orders were to close any potential target sufficiently to identify the ship and calculate its course and speed, while remaining undetected. This they were able to do. By 0845 the Arado had returned to the *Thor* and was hoisted on board. Meyer-Ahrens had not used the aircraft's radio to report the contact for fear of alerting the target. He proceeded immediately to the bridge to report to the Captain.

KMS Thor 1939.

'*Herr Kapitän,*' he said, saluting smartly, 'we have located a probable Allied merchant ship bearing 055 degrees, 90 miles from our present position,' he reported. 'She looks to be about four to five thousand tons and on a course roughly south-east, making about eight to ten knots. I was careful to remain at a safe distance and I'm sure we weren't spotted,' he concluded.

'Excellent,' Gumprich replied. He reached for the plotting board and grease pencil and began drawing the velocity triangle. He plotted the known factors: target bearing and range from his present position, and target course and speed, then he calculated the course *Thor* would need to steer and elapsed time taken to intercept the target at *Thor's* maximum speed of 18 knots. He worked quietly for perhaps ninety seconds then turned to the Watch Officer.

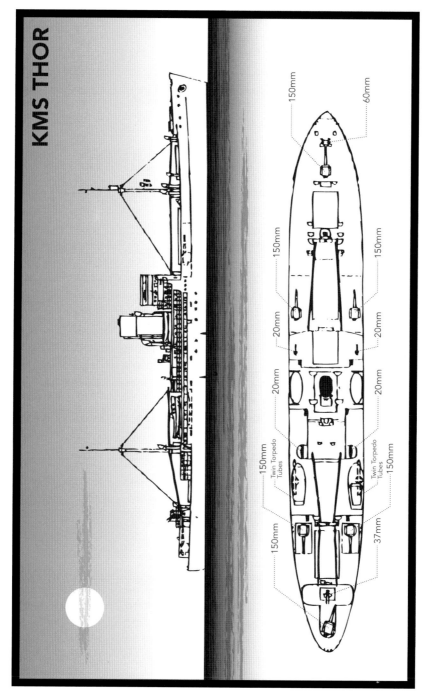

KMS Thor 1940.

'Bring the ship to 115 degrees and increase speed to 18 knots,' he ordered. 'That should bring us within gun range between 4 and 5 this afternoon.' Then to Meyer-Ahrens, 'Well done; but I want you to fly another sortie at midday to get an update on the target's position.'

'Very good, *Herr Kapitän*,' he responded, saluting again before turning away to attend to the task of refuelling, and checking the Arado for the coming mission.

SS WILLESDEN – SOUTH ATLANTIC

1635 hours, Wednesday 1 April 1942

Alex Runcie, who had the watch, expressed neither surprise nor concern when the lookout reported sighting the topmasts of another vessel, 80 degrees on the starboard bow. He rested his elbows on the bridge rail to steady his binoculars and made a slight adjustment to bring the vessel into focus. From the alignment of the masts he estimated the contact's course to be just south of east, which meant she would probably pass quite close. He went to the compass repeater on *Willesden's* starboard bridge wing and sighted through the azimuth ring to observe the stranger's bearing. It was 242 degrees. He checked again at 1645. The bearing was still 242 degrees, indicating that the oncoming ship was on a collision course or, at best, would pass very close. By now the funnel, samson posts and upper-works of the stranger were clearly visible and Runcie estimated the range to be about ten miles. He decided to call the Captain: 'Captain, sir, Officer-of-the-watch, I have an unidentified merchant ship 80 degrees on our starboard bow, range roughly 10 miles, closing,' he reported. 'If we both hold our present courses she will pass very close.'

'Very good,' Griffiths grunted, ungraciously, 'I'll come up.'

The Third Officer was still studying the oncoming ship through his binoculars as Captain Griffiths arrived on the bridge.

'That's odd,' Runcie said, 'she appears to be altering course away from us, yet she has the right-of-way.'

'I wonder what would cause her to do that,' muttered Griffiths, also studying the strange vessel through his binoculars, now hull up, at a range of about 8 miles.

David was off duty, relaxing in the officers' saloon, chatting to the First Mate over a cup of tea. Suddenly, the saloon windows, just a few feet from where the pair was seated, exploded inwards, showering them both with broken glass. Splinters of mahogany flew in all directions as the mess table disintegrated before their eyes. Seconds later there was a deafening roar as the attacking Arado, 7.9-mm cannons blazing, passed directly over the ship at a height of about 50 feet.

'Bloody hell! What was that?' David yelled as he hit the deck, performed a commando roll to the left, then dived for the screen door leading to the main deck, scalding tea, biscuits and crockery scattering everywhere. The pair headed for the bridge, two decks above. Eighteen seconds and two accommodation ladders later they arrived in a rush, taking in the scene in disbelief.

The helmsman was down in a pool of blood, clutching his stomach, moaning but still alive. There seemed to be no other immediate casualties but there was broken glass and splintered wood everywhere. Captain Griffiths stood gripping the rail, apparently unharmed, staring after the German aircraft, his face expressionless, saying nothing, doing nothing.

'We need to close up at action stations and man the guns!' the Mate yelled at Griffiths, having quickly assessed the situation. There was no response. He grabbed the Captain by the elbow and shook violently, 'Captain,' he yelled, 'we must take action – now!'

Griffiths slowly turned his head and focused his eyes in momentary recognition, 'Ah, Number One. Nasty business. Do whatever you think necessary.' Then the Captain turned away, sank to his knees, bowed his head and began reciting the Lord's Prayer. 'Our Father, which art in heaven, hallowed be thy name…'

The Mate stared in disbelief, but hesitated only a moment before reacting. He rattled out a stream of orders, firstly to the Third Mate: 'Alex! Get the lookout to take the helm, come hard a' port and put that bastard directly astern. Ring down "full ahead" then call the engine room and tell them we are under attack and I want every ounce of speed they can provide.'

The Arado was about three miles distant, turning for another run.

'Sound off Action Stations! and, David, man the Lewis gun and see if you can keep that bloody plane away 'til the gun crews close up, then get down to the 4-inch and stand by to engage that bloody Jerry ship as soon as she's in range,' indicating urgently towards the *Thor*, German ensign now flying and clearly visible, and headed directly towards them at full speed.

'Wilson,' he rapped at David Wilson, the apprentice on watch, 'make a note of our position and get it down to the wireless office quick as you can. Tell *Sparks* we're under attack from a German merchant raider and to get our position out with a QQQ message. Tell him to keep repeating it as long as he is able to transmit. Then get a couple of hands up here to take the helmsman down to the sickbay.' Runcie pressed the klaxon twice then broadcast on the ship's tannoy system. 'Hands to action stations. Hands to action stations, Guns crews close up. Close all watertight doors and hatches. The ship is under attack by an enemy aircraft and an armed merchant raider!'

Meanwhile, three quick strides took David to the port-side Lewis gun. He tore off the light canvas cover in a single motion, checked that the magazine was securely in place, cocked the weapon, then swivelled the gun on its spigot, searching for the approaching aircraft. *Willesden* was turning to port under full helm so it took David a moment or two to locate the Arado. When he did, the aircraft was about 3000 yards away, coming in straight and level, roughly fifty feet above the sea; grappling hook trailing behind and below. It was the pilot's intention to fly over the ship, between the masts, and drag away the main wireless aerial, preventing any radio transmissions. David was determined to prevent that. He steadied the gun, released the safety catch and concentrated on the oncoming aircraft that now filled the black, metal, spider-web sight. He squeezed the trigger. David was prepared for the sudden recoil and held the gun firmly, crouching lower and twisting to keep the approaching aircraft in his sights. He was aware of orange flashes from the Arado's machine guns and the impact of bullets striking the deck around him but he shut them from his mind. Every fifth round in the Lewis gun's magazine was a tracer and David could see the bullets clearly, streaming upwards towards the target. He adjusted his aim as

Arado Floatplane.

the Arado, now almost overhead, attempted to turn away at the last moment, put off by the gunfire and confused by the turning ship. David saw several rounds hit the aircraft but still it came on, its flight apparently unaffected. Just before it passed over *Willesden's* stern to bank away and prepare for another attack, David and the others on the bridge saw two black objects detach from the aircraft's wings and arc gracefully into the sea, less than fifty feet from the ship's side. The explosion, as the two 150-kilogram bombs detonated, seemed to lift *Willesden* bodily. Almost simultaneously, there were two resounding hammer blows on the hull as the shockwaves hit. Twin columns of water erupted high into the air, drenching those on the bridge, but doing little damage.

David ceased firing as the Arado opened the range to the west and only then did he look around to take stock. It was less than four minutes since the first attack.

The grim-faced figures of the Royal Naval Reserve, Able Seaman gunner whose emergency station was on the port Lewis gun, and his oppo on the starboard gun, emerged from behind a deck-locker where they had been taking temporary cover. 'Quickly!' David yelled, 'take over here.'

Without waiting for a reply David left the Lewis gun and headed aft, leaping down the ladders between the bridge and the after well-deck. Less than thirty seconds later, he was on *Willesden's* poop deck where he was greeted by the 4-inch Gun Captain, a Reserve Sergeant, Royal Marines, carried specifically for this purpose.

'4-inch closed up, cleared away and ready for action!' he reported.

'Very good,' David responded formally, quickly casting his eye over the gun's crew. Six of them were required to load and fire the gun.

David rapped out his orders to the Gun Captain: '4-inch, surface target, bearing right astern, estimated range, eleven thousand yards!'

The aimer and layer adjusted the gun's bearing and elevation and, when each could clearly see the target in their respective sights, they began tracking it, reporting back to the Gun Captain:

'Aimer – target!'

'Layer – target!' and the Gun Captain, in turn, reported back to David, '4-inch, target!'

David reported to the bridge that they were ready to engage, but the *Thor* was still outside *Willesden's* maximum effective range, so there was little they could

Kapitan zur See Gunther Gumprich, Commanding Officer of THOR - 1942.

do but wait. The German's aldis light was flashing, demanding that they stop transmitting and abandon ship. David correctly assumed that those on *Willesden's* bridge would read the message and take whatever action was appropriate – it was not David's responsibility or immediate concern.

Meanwhile the Arado was coming in for another run, machine guns blazing as before. *Willesden's* Lewis guns returned the fire but this time the pilot of the Arado was more determined and held his course, passing directly over the ship's funnel. The grappling hook snagged the main radio aerial, tearing it away.

In the Wireless Office *Sparks* took off his headset and slammed it on the desk. He had tried to transmit on several frequencies including the International Distress Frequency at 500 kcs, but each attempt was met by massive interference. He was being jammed by a very powerful transmitter that was very close – it could only be coming from the *Thor*. And now the main aerials were gone. The Radio Officer had grave doubt that any of his transmissions had got through.

David was studying *Thor* through his binoculars, judging distance in his mind. At roughly 10,000 yards there was a flash and a puff of smoke from the enemy vessel. David clicked the stopwatch in his right hand, counting off the seconds

– ten, eleven, twelve – a column of water erupted roughly 200 yards astern and 100 yards to port. A pause of roughly 10 seconds while *Thor's* gunners adjusted the range and bearing, then another flash, and another puff of smoke. This time the shell was 300 yards over, but on line. David heard the whine and involuntarily ducked as the shell screamed harmlessly overhead. The third shell fell almost alongside, throwing a column of spray over *Willesden's* forward well-deck. That was good shooting. The Arado was acting as a spotting aircraft, circling just beyond range of the Lewis guns, passing range and bearing corrections to *Thor's* gunners.

Thor fired again. This time there were three simultaneous flashes from her big guns. Having found the range they began pounding *Willesden* with broadsides; she could either be sunk or surrender. Still *Thor* was out of range of *Willesden's* gun. An incoming shell hit the officer's accommodation just aft of the funnel. David could wait no longer. He called the bridge, 'Bridge – 4-inch – permission to engage?'

There was a short pause while the communications sailor on the bridge conferred with the First Mate, then, '4-inch – From the Mate – Engage!' then he added, 'He said, just do your best and have a go at the bugger.'

David gave the order: '4-inch – Shoot!'

Then from the Gun Captain: 'Fire!'

The loading number reached across and pressed the red firing push, completing the firing circuit. Despite the small rubber plugs the gun's crew had inserted in their ears to prevent damage, the sound of the discharge at such close quarters was physically painful. The gun recoiled and the air was filled with the acrid smell of cordite. David counted off the seconds then raised his binoculars to observe the fall-of-shot. Damn! They were still some 400 yards short but it was much as he had expected. There was little else they could do but keep firing in the hope that *Thor* would stray a little closer to give them a chance of a lucky hit.

Willesden's single antiquated gun was no match for *Thor's* four-gun 15-cm broadsides. Outranged by at least 2000 yards it was simply a matter of time. The raider's shells were now regularly ripping into the ship, creating devastation. The after well-deck erupted into an inferno, following a hit on the diesel and aviation spirit, and another shell penetrated the hull at No. 2 Hold, starting a further fire in the forward part of the ship. The repair parties were overwhelmed.

At last, the order came down from the bridge to strike the ship's colours, cease firing and abandon ship. They had fired twenty-eight rounds without achieving a single hit. David ordered the gun's crew to make their way forward to the ship's lifeboats, now being lowered; however, with the well-deck fully ablaze this was no easy task. Grateful for his anti-flash gloves and headgear, David picked his way through the inferno, coughing and gasping in the thick, black, choking smoke.

The raider was still keeping up a steady rate of fire when, just as David reached the midships accommodation section, a shell hit *Willesden's* bridge, three decks above him. The effect was devastating. If the Captain and Mate were both dead, as they surely must be, David reasoned, he would be the senior surviving officer. He reached the bridge with difficulty and was confronted by devastation. There were two bodies; one the Cox'n and the other, a young sailor. Of the Captain and Mate there was no sign. David noted that the engine room telegraph register indicated 'Stop'. He called on the voice pipe but there was no response so he assumed the machinery spaces had already been evacuated. The ship was stopped and ablaze, down by the head and listing heavily to port: she could go down at any moment. There was nothing more David could do but to get the hell out as quickly as he could. The raider was still circling at about 6000 yards, keeping up a steady rate of fire.

Willesden had four lifeboats, any two of which, in accordance with the Board of Trade Regulations, were capable of accommodating the whole crew. By the time David reached the boat-deck the starboard lifeboats had been launched and were pulling away, to put as much distance as possible between them and the sinking ship. One of the port lifeboats was so badly damaged as to be useless, and the other was in the water, directly below the davits, but still attached to the ship by its falls. David encountered no one on his way down from the bridge and, after a quick look round, decided he must be the only person on board and still alive. He looked down at the lifeboat and recognised Alex Runcie in the stern-sheets, grasping the tiller. He yelled to attract his attention. 'Come on!' was the response from the boat, 'We'll wait for you!'

David reached out and, with both hands, firmly grasped one of the four manila lifelines hanging from the wire davit span. He launched himself into space and swung for a moment, then began to shimmy, hand over hand, down to the waiting boat.

Suddenly; a blinding flash. A momentary sensation of spinning, falling, total detachment, no pain, blackness, then nothing.

It was a little before sunset on 1 April 1942.

PART II
PRISONER OF THE GERMANS

1 April 1942–11 July 1942

GERMAN RAIDER THOR – SOUTH ATLANTIC

Thursday 2 April 1942

David's mind was confused as he struggled to regain consciousness, his body racked with pain. His chest and left shoulder were the worst. He tried to move his right arm to investigate but that was too painful. He groaned and stopped trying, exhausted even by the smallest attempted movement. He could feel by the motion and the slight vibration that he was still at sea but the smell was wrong, very clinical and antiseptic. Slowly, it came back: the attacking aircraft and the one-sided gun battle, the blazing ship, the lifeboat – then the explosion, and nothing.

Dr Fritz Lehmann, *Thor's* Senior Medical Officer, noticed the movement, 'Ah! So you're back with us?' The voice was foreign with a thick, clipped, Prussian accent, but the English was very good. David opened his eyes with difficulty. He was in a metal cot, gimballed to counter the motion of the ship. A white-coated figure was leaning over him. David tried to speak but the words came out as an incoherent croak.

'Here; I'll give you something to help the pain.' Lehmann leant over and injected 20 ml of morphine into David's right arm. Unconsciousness, bringing blessed relief, returned quickly.

David recalled very little of the next few days. Morphine controlled the pain but fuzzied his brain. *Thor's* medical staff were kind and competent. He received the very best medical attention. He learnt over time, from Dr Lehmann, and from members of *Willesden's* crew who were allowed to visit, that he had been brought on board the raider more dead than alive. The last shell fired by *Thor* had exploded close by, the resulting shrapnel causing severe lacerations to his chest and left arm. Other pieces of debris from the explosion were embedded in his legs and torso. He had fallen roughly 5 metres into the lifeboat adding broken ribs, lesions to his chest and legs and torn ligaments to an already horrific list of injuries. Dr Lehmann had operated as soon as he had been brought on board. He was able to save David's left arm – just.

On the second day he was visited by fellow prisoner Captain Griffiths, who told David that five members of *Willesden's* crew of forty-seven were dead. Three had gone down with the ship and two had been buried at sea from the *Thor* that morning, with full military honours. He also learnt that the raider had picked up the survivors from *Willesden's* lifeboats before dispatching the burning vessel with a single torpedo, fired at a range of about 1000 yards.

No mention was made of Captain Griffiths's behaviour on the bridge during the action and David was never to raise the matter.[3]

At one point, probably on the second or third day, David was awakened by the sound of *Thor's* heavy guns. This was accompanied by a change to the sound of the main engines and to the ship's motion. He suspected that another Allied merchant ship was under attack and he learned later that, on 3 April, *Thor* had intercepted and shelled the Norwegian freighter *Aust* of 5630 tons, out of New York and bound for Bombay with war supplies. Coincidentally, *Aust* had also bunkered at St Thomas and had shared adjacent berths with *Willesden* on 11 March.

The sinking of the *Aust* followed the pattern Gumprich had now set. The searching Arado found the ship and carried away her wireless aerials with its trailing hook before the raider engaged with her heavy guns. *Aust's* crew were ordered into the lifeboats while the *Thor* closed in to deliver the coup de grâce, on this occasion by the placement of demolition charges. Like *Willesden*, the *Aust* had attempted to return fire with her 4-inch deck gun but, also like *Willesden*, the encounter had been one-sided and the outcome predictable.

The Commanding Officer of the *Aust*, Captain Christoffer Tuften, and his complete crew of forty officers and men, remarkably all alive and accounted for, were taken prisoner aboard the *Thor*.

Having dispatched four ships in a period of ten days Gumprich was satisfied with his work but, as a direct result of his successes and by lingering so long in the same area, he was concerned that the wrath of the Royal Navy would soon descend upon him. The *Pagasitikos* and *Wellpark* were both overdue at their next ports-of-call, alerting the British to the raider's presence. Despite the temptation to remain in an area where he was having such success, Gumprich decided it was time to move on.

DURAL - NEW SOUTH WALES

Monday 6 April 1942

Howard Gunstone, leather schoolbag dangling precariously from his left shoulder, picked up a small stone from the dirt road just up from the corner of Galston

---

3   Captain Griffiths served out the war at Kawasaki Camp 1B near Tokyo, along with most other survivors from the Willesden. He was amongst the prisoners repatriated from Japan to Manila on HMS Speaker on 4 September 1945. His ultimate fate is unknown.

Road, where the school bus had dropped him, and threw it absent-mindedly at the milk churn, mounted horizontally on a stout fencepost, that also served as the mail box for 'Aunty' Madge's property, 25 miles or so north-west of Sydney. Madge Nichols was not related but was a friend of his mother's, from earlier days in Singapore. She had immigrated to Australia with her husband, Bill, some twelve months before the war and settled on the small property. They had been delighted to take in Helen and Howard when they had arrived as refugees from Singapore six weeks earlier. They had no children of their own and went out of their way to make it clear that Helen and Howard were welcome to stay as long as was necessary. They had not had any news of Helen's husband, John, since fleeing Singapore in January. Helen was therefore not keen to make any decisions about their future until she knew that he was safe. Howard had started at the Dural Public School at the beginning of March and had settled in well, despite some initial, good-natured ribbing over his Pommie accent.

Howard had no particular motive for throwing the stone except that it was what six-year-old boys do. It hit the milk churn with a very satisfactory *ding* and he chortled with delight as a small flock of galahs, distinctive in their grey and pink plumage, rose squawking from the roadside where they had been feeding, and flew off.

The house was roughly 200 yards from the road, through an avenue of orange trees, laden with fruit almost ready for harvest. As Howard turned into the driveway there was a cheerful, if somewhat breathless, 'Hold on there a minute!' and he turned to see the local telegram delivery boy, on his antiquated Post Office bicycle, freckle-faced and cap askew, pedalling frantically towards him from the direction of the village. He pulled up beside Howard with a sideways skid, meant to impress, and rummaged importantly in the leather pouch containing telegrams for delivery.

'Be a good lad and take this up to the house,' he said, as he handed over the small buff envelope addressed to Mrs H. Guy.

Howard took the telegram and started off towards the house, kicking a couple of stones on the way. He was greeted by his mother who was sitting on the veranda drinking tea with Aunty Madge. 'How was school today?'

'Not bad,' Howard responded, 'and the telegram boy said to give you this.' He handed over the envelope, which Helen tore open eagerly, hands trembling. She read quickly then grabbed Howard under the armpits with both hands and swung him off his feet and around in a circle. 'Daddy's safe!' she burst out, tears of joy running down her cheeks.

After bringing Howard back to earth she read the cable again, just to be sure.

'ARRIVED TRINCOMALEE SAFELY 2 APRIL AFTER EVENTFUL ESCAPE AND VOYAGE FROM SINGAPORE STOP HAVE BEEN POSTED TO NAVAL DOCKYARD BOMBAY AND EXPECT TO REMAIN THERE FOR DURATION OF WAR STOP SUGGEST YOU BOTH REMAIN WITH MADGE UNTIL I CAN JOIN YOU AT WAR'S END STOP LETTER FOLLOWS STOP BEST LOVE JOHN'

'Aunty Madge. Why is Mummy crying?' asked Howard.

'I expect it is because she's very happy,' said Madge.

'That's good,' Howard responded, without really understanding. 'Can I go and play now?'

'Of course you can,' Madge said, 'but mind you get changed out of those school clothes first.'

GERMAN RAIDER THOR - SOUTH ATLANTIC

Friday 10 April 1942

It was ten days since the loss of the *Willesden* and David was slowly recovering from his wounds. The heat below decks was oppressive, despite the ventilation provided in *Thor's* sickbay. However, after a week confined to bed he had been able to hobble out onto the upper deck with the aid of a sick-berth attendant and a cane, to spend time in the fresh air in a deck-chair beneath a small canvas awning. The danger of gangrene and blood poisoning was past and full recovery, except for a permanent stiffness in his left arm, was now simply a matter of time. The food and medical attention he received were both excellent and of a standard that David would have expected had *Thor* been a British ship.

Due to the nature and severity of his injuries, David remained accommodated in the ship's sickbay. What he learned of the ship and its operations was largely picked up through casual conversation with the medical staff, from the eight or so other injured prisoners who shared the sickbay with him and through regular visits by *Willesden's* First Mate and other members of the crew. In general, the other prisoners were also well fed and cared for, but their accommodation was a little more austere.

There were now 120 prisoners on board the raider. They were crowded together in uncomfortable conditions on the tween-deck, roughly amidships and a little below the waterline.

Thor's tween-deck was divided into three compartments by wooden bulkheads, each 6 metres by 8 metres. The ventilation was poor and the heat oppressive. Each prisoner was issued with a hammock for sleeping but, due to the lack of space, these were taken down and stowed away during the day. They were also each provided with a tin cup and bowl, eating utensils, toothbrush and a piece of saltwater soap. Each compartment had a single toilet but only two of the three had shower facilities. Because they were below the waterline, flushing the toilets was difficult and, more often than not, they became blocked and foul-smelling and presented a health hazard. A single hatchway in the centre compartment provided the only access to the prisoner's accommodation from the upper-deck. It had a steel hatch cover that was always closed and locked when the prisoners were below decks. They were allowed on deck for fresh air and exercise twice a day, one hour in the forenoon and another in the late afternoon. At all other times, and when *Thor* was in action, they were securely locked below.

The food was generally wholesome, well-cooked and adequate. Breakfast comprised black bread with artificial jam or honey and *ersatzkaffe*, an unpleasant-tasting coffee substitute. Lunch was generally a stew of potatoes, with peas or beans, and a little meat. In the evenings it was black bread again, with lard and perhaps a tin of sardines to share amongst five or six men and, of course, more *ersatzkaffe*.

David estimated the crew to be in the region of three to four hundred, mostly young men in their twenties. They were always polite and treated the prisoners properly and with dignity. Gumprich seemed to be a good captain, popular and well respected by his men. He certainly did not give the impression of being a Nazi and treated the prisoners more as fellow mariners who had fallen on hard times, rather than as hated enemies.

A little after midday on 10 April David was enjoying the fresh air on deck. The sky was overcast and the visibility poor but the weather was still warm enough, despite the fact that, for the last ten days, *Thor* had been making her way steadily to the south and east and was entering more temperate latitudes. There was a fresh breeze from the west, about Force 5, producing moderate waves. Although *Thor's* motion was not unpleasant, the prevailing conditions were well beyond the operating envelope for the Arado.

David was lost in thought when one of the sick-berth attendants hurried up to him. 'I'm sorry sir. I must take you below right away' and, without further explanation, helped David to his feet and assisted him back to the sickbay. As was normal when action was in prospect, an armed sentry materialised and positioned himself prominently at the sick-bay door, although David and his fellow patients hardly posed a serious threat.

Some thirty minutes earlier, in the small compartment adjacent to *Thor's* wireless office that also served as the ship's radar office, Electrician's Mate Koudelka, the radar operator on duty, was looking forward to the completion of his watch, when a small spike appeared on his 'A' scan display, barely visible against the background of the set's ground-wave clutter. Koudelka leaned forward in his seat and readjusted the set's tuning, then wound out the range strobe to align with the returning echo. He read the range against the scale: *19,000 metres and bearing roughly due south*, he noted, although the bearing accuracy of the set was notoriously unreliable. After several minutes the echo was much firmer and there was no doubt there was another ship out there. He called through to the officer-of-the-watch: 'Bridge – radar office! New contact, range nineteen thousand metres, bearing roughly south, classified surface ship.'

The watch officer moved quickly to the starboard rail and trained his binoculars in the direction indicated – nothing – but he doubted he would pick up another ship in these conditions at anything over twelve or thirteen thousand metres. He called the captain and Gumprich was quickly on the bridge. *Thor's* radar was incapable of determining the size, shape or identity of the contact – it could conceivably be a British warship – so without the Arado to provide identification, Gumprich decided on a more cautious plan than he would otherwise have adopted. He would track the target by radar until nightfall, remaining just outside visual range, then close in when darkness fell and attack without warning.

There was no moon and by 1940 it was almost dark. *Thor* had closed to 2500 metres with Gumprich manoeuvring the ship to keep her between the unidentified vessel and the setting sun. The target was a dark shadow against the rapidly fading light and so far had not been alerted to the raider's presence. They had tracked the ship on radar all afternoon and determined that its course was almost due west, proceeding at a steady speed of roughly 9 knots. This virtually ruled out any chance of it being a warship. Gumprich decided on a torpedo attack and at 1946 launched a single weapon at a range of 2400 metres – a sitting duck! Inexplicably the torpedo missed or, more likely, passed under the ship and failed to detonate. Gumprich cursed his luck and ordered his 15-cm guns into action.

As scheduled, *Kirkpool* had arrived in Cape Town on 17 March to take on fresh provisions and bunker coal, before continuing on to Lourenco Marques in Mozambique. However, while in Cape Town, new orders were received from the ship's agents, re-routing her to Durban, on South Africa's East Coast, to load coal for Montevideo, in South America. The passage to Durban, where she arrived on 28 March, was uneventful. On 31 March, loading complete, *Kirkpool* slipped her moorings and retraced her course, heading back, south of Cape Town, before heading westward for Montevideo.

By 10 April the ship was well out into the South Atlantic, in the vicinity of the Tristan da Cunha Islands, steaming westward at a steady 9 knots. The sea was relatively calm but with a long ocean swell and the weather pleasantly warm. Alfie and his mates had settled in to a regular watchkeeping routine and generally spent their off watch time on the focsle listening to tunes on the portable gramophone that Alfie had bought for half-a-crown (25 cents) in the second-hand shop in North Shields on his last shore leave.

On this day, Alfie was helmsman for the last dog-watch (1800 to 2000 hours). It was 1955 and he was looking forward to the arrival of his relief. The sun had set an hour earlier and darkness had come quickly. There was no moon and the sky was overcast. Alfie, legs slightly apart and braced against the gentle motion of the ship, moved the wheel easily to port and starboard, making minor adjustments to maintain the ordered course. The First Officer, Olaf Olsen, who had the watch, was a black outline in front of and slightly to Alfie's left. The only sounds were the creaking of the telemotor steering gear and the steady ticking of the bridge clock.

At 1958 the peaceful scene erupted into chaos and devastation. Without warning, there was a blinding flash followed by a violent shudder as the first of *Thor's* 15-cm shells thumped into the defenceless merchantman.

'What the bloody hell was that?' screamed the Mate, then, 'Sound the alarm for action stations!'

The raider pumped shell after shell into the defenceless vessel. Captain Kennington arrived on the bridge and tried to take in the situation. The ship was being pounded to bits – there was nothing that could be done. 'Stop main engine, abandon ship, everyman for himself!' he yelled.

As ordered, Alfie abandoned the wheel and headed for the boat deck. Now unchecked, the ship careered wildly to port and was in danger of colliding with the raider, but somehow this was averted. The situation on the boat deck was no better than on the bridge. The starboard lifeboat was hanging vertically in its davit, shattered and totally useless. At the port lifeboat, something was also radically wrong. The slip hook was jammed and the after falls were not manned. Men were frantically working to free the boat but without success. A burst steam pipe nearby added to the confusion, the noise of escaping steam making any form of communication almost impossible.

A blazing searchlight from the raider suddenly flooded the scene with unearthly light but still the shelling continued.

'Why don't you stop?' screamed Alfie into the darkness. 'Can't you see we're finished?'

Somewhere in the dark Alfie heard the voice of his mate, Ginger Robson;

'Look out; here comes the next lot!' as yet another salvo of shells thundered into the ship. The dead and dying were everywhere. Alfie felt so sick he wished the next shell would be a direct hit and finish him off altogether. Still the bombardment continued. Somehow a raft was launched and Alfie glimpsed Ginger, poised by the rail, ready to jump. 'Are you coming Roondie?' Ginger yelled above the noise, but not waiting for an answer before launching himself into space to the mercy of the elements.

Alfie couldn't swim and the thought of hurling himself into the blackness was terrifying. He watched the men diving overboard to gain the relative safety of the small raft. He had the option of drowning or facing the holocaust of the raider's shellfire.

Kirkpool was soon a battered burning wreck, listing heavily to port, and well down by the head. It was only a matter of time before she succumbed to the raider's relentless pounding.

Alfie was confused, his mind racing. Some driving instinct for survival told him he must get forward to get his lifejacket from his room in the focsle head. If he succeeded, perhaps there was still hope but it meant passing through the inferno raging in the ship's superstructure. The forward well-deck was awash. Smoke and steam filled the air; the noise and heat were terrifying. The fire had not yet reached the port alleyway so, with head down, Alfie made a mad dash forward. To his surprise he came across a group of men, probably about fifteen of them, trying frantically to launch the starboard raft, which was still intact. However, luck was not on their side. The men managed to get the raft over the side but, with the forward momentum of the ship, it was quickly washed astern to the dismay and anguish of those watching. In the chaos and confusion, Alfie was unable to fully recall the events that followed. His body was racked with pain but the instinct for survival drove him on.

The black seas were washing over *Kirkpool's* decks. The ship was clearly sinking and time was running out. Somehow Alfie made it to the sailors' quarters in the focsle head. He was knee-deep in swirling water. Bunks, shelves and personal belongings lay scattered in every direction. Miraculously, his life jacket was in its proper stowage where he had last left it, and he hastily put it over his head but in his haste he neglected to secure the tapes. He searched frantically for his wallet and seaman's knife without success. They were gone forever.

Back on the focsle, those crew members still on board were desperately trying to construct a raft from hatch beams and other material that lay at hand. Alfie joined them. He recognised the Second Engineer lying on the deck, washing backward and forward in the scuppers as the sea sloshed with the movement of the ship, his right side torn open with a terrible gaping shrapnel wound. His eyes flickered and he looked up at the men nearby. 'Put me away son,' he pleaded to the nearest but, of course, no one had it in them to do any such thing. They tried to make him comfortable; there was little else they could do.

The next minutes were a total blur. While some continued with the raft, others fetched a first aid kit and extra clothing that was quickly shared around. Alfie produced a container of water that was eagerly passed from hand to hand, each taking a gulp before passing it on. The Second Engineer died. Someone produced a torch and tried flashing the raider to tell them that there were still men alive on the *Kirkpool*, but there was no response. At least the shelling had stopped but exploding ammunition from *Kirkpool's* own gun added to the danger, confusion and noise. Lights flickered across the water but whether they were from the raider or survivors in the ocean, it was impossible to tell.

A large wave washed over the ship, taking with it their makeshift raft, with several men desperately clinging to it. Without conscious thought Alfie grabbed at the raft and held on. The next wave swept it away and he looked up to see the towering bulk of the doomed *Kirkpool* slipping away into the blackness. Alfie's next conscious memory was of cold, darkness, choking black oil and men in the ocean, some waving, some calling out and others silent and motionless. *Kirkpool's* Chief Engineer was amongst them. He took charge and tried to maintain morale by keeping the men together and calling encouragement. Time passed. There was no sign of the raider and the coldness of the water began to take its toll. Several of the men were forced to let go of the raft. They slipped away into the darkness, never to be seen again.

Alfie's body was numb below the waist. He could no longer raise his arms or kick his legs. The struggle was too much. He was about to let go when a large black mass materialised in the darkness, less than 100 metres away. He could feel the pulse of powerful engines through the water as the blacked-out raider loomed over them. The area was suddenly lit by dazzling light as the raider switched on its powerful searchlights. Someone called out in alarm, 'Look out; she's going to machine gun us!' but no such thing occurred.

Rope scrambling nets and ladders were hung over the raider's sides and Alfie, together with others in the water, splashed the last few yards and used their remaining strength to clamber to the ship's deck where they were met by willing hands.

As he climbed the last few feet there was another devastating explosion and Alfie turned his head to see a tower of flame erupt a mile or so behind him. *Thor* had launched a single torpedo to dispatch the crippled ship.

Sixteen of *Kirkpool's* crew of forty-six were dead, representing the greatest loss of life on any ship captured or sunk by the *Thor*.

⌒⌒

Thor's doctors and medical staff worked throughout the night treating the wounded and next morning David was greeted by a number of new faces in the sickbay. It was the *Kirkpool's* Second Wireless Officer, Malcolm Scott, himself badly wounded with shrapnel lodged in his back, who told David the story of what had happened on that dreadful night.

⌒⌒

On 21 April, *Thor* passed south of the Cape of Good Hope and entered the Indian Ocean. In a period of less than a month in the South Atlantic she had sunk a total of five Allied ships, having a combined displacement of 23,626 tons. They all carried vital war supplies that Britain could ill afford to lose.

NULLARBOR PLAIN – WESTERN AUSTRALIA

1130 hours, Monday 4 May 1942

Howard sat with his nose pressed to the window of the Trans-Australian, 'The Trans' as it was affectionately known, as it raced across the Nullarbor Plain. At 478 kilometres without a bend, this is the longest stretch of straight railway line in the world. The landscape was flat and featureless with patches of mallee scrub amongst a ground cover of spinifex, bluebush and saltbush, giving an overall olive complexion to the landscape, in stark contrast to the red dust of the desert and the brilliant blue of the cloudless sky.

'Look at that, Mum,' Howard turned to his mother and pointed excitedly as a flock of brightly coloured bluebonnet parrots rose from the scrub where they had been feeding and exploded into flight, startled by the passing train.

It was late Monday morning, and three days had passed since Helen and Howard had departed from Sydney's Central Station for the 4352 kilometre journey to Perth, where they planned to embark on the SS *Nankin,* bound for Bombay and scheduled to depart from Fremantle on 5 May.

Helen had thought long and hard after receiving John's telegram before deciding that, despite John's advice and protestations from Madge and regardless of the possible dangers, the family would be better off if they were all together in Bombay. Furthermore, she had to decide quickly as the Japanese were still advancing on every front and any delay might mean that the sea route between Australia and India would be cut. Helen was a determined and capable woman and, having made her decision, would not be persuaded otherwise. She set about putting arrangements in place, taking the bus into Sydney to visit the offices of Messrs Macdonald, Hamilton and Co. of George Street, Managing Agents for the Eastern and Australian Line; they were still running a passenger service to India and Helen was able to obtain passage for herself and Howard from Fremantle to Bombay.

There was great sadness when, on Friday morning, Uncle Bill heaved the same two well-worn suitcases that Helen and Howard had arrived with, back in February, onto the back of his old Ford 'ute' for the short trip to Sydney to catch the train, scheduled to depart from Central that afternoon. There were hugs all round with Aunty Madge trying unsuccessfully to hold back tears. 'Come on then,' said Bill, in a gruff voice designed to mask his feelings, 'best be off,' and with that, the three of them piled into the ute's front seat. Madge watched the trail of dust from the veranda as they turned onto the main road and disappeared in the direction of the city.

The train left on time and Helen and Howard settled in for the first leg of the long journey westward. They had to change trains several times over the next two days due to the gauge changes embedded in Australia's unique rail system. They had joined 'The Trans' in Port Augusta and it would take them as far west as Kalgoorlie before they changed for the final time for the run down to Perth. They had a small compartment to themselves, in second class, with comfortable bunks that folded away during the day. Helen was going over in her mind the progress of the war and the events of the last few months since fleeing from Singapore, wondering if she was doing the right thing, when Howard's comment about the parrots brought her back to the present.

'Aren't they beautiful?' she remarked. Just then, the guard passed through, calling them to lunch. 'Come on' said Helen, 'let's go and have something to eat.'

GERMAN RAIDER THOR - INDIAN OCEAN

Monday 4 May 1942

As soon as he awoke that morning, David knew something unusual was afoot. The sick-berth staff said nothing but there was a sense of anticipation. The atmosphere was quite different from the normal excitement and tension when a new target was discovered – this was more akin to a picnic or holiday atmosphere. The mystery deepened mid-morning when the ship's engines stopped and David was forbidden to take his normal spell on deck.

By David's reckoning, *Thor's* position was approximately 25°S, 80°E. He could visualise the position on a chart, putting them almost in the geographic centre of the Indian Ocean, roughly equidistant from Cape Town, Perth and Colombo, and on the main shipping route between Western Australia, Ceylon and India.

Thor's position was not a guess on David's part but a clever approximation, based on his knowledge of navigation and mathematics. He made a daily calculation of the ship's position, with no sinister purpose, but as a mental exercise born of curiosity and the need for mental stimulation. He arrived at his answer through the application of the principles of dead-reckoning and a basic knowledge of astronomy.

From the daily transit of the sun, he could estimate *Thor's* course and, based on his experience at sea, could make a good estimate of the ship's speed, and therefore the daily distance run. The problem was, with each passing day, small errors in his estimates were magnified to such an extent that after ten or fourteen days his calculations could be many hundreds of miles in error. He needed a simple way to directly estimate latitude and longitude, on a daily basis, then plot the position of the ship on a chart and overlay the results against his dead-reckoning calculations.

Rather surprisingly, the longitude problem was the easier to solve, and here the methodical Germans were unwitting helpers. With a meticulous need for precision, *Thor's* navigator advanced or retarded the ship's clocks one hour, each time the ship crossed one of the 15-degree meridians that divided the world into time zones. The changing of the ship's clocks therefore told David that they had moved 15 degrees further east or west, giving him a good estimate of longitude. Using this method, he correctly calculated that *Thor* had crossed the meridian of Cape Town on 21 April and passed into the Indian Ocean.

Estimating latitude was more of a problem because, to do this, he needed to know the angle of the sun above the horizon at the time of its meridian passage. Normally, as he had done when instructing *Willesden*'s young apprentices, he would use a sextant, but, of course, one was not available.

The answer came to him while convalescing in his deckchair on *Thor*'s upper deck. He noticed that the shadow of one of the guardrail stanchions ended by his foot and he realised that the higher the sun in the sky, the shorter the shadow, and also that the stanchion and its shadow on the deck formed a perfect right angle. Therefore, David reasoned, if he knew the height of the stanchion and the length of the shadow at the time of merpass, he could calculate the sun's altitude and therefore the ship's approximate latitude. He had previously noted that in *Thor*'s sick-bay, there was a graduated scale on one of the bulkheads that was used to measure patients' heights. Using this scale unobserved, it was a simple matter to mark off the distances on the walking stick the Germans had kindly provided to assist David in his convalescence. Each day therefore, while resting on deck, he would watch the shadow of the stanchion then, at the time of the sun's meridian passage, casually place his walking stick in a position to measure the shadow's length.

Knowledge of the ship's approximate latitude and longitude did not, however, allow him to accurately fix the ship's position. For this he needed a chart or map, neither of which was available. He therefore had to rely on his experience as a navigator and his memory of the latitude and longitude of key places, such as Cape Town, Colombo and Perth. By this method he was able to plot the positions of these places, and several other key navigational ports, on paper stolen from the Germans. It was by this means that he was able to determine that their position on this day was roughly in the geographic centre of the Indian Ocean.

Not only did the whole process occupy his mind but the knowledge gave him a small sense of power and a great deal of satisfaction that he was able, in a very minor way, to outwit his captors.

All this was going through David's mind because he was mildly annoyed that whatever was happening on this day was preventing him being in his position on deck to observe the sun's altitude.

Thor lay stopped throughout the day and from the noises coming to David in the sick-bay there was clearly a good deal of activity on deck. At about 1730, quite unexpectedly, he was told to gather the few belongings he had as, along with the other prisoners on board, he was to be transferred to another ship.

Somewhat shocked by the speed of events, David shook hands with Dr Lehmann and said goodbye, with genuine feelings of regret. Despite their opposing positions as captor and captive, David had received the best possible medical attention and, had circumstances been different, they could have become good friends. He was helped on deck by a sick-berth attendant to see another, somewhat larger ship lying stopped some 400 metres off *Thor's* starboard beam. He was to learn later that this was the German supply ship *Regensburg*, a cargo ship of about 11,000 tons, tasked with supporting *Thor* and other raiders and acting as a prison ship for their captives. The crews of both ships had been busy throughout the day transferring stores, spare parts and ammunition, using large inflatable rafts towed by the ships' motor boats. It only remained to transfer the prisoners. David and a number of the other wounded were unable to negotiate the swinging Jacob's ladders hanging over *Thor's* side so they were lowered into the waiting rafts using one of the ship's derricks and a Boatswain's Chair. As they pulled away, a cheer went up from the sailors on *Thor's* upper deck. The British and Norwegian prisoners in the rafts responded to the calls of 'Good luck' and the cheery waves. It was strange to realise that only a few short weeks previously, their ships had been sunk and shipmates killed by these same people: the camaraderie between mariners transcends the bitterness of war.

⌒〜

Conditions on board the *Regensburg* were similar to those on *Thor*. The prisoners were well treated and enjoyed the same food as the crew. The wounded, including David, were again accommodated in the ship's sick-bay, with the others in the tween-decks, which had been specially modified to act as prisoner accommodation. The forward tween-deck was a single compartment extending from No. 2 Hold through to No. 4 with the only entrance being by way of No. 3 Hatch. Living space was allocated to each of the captured ships' crews according to their numbers. A hammock was provided for each prisoner, slung from portable stanchions that were dismantled and stowed away in special racks each morning. Folding tables were provided for serving meals and for recreational purposes.

Ventilation was again a problem as their accommodation space was designed for the carriage of cargo, not prisoners. Air was provided through cowl vents and through the No. 3 Hatch, which was generally left open. There were no toilets or showers, necessitating a trip to the focsle head where the nearest facilities were situated. The prisoners had free access to the deck during daylight hours and had full use of the foredeck for exercise and recreation. An armed sentry was permanently positioned on deck, in the vicinity of the No. 3 Hatch, where a white line was painted across the deck from ship's side to ship's side. Prisoners were not allowed to cross this line to visit the midships or after sections of the vessel, except those whose duty it was to collect meals from the galley. During the hours of darkness, only one prisoner at a time was allowed on deck to visit the toilets.

The prisoners were required to keep their quarters clean, carry fresh water for their own use and prepare potatoes and other vegetables for their meals. These were taken to the galley for cooking.

The *Regensburg's* doctor and medical staff carried out a thorough check of all prisoners. The doctor expressed satisfaction with the progress of David's injuries and admiration that *Thor's* doctors had been able to save his arm. A good deal of flesh and muscle had been lost from above the elbow but the wound was clean and healing well. He was still unable to use the arm, or even bend it more than a few degrees. He began a program of physiotherapy, comprising exercise and massage, to strengthen the little remaining muscle and regain a better degree of mobility. It was still impossible for him to sleep in a hammock so, once more, he was allocated a cot in the ship's sick-bay. David was extremely grateful for the additional, simple comforts this arrangement provided.

⌒〜

It was now five weeks since David had been taken prisoner and, as his health improved, he came to give more thought to his circumstances and began to reflect on what the future might hold. There were times, alone with his thoughts, when he became quite depressed; he weighed the possibility of being intercepted by an Allied cruiser, and the battle that might ensue, or the dangers of running the British blockade in an attempted return to Germany. Thoughts of Muriel and the children were never far from his mind – *were they safe? what would they be thinking as the weeks without news stretched into months? would this damned war ever end? would the world really be a better place?* At times, it was many hours before he drifted into a fitful sleep.

FREMANTLE – WESTERN AUSTRALIA

1730 hours, Tuesday 5 May 1942

Captain Harold Stratford, Master of the cargo-passenger liner SS *Nankin* was born in Young, NSW on 2 March 1890. Slimly built, he stood 5 foot 8 inches; his nose had a pronounced beak and his eyes were a penetrating steel blue. He spoke in a quiet Australian accent, but with an air of absolute authority. He was standing on *Nankin's* starboard flying-bridge, looking on with satisfaction as the Port of Fremantle Pilot, a Master Mariner in his own right, passed the orders to get the ship underway. 'Slow ahead starboard. Port 30. Slow astern port,' he ordered.

The weight of the ship came on the steel wire spring, extending from the ship's bow to a point on the wharf adjacent to where they were standing. The combined action of the spring, the rudder and the twin propellers kicked the stern away from the ship's berth at the Overseas Terminal on Fremantle's Swan River.

'Slip the spring, slow astern both engines, sound three short blasts on the siren.' The Pilot rapped the orders out in quick succession and 7000 tons of steel backed gracefully away from the wharf, without the need to employ the Port Authority tug, fussing busily in attendance.

Helen and Howard stood together on A-Deck, along with most of the other First Class passengers, watching proceedings with great interest and waving to the small crowd on Victoria Quay who had gathered to farewell relatives and friends.

The *Nankin* was a fine vessel, but beginning to show her age. She was listed in Lloyd's Register as 7131 Gross Registered Tons. Her designed service speed was 12.5 knots. Built for the Far East trade in 1912 by Caird & Co Ltd of Greenock, she first saw service with the P&O Line before transferring to the Eastern and Australian Line, prior to commencement of the war. Her hull and funnel were painted black and the upper-works, predominantly the bridge and passenger accommodation, were painted white.

Early in 1941, the ship was defensively armed in Melbourne's Williamstown Dockyard with a single 4-inch gun fitted to the Poop deck aft and two Vickers machine guns, fitted either side of the bridge.

Nankin was designed to accommodate a total of ninety-four First and Second Class passengers with another hundred in Third Class. On this voyage she carried seventy-four in First and Second Class and a further eighty-eight in Third: twenty-six were women, three were children (under twelve years old) and nine were infants (under five). There were eighteen Naval passengers and five Army. *Nankin* also carried a crew of 160, making a total of 322 on board for the voyage to Colombo and Bombay. The ship's manifest showed she was carrying general cargo to support the British war effort in India. It was largely comprised of flour, frozen meat, butter and general stores but included some 400 boxes of .303 rifle ammunition for Britain's Indian Army. She carried a deck cargo of bailed wool and drums of creosote. Also, tucked away in a locked steel cage in the No. 2 hold tween-deck, were 120 bags of mail.

'Stop both engines, slow ahead both engines, steer 205,' ordered the pilot. The ship slowly gathered way and with one final *whoop!* of the siren the shoreline began to slip past. They stopped briefly just beyond the North Mole to disembark the pilot.

Captain Stratford ordered course to take the ship north of Rottnest Island and out into the Indian Ocean.

Helen and Howard stood by the rail in the fading light until the last deep blue line of the Australian coast disappeared from view to the east. It was getting cold and Helen involuntarily shivered, perhaps as much in apprehension as from the cool evening air. There was a moment of doubt: *have I done the right thing? Should we have stayed on in Dural rather than face the uncertainty ahead?* She shrugged: *too late now.* She took Howard by the hand. 'Come on; let's go and get ready for dinner; see if you can find the way back to the cabin without help,' and off they went.

BARRY – GLAMORGANSHIRE

Thursday 7 May 1942

It started out as a pleasant enough morning, partially overcast but not cold. Donald and Andrew were in the backyard, playing aeroplanes. 'I'm a Spitfire,' Donald announced, arms extended and making the appropriate *rat-tat-tat-tat* noises as he bore down on his little brother who, at a little less than three years old, was more interested in poking a small green caterpillar with a piece of stick than Donald's antics. Muriel was folding laundry in the kitchen, watching the boys through the back window. There was a knock on the front door and she was still smiling at the thought of the boys' games as she opened it.

The postman stood there, hand extended, thrusting an envelope towards her, 'Special delivery for Mrs Millar.' His head was slightly bowed to avoid direct eye contact – he had brought too much bad news to too many families since the beginning of the war to look the recipients directly in the eye.

The blood drained from Muriel's face and she grabbed at the door jamb for support before gathering herself to take the envelope from the boy. With hands trembling, she tore it open. It was from Watts, Watts & Company, *Willesden's* owners. She read quickly:

> 'Dear Mrs Millar,
>
> 'We regret to advise that the vessel in which your husband was serving is overdue and your husband has been officially posted as 'Missing'. At this time we remain hopeful that he and the other crew members may have been captured and are being held as prisoners-of-war. We are pursuing inquiries through the Red Cross and other organisations in an attempt to determine if this is the case.
>
> We realise the anxiety this will cause and assure you that we are doing everything in our power to obtain news of the vessel and its crew and will keep you fully advised.
>
> Yours faithfully
>
> Watts, Watts & Co. Ltd.

Muriel stumbled to the sitting-room and collapsed into a chair, unable to stand or hold back the tears. 'Please God let him be alive,' she sobbed.

SS NANKIN – INDIAN OCEAN

Friday 8 May 1942

During the first few days at sea the passengers cautiously sounded each other out, showing interest in their fellow travellers but not wishing to intrude, forming groups and making friends as people thrown together in such circumstances inevitably do. They were a varied lot, comprising a number of unaccompanied women who, like Helen, were joining their husbands. Most of the men were civil servants, business personnel or military, some with families and some, but not all, of whom were taking up positions in Ceylon or India. There were also three ministers of religion taking up missionary posts abroad. One of the more influential passengers was Mr Gerald Stewart, who was to take up the position of Deputy Commissioner in the Indian Civil Service. However, despite rank or status there was a common bond: they all faced an uncertain future.

SS Nankin.

A nearby cabin to Helen and Howard's was occupied by Mrs Madeline Charnaud, travelling with her eleven-year-old son, Michael. In her mid-forties, dark-haired, tall and very attractive, Madeline was a very imposing woman with a distinct air of confidence and authority about her. Her husband, Mr Fredrick Charnaud, owned a tea plantation in Ceylon and Madeline and Michael were

on their way to rejoin him following an extended break in Australia. Despite the differences in their ages, Michael and Howard quickly became friends and spent much time together, exploring the ship and playing games. It was a comfort to Helen to know that Howard was in good company and the pair seemed to be enjoying the adventure immensely.

Due to the many similarities in their backgrounds and circumstances, Helen and Madeline also became good friends.

Madeline Charnaud 1939.

Boat drill and emergency stations were exercised regularly but, despite the gloom of war, the passengers saw no immediate threat to their wellbeing. The sea was calm and, as *Nankin* steamed steadily north, the weather became warmer and more pleasant.

Of course, most of the conversations, amongst passengers and crew alike, centred on the progress of the war, and there was much discussion on the Japanese advance through the Pacific. Little could they know that, at that very moment, Japanese and Allied fleets were locked in the decisive battle of the Coral Sea just off Australia's North-East coast.

It was a beautiful evening and, to those on the *Nankin*, the war seemed very remote.

GERMAN SUPPLY SHIP REGENSBURG - INDIAN OCEAN

Saturday 9 May 1942

David and the other prisoners quickly adapted to the changed circumstances on their new prison ship. It did not take long for David to return to his mind game of estimating the ship's position, and he quickly established that they were going nowhere; the ship was holding an almost stationary position in mid Indian Ocean. This led David to suspect, quite correctly, that *Thor* was hunting the sea lanes for new victims while *Regensburg* waited in the wings to take on more prisoners and provide logistic support.

SS NANKIN – INDIAN OCEAN

0804 hours, Sunday 10 May 1942

Captain Stratford was puzzled. Along with the others on *Nankin's* bridge he had his binoculars trained on a small object, roughly 10 degrees above the horizon, travelling quickly ahead of the ship from right to left. There was no doubting it was a small aircraft, but it was too far away to distinguish any identification markings. The nearest land was 1200 miles away, at Carnarvon on Australia's West Coast, and there was no possibility that a small plane could travel that distance. It therefore had to have been launched from a ship, somewhere in the vicinity. Stratford judged the aircraft, a single engined floatplane, to be at about 8000 feet and it was circling the ship at a distance of about 12 miles, with no apparent intention of approaching closer. After ten minutes or so, it disappeared in a westerly direction, as mysteriously as it had appeared.

Stratford went over the possibilities in his mind: aware that most Allied cruisers carried reconnaissance planes, he was fairly certain that this was just such an aircraft. However, if that was the case, why hadn't it approached closer; and why hadn't he been briefed on the presence of an Allied warship in this area, prior to sailing from Fremantle? *Should I break radio silence and check? No – surely it has to be one of ours?* First Officer, Burnham Dun, agreed. They discussed the possibility of the aircraft being from an enemy armed merchant raider but there had been no reports of such a vessel operating in this area since the *Sydney–Kormoran* incident the previous November, so they rated the possibility as being highly unlikely. Even so, a lingering doubt remained. 'It's almost certainly unnecessary,' Stratford said, 'but let's exercise Boat Stations one more time, and we'll alter course as well – just for peace of mind.' Stratford left the bridge, asking to be called if the aircraft returned or if anything else unusual occurred.

The rest of the morning passed quietly and, a little after midday, the Officer-of-the-watch recorded the ship's noon position in the deck-log: 'Latitude 27°03´S, Longitude 90°08´E.'

At 1435 Officer Cadet Hulbert, who was standing watch with *Nankin's* Second Officer, knocked on the door of Stratford's day cabin. 'Mr Rozea's compliments sir,' Hulbert blurted out breathlessly, 'and he thinks he can hear an aeroplane, but he can't see anything because of the low clouds.'

Captain Stratford made to stand up but before he reached his feet the world exploded. Machine gun bullets tore through the light steel bulkhead on the port side of the cabin, leaving a trail of devastation. It was a miracle that both survived the flying glass and splinters unharmed. Stratford dived for the door and raced to the bridge, taking in the situation at a glance. There was a ship on the starboard bow at a range of about eight miles and the same seaplane they had seen earlier in the day was on *Nankin's* port bow. Both were headed directly towards his ship. *Nankin* was turning under full helm. Second Officer Rozea believed, erroneously, that the aircraft had launched a torpedo and he had ordered the course change in an attempt to avoid it.

'I have the ship!' barked Stratford, formally taking control from the Officer-of-the- watch, then, 'Ring down "Full Ahead."'

He allowed the turn to continue until the unidentified ship was directly astern. 'Steer 215 degrees,' he ordered, then to Rozea, 'Call the engine-room and tell them to give me every ounce of speed they can and also to prepare demolition charges in case we need to scuttle the ship,' then to Hulbert who had followed the Captain back to the bridge, 'Sound off "Action Stations" and "Take Cover."'

The attacking aircraft closed again in an attempt to tear away the wireless aerials, but was frustrated by return fire from *Nankin's* machine guns and small arms. The aircraft, Nazi markings now clearly visible, stayed close and low, darting in with bursts of cannon fire as the opportunity presented.

Helen was resting in her cabin when the 'Take Cover' alarm sounded. The noise of the attacking aircraft and the sound of gunfire galvanised her into action. Her first thought was for Howard whom she had not seen since lunch when he announced that he was going up to the boat deck to watch the flying-fish which had appeared for the first time that morning. He was filling in time while waiting for Michael, who was receiving a chess lesson in the First Class Saloon. Helen

Captain Harold Stratford.

grabbed their life-jackets and headed for the upper-deck where she hoped to find the boys. She saw Madeline Charnaud in the press of passengers making their way to the First Class lounge – their designated emergency station. 'Have you seen the boys?' Helen gasped.

'Michael was having a chess lesson,' Madeline responded, 'then I think they were planning to meet up on the Boat Deck.' Together they pushed through the press of people towards the companionway leading to the Boat Deck, where they found the two boys, pointing excitedly at the attacking aircraft with little apparent concern or understanding of the danger. 'Is it a Jap?' asked Howard, calling on the only knowledge he had, gained from his experiences during the flight from Singapore.

'Of course not,' said Michael knowledgably, 'It's a Jerry. You can tell by the black crosses on the wings.'

The Arado was closing fast and Helen could see the stabbing red tongues of flame as the twin machine cannons continued to spit out a hail of bullets. The two women flung themselves at the boys and dragged them to the shelter of the ship's superstructure. Bullets ricocheted off the steel and exploded around them as the aircraft roared low overhead. Two of the ship's Indian passengers, caught on the open deck nearby, were killed instantly.

The noise, combined with that of the *Nankin's* return fire, made communication almost impossible. As the aircraft passed, the two women grabbed the boys and raced for the relative safety of the ship's interior before making their way to the lounge where the other passengers were gathering – anxious but calm.

Chief Steward McIntyre was in charge, and together with the ship's doctor, Dr Laing, and the stewardesses, went about the business of assisting mothers and infants with life jackets, comforting the children and passing on what little information they had about what was happening. Two of the First Class passengers were caught in the Arado's fire and received slight wounds from flying shrapnel.

On *Nankin's* bridge the situation was deteriorating rapidly. Stratford ordered radio silence to be broken. Distress messages were transmitted continuously on a variety of wavelengths but with little chance of getting through due to continuous jamming by the raider. At 1438, at a range of about 13,000 yards, *Thor*, for she was the unidentified vessel, opened fire with her main armament, but the shells fell short and wide. Captain Stratford ordered *Nankin* to commence zig-zagging, and return fire with her 4-inch gun, but the gesture was futile and only served to place the passengers in danger while marginally delaying the inevitable. By 1500 *Thor* had found the range and high explosive shells were bursting all round, subjecting the ship to a rain of shrapnel. A direct hit penetrated *Nankin's* hull abreast of No. 1 Hatch, just above the waterline. *Nankin's* gunners fired a total of twenty-eight rounds in reply, but all fell short. Resistance was pointless and could only result in further loss of life.

Stratford ordered; 'Cease firing; strike the colours,' and 'Abandon ship!' Safety of the women and children were now his primary concern. At 1510 the ship was stopped and he passed the word to the engine room to start the timers that would detonate the scuttling charges. They were set for 30 minutes; sufficient to allow all passengers and crew to get clear. Captain Stratford left the bridge to collect the secret codes and confidential documents kept in the safe in his cabin. These, together with the cryptographic key cards from the wireless office, were cast overboard in a specially prepared, perforated steel chest. Stratford gave no thought to the 120 bags of unclassified mail in the tween-deck locker. At 1510, *Nankin* transmitted:

'*Nankin* abandoning ship: position 26°43′S, 89° 47′E.'

Despite *Thor's* attempted jamming of the signals, the message was picked up by the Australian Navy's long-range receivers at Carnarvon, then relayed to the main communications station at HMAS *Harman* in Canberra. It was the last message received from the ship.

Nankin's crew escorted the passengers to the boat deck to begin the task of loading and launching the boats. There was no evidence of panic during the action or while disembarking. Mothers and children stood quietly in line with the able-bodied men providing assistance as required.

Howard clutched his mother's hand as they waited their turn. He was very frightened and choked back tears. Helen tried to reassure him that all would be well but she was far from convincing. There had been no time to return to the cabin to retrieve valuables or other possessions. They scrambled into the boat with only the clothes they were wearing.

In another lifeboat, Michael was also trying desperately to be brave. However, the noise of gunfire, the roar of the attacking aircraft, the anxiety transmitted through the other passengers and the discomfort of the lifeboat, were all too much for the eleven-year-old. Hands clasped firmly over his ears and head buried in the folds of his mother's dress, he tried to shut the noise and chaos from his mind.

While the boats were being launched, *Thor* kept up a steady rate of fire, ceasing only when the boats were clear of the ship. The Arado flew over the scene in tight circles, until *Thor* came up, but made no attempt to continue the attack or interfere with the boats once they were clear.

By 1520 passengers and crew were all safely embarked in the lifeboats. Miraculously, the only casualties were the two Indian Lascars killed and the two First Class passengers wounded by *Thor's* aircraft.

Gumprich brought *Thor* to the scene at maximum speed, stopping the ship near the lifeboats and less than 200 metres from where *Nankin* lay abandoned, wallowing ungainly in the long, lazy swell. Gumprich suspected that Stratford would attempt to scuttle the ship so, even before the *Thor* had stopped, her motor launch was lowered to the waterline, emergency repair gang embarked and ready to board the *Nankin*.

The lifeboats were moving away from the *Nankin* in a tight little group. Stratford estimated that they had 10 or 15 minutes before the scuttling charges detonated, and he needed to be certain that the boats were well clear. However, the repair team in *Thor's* motor launch had other ideas. They intercepted the lifeboats and took Stratford on board the launch, together with *Nankin's* Chief Officer and Thomas Brown, the Chief Engineer. Then, choosing the nearest lifeboat to the *Nankin,* which happened to contain many of the women and children, took it in tow and made as if to head back to the jumping ladder, still clanging against the abandoned ship's hull as the *Nankin* rolled in the heavy ocean swell.

Thor's Second Engineer was in command of the repair gang. He had a pleasant enough demeanour and Stratford judged that he was probably in his early thirties. He spoke good English with a pronounced German accent. He addressed himself to Captain Stratford in a polite but formal manner, leaving no doubt as to who was in command. 'Captain,' he said, 'it's very probable that you've placed demolition charges to sink your ship. I would be pleased if your officers would accompany my men and assist them in locating the devices and rendering them safe. Meanwhile, the motor launch and your lifeboat will remain with us.'

Stratford looked to his Chief Engineer, 'How long have we got Chief?'

'I would think about seven minutes sir,' Brown responded.

Checkmate, thought Stratford. He had no decision to make; then turning to the German, 'We have very little time. If I give you my word that my officers and I will cooperate, will you allow the lifeboat to move off to a safe distance?'

'Of course,' the German responded, 'I accept your word as an English captain.'

The lifeboat moved away and the repair team, with the help of *Nankin's* officers, set about the task of defusing the scuttling charges and repairing a number of pipes and valves, damaged by *Nankin's* departing crew.

Meanwhile, *Thor* had recovered the Arado and was busily taking on board *Nankin's* passengers and crew. The No. 2 lifeboat had been damaged by shrapnel during the action and was leaking badly. The boat was awash and barely afloat when it reached *Thor*. A number of *Thor's* sailors clambered into the boat, waist-deep in water, to pass up the women and children to waiting arms on the deck above. Now the action was over the officers and crew of the raider could not have been kinder or more helpful. Indeed, they were rather shocked and embarrassed to discover the presence of so many women and children, and babes in arms. As they came on board the raider, the survivors were wrapped in blankets, taken below and fed.

GERMAN RAIDER THOR – INDIAN OCEAN

0800 hours, Thursday 14 May 1942

Gumprich swept the horizon with his binoculars and gave a grunt of satisfaction as he picked out the familiar silhouette of the *Regensburg*, some ten miles to the north-west, precisely where he expected her to be. The *Nankin* and her cargo were far too valuable to be consigned to the bottom in the manner of *Thor's* other victims, so Gumprich had taken what fresh provisions and stores he needed to meet his immediate requirements and planned to transfer further stores, as well as the prisoners, to the *Regensburg*, leaving *Thor* free to search for further victims.

Gumprich had returned fifty-nine members of *Nankin's* crew, to operate the ship under the control of his own prize crew, until such time as she could be delivered to the appropriate German authorities. The two ships had stayed together since *Nankin's* capture.

It was an extremely busy day for everyone, and David watched proceedings with great interest from his position on *Regensburg's* upper deck. The three ships, *Regensburg*, *Thor* and *Nankin*, lay stopped about 400 metres apart. There was almost no wind and the sea was calm. Boats were lowered from all three vessels and, supplemented by several large inflatable rafts, were used to transfer prisoners and stores.

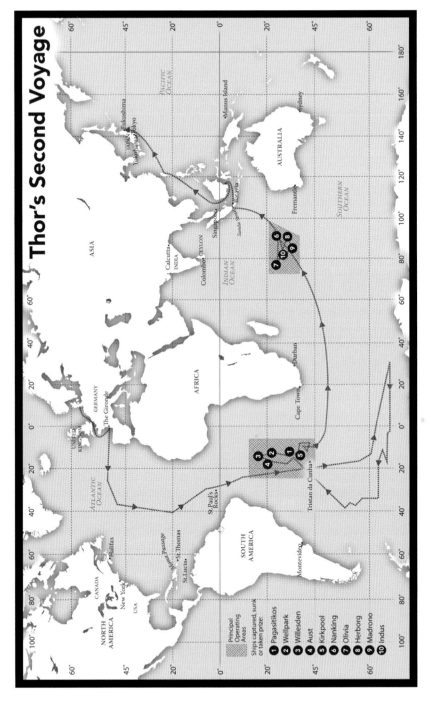

Thor's Second Voyage 30 November 1941 - 9 October 1942.

Firstly, *Nankin's* passengers and crew, apart from those returned to the *Nankin* to assist in the operation of the ship, were ferried across to the *Regensburg*. The women and younger children, and Cadet Crocker who was suffering from a heart complaint incurred since capture, were hoisted aboard by basket.

At six years old, Howard was determined to tackle the scrambling nets on his own, but the movement of the lifeboat and rolling of the ship made the transfer hazardous. Howard grabbed for the nets but, before he could start climbing, the lifeboat lifted on the ocean swell and was thrown towards the side of the ship. David, watching from the deck, suddenly realised that this small boy was about to be crushed. Without thought for the discomfort in his partially healed arm, he scrambled over the side and reached down to grasp Howard under the arm, lifting him bodily upwards to safety, seconds before lifeboat and ship were hurled together in a sickening crash.

Mrs Maria Mok, a British Chinese who was travelling to Colombo with her husband and family, also needed special care. Her husband was a fitter who was to have joined the Naval Dockyard at Trincomalee. With them they had three infant children, the youngest of whom had been born on the *Thor* just two days previously and delivered by Dr Lehmann, much to his delight and that of *Thor's* medical staff, who smothered both mother and child with the best possible attention. With her two other children, aged eighteen months and two and a half years, Maria Mok needed all the assistance she could get and the other women pitched in, to the extent they were able.

Once the prisoners had been safely transferred, the boats set about the task of replenishing both *Thor* and *Regensburg* with fresh provisions from the ample supplies in *Nankin's* fridges and storerooms. After many months at sea, the fresh meat, fruit and vegetables caused great excitement amongst the crews of the two German ships.

Next morning, 15 May, *Thor* departed in search of new victims. Meanwhile, *Regensburg* took *Nankin* in tow, although it was not clear whether the latter's engines were giving trouble or it was an attempt to economise on fuel. Either way, the two ships made their way slowly north.

KMS REGENSBURG – INDIAN OCEAN

Saturday 16 May 1942.

Since the arrival of the prisoners from the *Nankin*, accommodation on board the *Regensburg* had become crowded. The male prisoners joined the survivors from the three British tramps and, with the crew of the Norwegian *Aust*, shared the forward tween-deck. There were 255 male prisoners in all, sharing the primitive and limited facilities. The thirty-nine women and children from the *Nankin* were accommodated in the after part of the ship in No. 5 tween-deck, sleeping in hammocks in conditions similar to the men. All the prisoners were allowed on deck between daylight and dusk and, for two hours in the forenoon and afternoon, the women and children were allowed forward to mix with the men.

Over the first week or so, the crews of both ships worked hard, continuing to strip the *Nankin* of all food, stores and equipment that might be useful to the Germans over the coming months. The deck cargo of creosote was jettisoned and sunk by rifle fire. The wool from the hatch covers was moved into the space provided, giving access to the cargo in the holds. The 400 boxes of ammunition and the shells for *Nankin's* 4-inch deck gun, of little use due to the difference in calibre from the German weapons, were also jettisoned. However, the flour, frozen meat, steward's stores, deck and engine room stores, as well as fittings and furniture from cabins and public rooms, were all laboriously ferried across to the *Regensburg* using the boats and the inflatable rafts. Also included in the transfer were the 120 bags of mail that had been tucked away in the locked steel cage in *Nankin's* No. 2 Hold.

Each day, as a gesture of goodwill, a limited number of prisoners were allowed to return to the *Nankin* to recover cabin baggage and personal possessions. Audrey Jeffery, a young woman travelling alone, who had been on her way to take up a position with the Lutheran Church Mission in India, used the opportunity to recover the small, portable sewing machine she had brought with her, little realising how fortunate that decision was in the context of the events that lay ahead.

It was a busy time for all.

David observed all this activity with great interest but, initially, it had very little effect on his daily life, except that there was a marked improvement in the standard of food provided to the prisoners since the capture of the *Nankin*. Also, he and the other prisoners already aboard the *Regensburg* caught up with the news and the general progress of the war from the new arrivals.

On the second day after the arrival of the *Nankin* prisoners, David was back at his old task of measuring the length of shadows on *Regensburg's* deck in order to estimate the ship's position, when he was startled by an unexpected voice at his shoulder: ' Hello mister. What are you doing?'

David gave a start and turned, to be confronted by a small boy, head slightly to one side, studying his seemingly very strange behaviour. The boy, about six years, had a pleasant demeanour, sparkling blue eyes and an untidy shock of thick blond hair. He immediately recognised him as the boy he had hauled over the *Regensburg's* side two days previously.

David took to him straight away. 'Hello,' he said, in a friendly tone, 'I'm trying to work out where we are. What's your name?'

'Howard,' came the response, 'Howard Gunstone. Mother and I were going to join my stepfather in Bombay but the Germans stopped us. But why don't you use a map?' – all in one breath.

David laughed for the first time in many weeks. 'I wish I could,' he said, 'but sadly I don't have one, and the Germans won't lend me one either. How old are you Howard?'

'I'm nearly seven,' said Howard proudly. 'My friend Michael has got a map. He's shown it to me – and he's eleven,' he added, as if for extra conviction.

'Howard. Come away and don't annoy the gentleman.'

David turned towards the new voice to see a very attractive dark-haired woman, probably aged in her early thirties, with kindly brown eyes, anxiously taking in the scene and moving hurriedly towards them.

David rose quickly and turned towards her, 'He's no bother. We were just getting to know each other.' He extended his hand, 'David Millar,' he offered, 'my ship, the *Willesden*, was captured and sunk by the *Thor* about six weeks ago. I must say it's nice to see some new faces. It's just a pity the circumstances weren't a bit more pleasant.'

Helen took the extended hand. The grip was firm and warm. 'Helen Guy,' she said. 'Please chase him off if he's being a pest.'

'Not at all,' said David, 'but I *am* interested in his friend Michael and his map. Can he possibly have one?'

'I think he has a school atlas,' said Helen, 'he was using it on the *Nankin* to keep track of the voyage. I saw him showing it to Howard before we were captured. I'll ask his mother if he still has it if you like.'

'I would be delighted if you would,' David responded, 'and I should be rather discreet about it if I were you. I don't think the Germans would be pleased if they knew we had maps and were keeping track of our position.'

Helen smiled broadly. 'I'll see what I can do,' then, 'Come on Howard, time to go.'

The following afternoon, David had just taken up his customary position on *Regensburg's* upper deck when he saw Helen strolling casually towards him, deep in conversation with another woman, a little older than Helen, probably in her mid-forties, slightly taller and with dark hair and a pleasant, kindly demeanour. Two boys trailed behind them. 'Hello again,' said Helen as they approached, 'this is Madeline Charnaud and her son Michael.'

David scrambled to his feet. 'Pleased to meet you both. I'm just sorry it had to be in these circumstances.'

Madeline took David's extended hand and smiled broadly. 'Helen tells me you're able to calculate the ship's position by measuring shadows?'

'I try,' said David modestly, 'mainly as a mental exercise, but it also gives me a sense of satisfaction to know I am putting one over on the Germans.'

Madeline looked around quickly to ensure there were no unwelcome eyes observing them, then reached into the folds of the light cardigan she was wearing and produced a school atlas. 'Would this be any help?' she said, grinning broadly, as she offered the atlas to David.

David took the book and quickly stuffed it inside his shirt. 'My word,' he said enthusiastically, 'with the information in the atlas I should be able to calculate where we are within a hundred miles or so, even in mid-ocean.'

'Could you show me how to do it?' asked Michael, who had been following the conversation closely and was curious to know how David was able to work out the ship's position.

David thought deeply for a few moments before turning to the two women, breaking into a broad grin. 'I've got an idea,' he announced, 'Suppose I offered to teach the two boys mathematics. It would be a natural enough thing to do because, after all, they really do need to keep up their schooling. I really would teach them maths and if Michael is still interested I could use the opportunity to teach him some basic navigation as well. It would also be a splendid cover for me to do my calculations. We'll need to be totally up front about it and tell the Germans exactly what we're doing – well perhaps not exactly, but at least ask them for permission to start maths classes for the boys. I'm sure they won't object, because the prisoners from the *Aust* are already running classes in Norwegian, and a number of other groups have also been formed to give talks on a whole range of subjects. It helps break the boredom. We might even be able to con Jerry into providing pencils and paper. What do you think?'

'I think it's a splendid idea,' said Madeline. 'One of the other passengers from the *Nankin*, a Miss Biswas, is a schoolteacher, and we've already spoken to her about starting up classes for the children. If you were to teach them mathematics I'm sure it would fit in splendidly; but are you sure it wouldn't be too much trouble?'

'No trouble at all,' said David, 'it would give me a real purpose and I would enjoy it very much. If you both agree then, perhaps we could talk to this Miss Biswas and see if we can't work out some sort of a program.'

'Seems like it's settled then,' Helen chipped in, 'and I'm sure the boys will enjoy it,' and with that they parted company, agreeing to meet again the following day.

In the following few weeks, life on board the *Regensburg* settled into a steady routine for prisoners and crew alike, with very little out of the ordinary to break the monotony. It was clear to David, from his daily calculations, that they were still going nowhere, so he assumed, correctly, that *Thor* was still lurking somewhere in the vicinity.

The day after he had spoken to Helen and Madeline, David had met with Subasini Biswas, a middle-aged British Indian woman who was returning home after a period in Australia. She readily agreed to set up classes for the boys, with David being responsible for mathematics. Separate arrangements were made for Howard and Michael due to the disparity in their ages and it was agreed that David should have each of the boys for an hour, on alternate afternoons. Captain Stratford, who was acting as spokesperson for all the prisoners, approached *Regensburg's* captain who readily agreed to the arrangement. As far as he was concerned, anything to keep the prisoners occupied made life easier for all.

⌒⌿

On 25 May there was a sense of expectation amongst the crew and a little after midday *Thor* again appeared on the scene. The three ships lay stopped and the tow-line between the *Regensburg* and the *Nankin* was disengaged. The process of transferring further supplies from the *Nankin* to the *Thor* then commenced. The work continued until late evening, then again on the forenoon of 26 May, completing in the early afternoon. No prisoners were transferred from the *Thor*, so it was assumed that she had not met with further success.

The three ships remained in company until the evening of the 28th then, without warning, *Thor* and *Nankin* increased speed and quickly disappeared to the north-west. This time, there was much cheering and blowing of sirens as the ships parted company, indicating to David and the other prisoners on *Regensburg* that it was probably for the last time. The sense that orders had been received and were being implemented was reinforced when *Regensburg* also increased speed and set course to the south-west.

The prisoners on the *Regensburg* were never to see *Thor* or the *Nankin* again.

For the next three days, *Regensburg* continued steadfastly to the south-west, making good, in David's estimation, some 300 miles a day. Clearly the ship was going somewhere with a purpose and, as the Cape of Good Hope was the only land that lay in that direction, speculation amongst the prisoners was rife that they were returning to the South Atlantic, or perhaps the ship was headed home to Germany?

On the morning of 31 May a change in the pitch of the engines alerted the prisoners that the ship was slowing and, when they were prevented from going on deck for morning exercise, speculation was again rampant. At 1400 the prisoners were allowed on deck where they found the *Regensburg* stopped and attached by a heavy wire to the stern of another ship. As they watched, a large leather hose, supported by buoys, was floated down to the *Regensburg* and taken on board at the foremost part of the ship. It was quickly connected to a fitting on the fore-deck; pumps were started, and *Regensburg* commenced taking on fuel.

Late in the afternoon *Regensburg's* captain sent for Captain Stratford and announced that a number of the prisoners were to be transferred immediately to the other ship, which he identified as the German cargo–passenger vessel *Dresden*.

'Here is a list of those to be transferred. They're to be ready in two hours' time. Tell them not to worry about their personal baggage. Arrangements will be made to transfer that separately.'

Captain Stratford took the list and ran down it quickly, checking names. His was the first name on the list that included all the First and Second Class, non-military male passengers from *Nankin*, as well as all the women and children. Also on the list were *Nankin's* stewardess, Purser, Chief Steward, Cadet Crocker (still suffering from heart problems) and all the sick and wounded from the three British tramps. Roondie and his mate Ginger, were listed, along with David, the sole representative from the *Willesden*. They totalled 105 in all. No explanation was given for the transfer or the rationale for who was included or excluded; however, it was clear to Stratford that those remaining on *Regensburg* were all the fit and able men from the three British tramps, all of the Norwegians from the *Aust* and the military personnel, whereas those being transferred to the *Dresden* were generally the women and children, the male non-combatants, the sick and the wounded.

It took David a few minutes to gather his meagre belongings and stuff them into a flour sack that he kept for just such a purpose and, after a quick farewell to other members of *Willesden's* crew who were to be left behind, he was ready. The women and children, together with the wounded, were transferred first. A stout manila rope, from which a wicker basket was suspended, was passed between the two ships. At the *Dresden* end, the manila passed through a block attached to the ship's superstructure and was held by thirty seamen acting as a 'spring' so that the basket did not drop into the sea, or the manila break, as the ships rolled apart and together in response to the long westerly swell. The process was slow, laborious and intimidating for the women, but both Michael and Howard found it exciting. The able-bodied men were transferred using the ships' boats and the large rubber rafts, which could carry twenty people at a time. It was well after 2200 before all the prisoners were across. It was too late to sort out permanent accommodation for the women and children so they all dossed down on mattresses laid out on the deck in the ship's lounge. The men were accommodated forward in two compartments under the focsle head, some in hammocks and the rest on rough straw mattresses thrown on the deck.

The crews of both ships worked hard throughout the night transferring the prisoners' baggage from the *Regensburg*, together with supplies of flour, butter, frozen meat and other stores, previously part of the *Nankin's* cargo.

The frantic activity continued into the following morning and it was 0830 before the *Regensburg* completed refuelling, disengaged from the *Dresden* and steamed away in a north-easterly direction. The prisoners waved and called encouragement to each other as the two ships separated, each promising to notify authorities of the other's existence should circumstances permit.

KMS DRESDEN – INDIAN OCEAN

Monday 1 June 1942

The crew of the *Dresden* took several more hours to recover the refuelling hose and boats and at 1100 she too made off to the north-east, at about 10 knots.

The ship itself, prior to being called up for military service, was owned by the Nord Deutsche Lloyd line and before the war had operated on the Hamburg–Argentine route, carrying both passengers and general cargo. She was similar in appearance to the *Nankin*, having a prominent midships superstructure with lavish accommodation for up to sixty passengers but, at 11,000 tons, was significantly larger. Unlike the *Regensburg*, she had not been modified for the carriage of prisoners and retained her normal peacetime configuration.

The prisoners spent their first day on board adapting to their new circumstances. They were examined by the ship's medical staff; names, birthdates and other personal particulars were, yet again, carefully recorded. They were allocated accommodation according to their status: the women and children, who were not seen as a threat, were allocated cabins in the midships section. With adequate meals, served in the main dining room, and access to the ship's swimming pool, this gave them a false sense of wellbeing. As Madeline Charnaud remarked, the accommodation was superior to that provided as paying First Class passengers on the *Nankin*!

The men were less fortunate. They were crammed into two storerooms in the fore part of the ship, each measuring roughly 4 metres by 5 metres, providing sleeping space for thirty-two men. The only fresh air came from one small ventilator. The heat was almost unbearable. After strong representation to the captain, a staunch Nazi by the name of Jaegar, awnings were spread to provide some slight relief. A rough, wooden, makeshift toilet was erected against the focsle bulkhead, providing the only such facility for the sixty-four men.

Now, over two months since the sinking of the *Willesden*, David's wounds were healing well, to the extent that he was strong enough to be accommodated with the men.

The women and children were allowed to mix with the men twice each day on the fore-deck that also served as the men's recreation space. In a similar arrangement to that on the *Regensburg,* a 'no go' zone was established at night by stretching cargo nets across the deck from rail to rail, about 20 feet aft of the focsle bulkhead. The men were not allowed aft of this bulkhead except to visit the toilet and, then, only singly.

At night, two guards, armed with Lugers, machine guns and grenades (which seemed excessive) were posted on deck to police the 'no go' zone. On the night of 6 June, one of *Nankin*'s passengers, a Canadian missionary of German extraction by the name of Gerhard Baergen, not knowing that there were already two prisoners waiting to visit the toilet, stumbled out onto the deck, still half asleep and intent only on completing the business at hand, without heed or thought for what was going on around him. One of the guards, suddenly aware that there were several men moving close to him in the darkness, panicked, '*Halt! Wer dort geht?*' (Halt! Who goes there?) he called. Receiving no reply, the guard opened fire with his machine gun, spraying bullets with reckless abandon. Luckily nobody was hurt but had the bullets been a little higher and to the right they would have entered the open doorway of the men's accommodation with catastrophic effect.

Meanwhile, Gerhard, having completed his task, returned to his hammock and turned in, without saying a word, and apparently completely oblivious that anything untoward had happened. This was even more remarkable due to his German ancestry and his ability to speak fluent German. Thereafter, the offending guard was assigned to the galley.

David was soon back at his old task of calculating the ship's position and, as the days passed, it became apparent that they were continuing to make steady ground to the north -east, with some specific destination in mind. David discussed his findings with Captain Stratford, also a skilled navigator, who had spent many years on the Australia–Far East run and knew these waters intimately. 'It seems to me,' David said, 'that we're heading for the East Indies (Indonesia) and *that* either means another rendezvous, or a final destination somewhere in the Far East – maybe even Japan.'

'I agree,' Stratford responded, 'and from what I know of the Japanese being in their custody is not a pleasant prospect. Best say nothing to the others until we're sure. No point in stirring up unnecessary concern at this stage.'

'Agreed,' said David.

KMS DRESDEN – INDIAN OCEAN
Friday 12 June 1942

Life on board *Dresden* settled into a steady routine and, in the circumstances enjoyed by the women and children, it was difficult to remember that they were still at war. Madeline had been a fluent German speaker as a child and it was not long before it all came back, and she was able to mix and converse with *Dresden's* officers. Likewise, most of the ship's officers spoke some English, to a greater or lesser degree, and expressed a great deal of sympathy for the British prisoners. They were very much aware that, at any moment, they might be intercepted by a British cruiser and the situation and circumstances quickly reversed.

The children, in particular, were well looked after by the crew who, no doubt, were thinking of their own families whom they had not seen for many, many months.

It was an artificial situation that could not last. Captain Jaeger became increasingly agitated and complained that the women prisoners imagined they were still passengers. Matters came to a head on this particular Friday when one of the women asked if beer might be served with lunch. To compound matters, some of the women refused the soup served with lunch because there was supposedly a film of grease on its surface.

Jaeger was furious. All of the prisoners, men, women *and* children, were mustered on the fore-deck with Jaeger positioned above them on the hatch of No. 1 Hold, legs astride and hands on hips, glaring down. The German captain berated them, without pause, for five minutes, working himself into such a state that he was in danger of losing control. He produced photographs of his own family and accused Churchill of indiscriminate bombing of innocent women and children. He dealt with the 'beer and soup' issue at length, forcefully reminding the prisoners of their status, and how lucky they were to be in German hands. Then came the startling news: 'When we arrive in Japan you will be turned over to the Japanese,' he spat out angrily. 'When all you have to eat is fish and rice, you may well remember the nourishing food and treatment you received on board *Dresden*.'

Jaeger stormed off and, chastened, the prisoners remained, huddled in little groups, discussing the implications of the startling announcement. Harold Stratford, as ex-Captain of the *Nankin*, was their natural leader and he moved amongst the groups trying to reassure them, but the anxiety remained and a sense of despondency enveloped them all.

Later that day, land was sighted to the north. From previous voyages, Stratford recognised it as the southern approaches to the Sunda Strait that separated the islands of Sumatra and Java. For David, it was the first land he had seen since departing from St Thomas three months previously. He had predicted the sighting, which confirmed his daily calculations. It gave him great satisfaction to have reckoned the ship's position with such accuracy.

Once clear of the Straits, *Dresden* altered course to pass south-east of Borneo and into the Celebes Sea, via the Makassar Straits, ruling out Singapore as a possible destination and reinforcing Jaeger's contention that they were headed for Japan. This was confirmed that evening when the ship was challenged by a Japanese Navy patrol vessel. David and Harold Stratford were on the fore-deck discussing the events of the day when the vessel approached, aldis light flashing the recognition challenge. Much to the amusement of the two British officers, it became quickly apparent that the Japanese vessel could not communicate in German, nor could the *Dresden* communicate in Japanese. The only common language understood by both was English. David and Stratford, both of whom were able to read morse, had no difficulty in reading the flashing light. In answer to the Japanese challenge Captain Jaeger responded; 'German vessel *Dresden*. Bound for Yokohama.'

'Well, that settles it,' David remarked. At least their ultimate destination was finally confirmed.

⌒〜

On 14 June they crossed the equator and, despite the circumstances, captors and captives alike entered into some light-hearted fun, as King Neptune, in the form of a German sailor, resplendent in yellow wig and carrying a fearsome-looking trident, clambered over the ship's side to perform the mysterious rites of initiation. Food and beer were plentiful. It was towards evening and the weather was pleasantly warm and the sea calm. Laughter rang throughout the ship as 'victims' were greased and lathered before being tipped backwards from the 'initiation chair' into the ship's swimming pool.

Michael and Howard watched proceedings with delight, laughing uproariously at the antics of Neptune and his helpers.

David stood to one side, watching the ceremony with Helen and Madeline and two of the German officers. *How strange the circumstances of war,* he thought, *surely we have more in common with our enemies than separates us?*

The two mothers, delighted with the obvious enjoyment of the children, pointed out King Neptune's 'doctor' and 'barber' as they performed their mysterious rites.

For a moment, but only a moment, there was no war, there was no killing; there was only a group of happy, laughing people, drawn together by a common destiny, locked in time, in these circumstances and at this place.

Almost before the realisation that it existed, the moment was past. The ceremony was over. The women and children returned to their quarters and the men to their prison in the focsle head. Captor and captive resumed their respective roles.

Meanwhile, *Dresden* ploughed on resolutely to the north, and Japan.

As each day passed the presence of the Japanese became more and more apparent. First there were the larger cargo ships, then the coasters, the rising sun displayed prominently from their ensign staffs. Occasionally, a plane flew over, swooping low for a closer look, so Jaeger had large black swastikas, against a blood-red background, spread out on the covers of No. 2 and No. 4 Hatches, so there could be no doubt as to their identity. They were constantly on the lookout for American submarines but luck was with them and they passed through the blockade lines unscathed.

On the morning of 23 June the sea was glassy calm and, as the early sea-fog was burnt off by the sun's warmth, a small group of fishing vessels was revealed. They were nestled in the lee of a substantial island that loomed quite suddenly out of the rapidly dissipating mist. Bare-legged men, dressed in khaki shorts and shirts and wearing wide brimmed, straw coolie hats, could be seen tending their nets. They barely looked up as *Dresden* passed. From previous visits, Captain Stratford recognised the island as O-Shima, guarding the approaches to the Gulf of Tokyo, some fifty miles south of Yokohama. Two Japanese patrol boats provided an escort for the final few miles and, after anchoring off the port overnight, *Dresden* moved into the Inner Harbour and shackled to a mooring buoy where she remained, without further information or explanation, for the next nine days.

The port was busy. During the morning and afternoon exercise periods David noticed the presence of a number of ships, including a large transport packed with troops and flying the Japanese Rising Sun. It departed on the second day, presumably to reinforce or replace some Japanese garrison in one of the newly acquired territories. A number of German ships were also in evidence but the reason for their presence was not clear. Still, the *Dresden* swung idly around her mooring buoy, with no apparent purpose.

GERMAN EMBASSY – TOKYO

Monday 29 June 1942

The small group sat gathered around the large mahogany table in the Ambassador's opulent office. The Ambassador, His Excellency Herr Otto, had called the meeting to discuss the future of the civilian prisoners on the *Dresden* and another German ship, the *Ramses,* both of which were currently berthed in Yokohama harbour. Also present at the meeting were Germany's Senior Military Attache in Tokyo, *Vizeadmiral* Paul Wenneker, and his Naval Assistant, *Kapitän zur See* Sauerland, together with the Captains of the two vessels in question, Jaeger of the *Dresden* and Falke of the *Ramses*. Ambassador Otto had a number of official papers spread before him. 'I regret,' he addressed the group, 'that Berlin has been less than helpful in providing direction on the disposal of the civilian prisoners, especially the women and children. The matter's considered to be a local problem and it's been left to me to find a solution.'

Admiral Wenneker spoke, 'As you are aware Herr Ambassador, these civilians are no threat to Germany. The preferred option would be to repatriate them through a neutral country in exchange for our own people in similar circumstances. There have been preliminary discussions on this through the Protecting Power and there is already precedent for such an exchange. You'll recall the recent one in Madagascar using the Swedish Mercy Ship *Gripsholm*.' He paused before going on, 'Negotiations here are proving more difficult and there's no certainty about the outcome. The problem is that Germany still holds responsibility for their custody and wellbeing. We really don't need it.'

He went on, 'Both *Dresden* and *Ramses* are urgently required for other, higher priority, tasks. We can't keep using them as civilian prison ships.'

Kapitän Jaeger of the *Dresden* spoke, 'That's right. I'm scheduled to sail in a few days' time so, for me, relocation of the prisoners on *Dresden* is now urgent.'

There was silence for several moments, then Wenneker spoke again; 'We agree that they should be repatriated – perhaps with one or two exceptions. Not only would it rid us of the problem, but it's consistent with our obligations under the Geneva Convention. However, the arrangements will take time and, in the meantime, we can't afford to keep them aboard the two ships.' The others nodded in agreement.

'Go on,' said the Ambassador.

'What I propose,' said Wenneker, 'is this. To allow *Dresden* to meet her commitments, we transfer all prisoners to *Ramses* as soon as we can. Then we ask the Japanese, probably through the Interior Ministry's Security Bureau, if they'll provide somewhere to keep the prisoners until repatriation can be arranged, hopefully before too long.' He paused, 'You may need to telephone the Minister yourself, Ambassador. This won't absolve us from our obligations, and the Japanese may insist that we pay for the support of these people, on the basis that they're holding them in custody on our behalf.'

'That seems the only practical way forward,' agreed the Ambassador, 'and I agree we ought to pay the cost of their support,' he paused, 'I still feel very uncomfortable turning women and children over to the Japanese, even on a temporary basis. We'll ultimately be held accountable for their safety. Still, I see no alternative.'

'Admiral,' he continued, 'I'll leave you to organise the transfers, and I'll contact the Minister right away, but I want to emphasise to you all, the custody and treatment of women and children is a very sensitive issue and we must keep this matter secret, at least until such time as repatriation has been agreed. This includes the provision of names of the prisoners to the Protecting Power, or the Red Cross. Are there any further questions?'

There were none. 'In that case we are agreed,' said the Ambassador. 'Thank you gentlemen, for your attendance.'

The group rose and dispersed.

CONVENT OF THE CONGREGATION OF NOTRE DAME FUKUSHIMA – JAPAN

Tuesday 30 June 1942

Sister Saito, one of five French Canadian nuns at the convent, was busy about her duties in the administration office adjacent to the main entrance, when the telephone on the wall rang shrilly. She lifted the earpiece from its cradle, and leaned towards the mouthpiece. '*Notre Dame Shudoin de gozaimasu*,' she said, speaking fluent Japanese.

The caller was Father Hayasaka from the Sendai diocese, which had jurisdiction over the Fukushima Convent. He spoke quickly but his voice was troubled, 'I have been summoned by the Interior Ministry in Tokyo, where I am now,' he said. 'They intend to appropriate the convent as a detention centre for enemy nationals, including women and children. Regrettably, we have no right to refuse.'

'I understand,' Sister Saito replied, 'but where are we to go?'

'Arrangements will be made for you to move to the convent in Aizuwakamatsu City,' Father Hayasaka replied, 'and you must vacate the Notre Dame Convent within ten days. I understand the disruption and distress this may cause, but there's no alternative.'

'Thank you for letting us know,' Sister Saito responded, 'I'll inform the Mother Superior right away.' She replaced the earpiece and went quickly to seek Sister Louis de Sacre Coeur, and advised her of the call.

The nine convent Sisters, five French Canadian and four Japanese, who made up the little community were gathered and told what had to be done. They quickly made ready, and the things they were not able to take with them were stored in the attic on the second floor.

Although disruptive and unsettling, the move to Aizuwakamatsu did not impose undue additional hardship on the Sisters as, since the outbreak of war, the Japanese had viewed all such Christian institutions with great suspicion. The Kindergarten and Clinic, which gave the convent its principal raison d'etre, had been forced to close, and the building itself was regularly searched and kept under surveillance by the Prefecture Police. Books and documents had been seized and were only returned after careful scrutiny. The Sisters were also required to sign oaths that they would not partake in espionage activities.

On 9 July the Sisters were taken to Fukushima railway station in the Police Prefecture lorry. They boarded the train for Tokyo and Aizuwakamatsu, passing the beautiful Lake Inawashiro on the way; however, they had no time or inclination to enjoy the grandeur of the scenery. As they left the convent in Fukushima, Sister Saito reflected momentarily on the possible consequences of this terrible war and gave silent prayer for the safety and wellbeing of those unknown souls of whatever race, religion or ethnic background who might occupy the convent they had just vacated.

KMS DRESDEN – YOKOHAMA HARBOUR

Friday 3 July 1942

Action at last! *Dresden* slipped from the mooring buoy and, with the assistance of two small harbour tugs, manoeuvred alongside the main wharf. Without further explanation, the prisoners were ordered to gather their belongings and muster on the wharf, adjacent to the ship. Escorted by a guard made up of sailors from the *Dresden,* they were taken a short distance along the wharf to another German ship, the *Ramses,* and herded on board.

Again, the women and children were quartered in the ship's very comfortable passenger accommodation space, amidships, but only those women who also had husbands on board were allowed forward to speak with the men. As previously, the men slung hammocks in the spacious, but badly ventilated, No. 2 tween-deck. It was oppressively hot during the day as the summer sun blazed on the steel deck above. In recognition of his status as the internees' representative, Captain Stratford was provided with a separate small space, fitted with a bunk, desk and chair, for his personal use. David bunked in with the other male prisoners in the tween-deck. They quickly became aware that there were other prisoners aboard the *Ramses,* but who they were, or where they came from, was a mystery. They were being held in another part of the ship and contact with them was prohibited.

In the following days there was much activity aboard the ship, making it clear to David and the others with naval backgrounds, that she was preparing for sea. Drums of what appeared to be whale oil were loaded from lighters alongside. The bridge area was armoured and strengthened for the fitting of defensive armament and temporary wooden showers and toilets were erected in the forward and after well-decks. A further galley was constructed abaft the funnel. Every indication was that the ship was being prepared to carry prisoners on a long voyage. Excitement ran high and each day rumours of possible destinations rapidly spread through the prisoners' ranks. Talk of repatriation was rife. Perhaps they *would* be home by Christmas?

English versions of the local newspapers were made available by the Germans so David and his fellow prisoners, at least for now, were able to keep track of the progress of the war, but only as viewed by the enemy. In particular, they became aware of the outcomes of the Battle of the Coral Sea on 7 May and the Battle of Midway on 4 June, both of which were heralded as great victories for the Japanese. They also read of Allied shipping losses in the Atlantic, the fall of Tobruk in the Western Desert on 21 June and the mounting pressure on El Alamein, as Rommel and his *Afrika Korps* pushed forward.

YOKOHAMA HARBOUR

Tuesday 7 July 1942

Without ceremony or undue attention being paid to her, the German supply ship *Regensburg* slipped into Yokohama Bay and dropped anchor. Still on board were Captain Tuften and the Norwegian crew of the *Aust*, the fit seamen from the *Wellpark, Willesden, Kirkpool* and *Nankin*, as well as a number of British military personnel who had been taking passage on the *Nankin*. A keen observer on board *Regensburg* may have noticed the *Dresden* and the *Ramses* amidst the forest of masts of ships lying alongside the quay. However, the *Regensburg's* arrival was unnoticed by David or any of the other prisoners then aboard the *Ramses*.

Several days after her arrival, a motor launch flying the German flag pulled alongside *Regensburg*. The 120 bags of mail, previously carried in the *Nankin*, were transferred to the launch, transported ashore, and delivered to the German Embassy in Tokyo. It was later revealed that included in the mail were four 'Most Secret' Weekly Intelligence Summaries which, theorists claim, had they been discovered by the Germans at the time of *Nankin's* capture, could have changed the outcome of the war. [4]

KMS RAMSES – YOKOHAMA HARBOUR

Friday 10 July 1942

It was late afternoon and the prisoners were mustered in *Ramses'* forward well-deck. Standing on the No. 2 Hatch above them were five men: the Captain of the *Ramses*, Captain Falke, and the German Naval Attache, Captain Sauerland, who had arrived on board a little earlier, accompanied by three officials from the Japanese Interior Ministry. Two of the Japanese were wearing business suits and the third, dressed in a black uniform with his hand resting on the hilt of an impressive sword, was a senior police officer from the Fukushima Prefecture.

Captain Sauerland stepped forward, looking quite uncomfortable. 'I have to inform you,' he said, 'that pending implementation of plans for your repatriation, temporary arrangements have been made for your custody to

---

4   The author has researched this claim in depth and while accepting that there was a massive security breach, the summaries were very general in nature and already outdated at the time of Nankin's capture. It is the author's professional opinion that the importance attached to these documents is greatly overrated.

be transferred to Japanese authorities. This was not the wish of the German government but, in the circumstances, there was no other choice. You will remain German prisoners but will be in the custody of the Japanese police, and treated as civilian internees. The Japanese authorities will be responsible for your custody and day-to-day supervision.'

Captain Sauerland turned away, head slightly bowed, troubled with the burden of guilt that these women and children were to be handed over to the Japanese. Still, he consoled himself with the thought that this was war and these people were the enemy. Unfortunate as it was, there was little else he could do.

One of the Japanese officials from the Interior Ministry then stepped forward and addressed the prisoners in broken English: 'The Japanese Government does not wish to make war on women and children and innocent people. Even although your governments continue to act aggressively towards us, the Japanese Government still wishes you no harm and would want to return you all to your own countries. We cannot return you at this time because of illegal acts by American and British aggressors who sink our ships carrying wounded soldiers and innocent people like yourselves. Until it is safe to return you to your own countries you will stay in pleasant surroundings in the countryside where you will enjoy pleasant walks in lovely gardens.'

With that, the officials moved away, leaving the internees to huddle in small groups to discuss the implications of what they had just heard. Some were optimistic, taking the speakers at their word, and thought they would soon be released. Others, like Captain Stratford who knew the Japanese well, were less so.[5]

As the German Naval Attache was about to leave the ship, Madeline Charnaud, speaking fluent German, stepped forward and confronted the officer. 'Excuse me sir,' she said, 'but I do not trust the Japanese. I have a small parcel of family jewels. Would you please keep them in the Embassy safe and return them to me when this war is over?'

Somewhat staggered by the nature and audacity of the request, Sauerland at first refused; however, Madeline was very persuasive: 'Sir,' she said, 'if the situation was reversed and a German lady made the same request to an officer of the Royal

---

5   Although the war with Japan was in its early stages, rumours, still largely unsubstantiated, of maltreatment of prisoners had already begun to circulate before Nankin had left Australia. These, together with differences in appearance, language and culture, and unguarded comments by their German captors, were sufficient to cause anxiety amongst many of the internees.

Navy, he would not refuse.' Madeline's argument was persuasive and eventually, but still under protest, Sauerland took the package and departed.

The prisoners were instructed to gather their belongings and a little over an hour later they were herded down the gangway and mustered on the wharf, adjacent to the ship. Here they were joined by thirty-three crew members, thirty-two men and one woman, from a Greek ship, the *Pagasitikos,* that had been sunk by the *Thor* in the South Atlantic on 23 March. Distress calls from this ship had been picked up at the time by the *Willesden.* The Greeks were also being held on the *Ramses* and turned out to be the mysterious group with whom those from the *Dresden* had not yet come in contact. They had arrived in Yokohama a month earlier via the *Thor, Regensburg* and the German supply ship *Tannenfels.*

It was clear that the Germans had now transferred responsibility for the physical custody of the prisoners to the Japanese, for the crew of the *Ramses* played no further part in proceedings but simply looked on, concerned about the fate of those who had, shortly before, been prisoners in their care. Many of them turned away, unable to watch as the women and children, with their pitiful few belongings, gathered on the wharf.

David and the other prisoners were now under the control of fifteen Japanese from the Special section of Prefectural Police, who had arrived from Fukushima by train that afternoon for the purpose of escorting the prisoners back to the internment camp. Their uniforms were entirely black. They wore black, loose-fitting trousers that ended just below the knees, with their lower legs bound with black webbing putties, and black, military-style boots. They also wore loose, long-sleeved, tunics, high-necked and fastened down the front with four metal buttons. Each had a black, tram-conductor cap, with a shiny black peak, that fitted snugly just above the ears. Finally, they all wore a thick leather belt from which was hung an impressive military-style sword.

It formed a sombre and intimidating picture as the prisoners were divided into groups in the gathering darkness. Most alarmingly, and without explanation, the women and children were separated from the men, wives from husbands. The Japanese guards tried to form them into lines so that the prisoners could be counted. 'Atsu-mari!' (line up) they screamed but the words were meaningless and had little effect except to cause further confusion. The Japanese spoke no English or Greek, the Greeks spoke no Japanese and very little English and the English spoke neither Japanese or Greek. The sprinkling of Arabs, Malays, Africans and Chinese confused the language problem even further. The prisoners were tired, confused and apprehensive. The guards were on edge and overly anxious. Tempers frayed and it was late before the 137 men, women and children were finally counted and their possessions meticulously checked for anything suspicious.

Audrey Jeffries' portable sewing machine attracted a great deal of interest but was eventually allowed to remain in her possession.

They were all herded aboard four blacked-out, waiting buses. It was a 10-minute drive through the darkened streets to the Yokohama Railway Station. The local population, most of whom had never previously seen a European, looked on with wonderment and awe as the internees were hustled from the buses to a waiting train. A short journey to Tokyo followed, where they changed trains at Ueno Station to the *Touhoku* (North-Eastern) line.

The women and children were still kept separate and were in ignorance of what was happening to the men. Howard and Michael stayed with their mothers, tired, hungry and confused. David was in another carriage with most of the male passengers from the *Nankin*. 'Roondie' and 'Ginger' were in a third carriage with the rest of the *Kirkpool* lads and the Greek seamen from the *Pagasitikos*. Alfie was having a great deal of trouble with his right arm that had been causing him problems since the loss of the *Kirkpool* three months previously. It was swollen at the elbow and causing excruciating pain. No matter what position he adopted, he couldn't obtain relief. The doctor on the *Ramses* had given him a sling prior to their departure from the ship, but it provided little comfort.

The train from Tokyo rumbled northwards throughout the night. The carriages were in darkness and the prisoners huddled together for mutual protection and comfort but, despite their exhaustion, few slept, some through apprehension of what might lie ahead and others, like Alfie, due to pain from injuries. Whispered conversations halted abruptly as the nervous guards, constantly patrolling, periodically passed through to check the prisoners. At times throughout the night, as circumstances and hunger dictated, the prisoners picked at the black bread and tinned fish that had been provided by the crew of the *Ramses* prior to their departure from Yokohama, not knowing where their next meal might come from.

Dawn broke, and still the train rumbled northwards. The scene outside had changed. Gone was the vista of the built-up urban and industrial areas of Japan's greatest city, replaced by pastoral countryside and rolling hills. To the left David could see the distant Azuma Mountains and after crossing the Arakawa River, tributary to the impressive Abukuma, the train eventually rumbled in to Fukushima's Main Station. It was 0740 on Saturday 11 July 1942. The journey from Tokyo had taken eight hours.

The train had barely come to a halt before the Japanese guards were hustling the prisoners onto the platform. The women and children were still kept separate and herded into a waiting bus and whisked away. The men were formed into pairs, to the shouts of the Japanese guards, '*Atsu-mari! Atsu-mari!*'

There were ninety-one men in all and when they were eventually formed into something resembling two lines the counting began. '*Ichi, ni, san, shi,*' the sergeant in charge strutted up the line calling the numbers out loud, pointing his bamboo cane at each pair of prisoners as he passed, '*go, roku, shichi, hachi, ku, ju,*' and so on down the line. The prisoners were too tired and miserable to cooperate and shuffled about, changing positions, some deliberately, but mostly due to ignorance of what was happening. The first two counts were abandoned due to total confusion. The third count came to eighty-six, and the fourth, ninety-four. The guards were getting angry, adding further to the confusion. It was half an hour before the sergeant was finally satisfied that the numbers were correct and the men shambled off towards the town in response to the unintelligible screams of '*Mae susume!*' (Quick March!)

It was a clear day with a bright blue sky and although early the internees could already feel the heat of the early morning summer sun, promising a scorcher of a day to come. They presented a strange sight as the odd, shambling procession departed the railway station and wound through the streets of central Fukushima. Again the local inhabitants looked on in wonderment, many having never previously seen a European. Gradually, the larger buildings that formed the city's civic centre gave way to single-storey shops and smaller dwellings. The built-up area gave way to paddy fields and unsealed dirt roads.

After a mile or so they approached a large, two-storeyed, Gothic-style building on the outskirts of the city. Recently constructed and European in character, it was set in its own grounds, and surrounded by a high wall. Without pause, the straggling line passed through the open gates, that clanged shut as the last of the prisoners passed through. There was a sense of relief as the men noticed that the bus that had taken the women and children from the station, although now empty, was parked in the forecourt. The men came to a dusty halt opposite the building's main entrance.

Well, mused David, *wherever we are, we seem to have arrived.*

Lost at Sea Found at Fukushima

PART III
INTERNMENT IN JAPAN
11 July 1942–16 August 1945

The Congregation of Notre Dame is an order of Catholic nuns based in the Canadian City of Montreal. In 1932, in response to a request from Pope Pius II, five Sisters, led by a Sister Arcadius, set out from Montreal on the ship *Empress of Asia* to propagate the faith and promote Christian education and charity in Japan. They arrived in Tokyo on 19 October and, the following day, set out by train for the rural city of Fukushima, roughly 150 miles to the north of the capital, and the place selected by the Bishop of Hakodate for the construction of a new convent. A site comprising approximately two hectares of rice paddy in the Hanazono Cho district on the outskirts of Fukushima was chosen, and negotiations began with the numerous owners for the purchase of the land.

A Czechoslovakian architect, resident in Yokohama, was engaged to design the building under the direction of Sister Arcadius. The European character that he brought to the design was very much apparent in the completed structure. The construction itself was contracted to the firm of Seki Engineering, also based in Yokohama. Work began in October 1934 and the building was completed in May 1935, at a cost of ¥300,000.

The Sisters took up residence on 17 May.

FUKUSHIMA

Saturday 11 July 1942 – The First Day

The convent was a grand, two-storey, structure of ferro-concrete. The ground and first floors had large, outward-opening bay windows, painted grey, in contrast to the brilliant white finish of the stucco-coated walls. The roof, enclosing a spacious attic, was finished with terracotta tiles. Projecting dormer windows, also painted grey, were spaced at regular intervals along the length of the building, front and back.

The building was laid out on a north–south axis in the shape of the letter 'E' with the front of the building and main entrance at its centre, facing west, and the arms of the 'E' extending due east. The grounds were rectangular and surrounded by a 2.5 metre brick and stucco wall, surmounted by coiled barbed wire, hastily erected at the direction of the Chief of the Special Branch of the Prefecture Police for Fukushima. The main gate was wrought iron. It was kept locked and permanently manned by a Japanese guard, also provided by the Police Prefecture. Three smaller gates in the perimeter wall were permanently locked and never used.

The gardens were extremely pleasant, with junipers, pomegranates, firs, rhododendrons, pines and camellias in abundance. Donated by parishioners when the building was constructed, the plants were now well established. Well-maintained vegetable gardens, providing ample fresh produce, occupied most of the remaining available space inside the walls.

David and the others quickly took this all in as they stood in the morning sun, waiting in the forecourt in front of the main entrance. They reacted with pleasant surprise, even mild excitement; perhaps the Japanese officer who had addressed them in Yokohama had been telling the truth? Perhaps they *would* live in comfort until repatriation could be arranged? Optimism ran high and excited chatter broke out as they were hustled into the building and herded into the large assembly hall located on the ground floor.

The hall was spacious and easily accommodated the prisoners, including the women and children, who were also present but still kept separate. This was the first time since capture that all 137 internees had been gathered together in one place, at one time and, as they waited, David reflected on the diversity and varied backgrounds that this strange group comprised, thrown together as they were by the circumstances of war (see Appendix 3).

There were ninety-one adult males, thirty-four adult females and twelve children, ranging in age between two months and eleven years. By nationality and ethnic background, there were 115 holding British passports but, of these, only seventy-six were citizens of the United Kingdom. The rest comprised five Australians, two Canadians, seventeen British Chinese, two Indians, two Malays, two British Africans and two British Arabs. In addition, there were twenty Greeks, a Portuguese and an Armenian.

Seventy-five of the prisoners were ex-passengers of the *Nankin*. The remainder were crew members from other ships captured by the *Thor*: thirty-three from the *Pagasitikos*, seventeen from the *Kirkpool*, six from the *Wellpark* and five from the *Nankin*, with David being the only person from the *Willesden*.

By social status the sailors ranged from ships' captains to the 'black gangs', who stoked the coal for the ships' furnaces. The *Nankin* passengers included high-ranking officials of the British Foreign Office, company directors and tea planters, down to junior clerks and officials. There were also several missionaries, and many of the *Nankin* passengers were accompanied by wives and children.

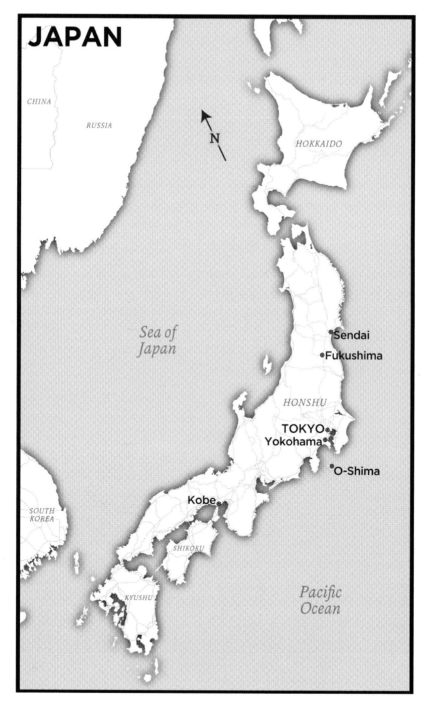

JAPAN - Location of Significant Features.

Add to this the fact that their captors were Japanese, with little or no understanding of the diverse cultures or command of the English or Greek languages, and it was easy to conclude that the administration of the camp would be a complex matter, requiring a great deal of patience and understanding, by captors and captives alike.

David's thoughts were interrupted when three Japanese men entered the assembly hall and mounted the stage. Two of them were in black uniforms, clearly identifying them as senior police officers. The third was a short, grey-haired, middle-aged man in dark trousers and a white short-sleeved, open-necked shirt. He wore round, heavy, metal-framed glasses. As they entered, the dozen or so Special Police who had escorted the prisoners from the railway station and whom were now spaced at intervals around the hall, bowed stiffly from the waist, indicating the importance of the new arrivals. David and the others watched with amusement and seeming indifference, but the low chatter ceased as the new arrivals mounted the stage. The prisoners turned towards them with an air of expectation.

The grey-haired civilian stepped forward and spoke in a loud voice. His English was passable and he spoke with a broad American accent. 'My name is Mister Midorikawa,' he said, 'my wife and I are to be interpreters during your time in this camp. So far you behave very badly and not show proper respect for Japanese people. Whenever in presence of Japanese officers or guards you must be silent and bow respectably. I must remind you that you are defeated people and must not show pride but must show respect at all times. If you do not do this you will be punished.'

Midorikawa half turned and gestured towards the two uniformed officers beside him. 'This is Inspector Nakao Masatake, the Chief of the Special Branch of Police from Fukushima. With him is Commandant Nemoto Kô who is in charge of this camp. They are important officers who will be responsible for your wellbeing. You will show proper respect by bowing to them now. Japanese word for bowing is *keirei*. Whenever Japanese say *keirei* or whenever you are in presence of Japanese officer or guard, you must show proper respect.' Midorikawa took a deep breath and yelled '*keirei*,' hissing through his teeth and expelling his breath with great force.

Very little happened. A number of the prisoners shuffled their feet, looked at the floor or looked around sheepishly to see how the others were reacting. A low, resentful murmur spread throughout the group. Midorikawa was angry and began to shake; in danger of losing control and the all important 'face', he was uncertain what to do next. The guards around the perimeter of the hall moved a step forward, swords still sheathed but hilts firmly gripped and thrust forward.

The situation was explosive and nobody was sure what would happen next. There was a hasty exchange between the interpreter and the two police officers, following which, Captain Stratford was called forward. Nakao and Nemoto also showed signs of anger, but maintained their composure.

Midorikawa addressed Captain Stratford directly; 'Your people behave very badly. If they continue to act in this matter and disobey instructions you will all be severely punished. Life for you here will be very bad. You have last chance to obey instructions now.'

Stratford remained calm and stood his ground. However, through his many previous visits to Japan, he understood something of the Japanese psyche and was aware that little would be gained by forcing an early confrontation, particularly one that might endanger the safety of the women and children.

He turned to the assembled internees and spoke in a quiet but authoritative voice: 'As you know, it's not our custom to bow to each other, and indeed, some of us may see it as degrading. However, it's the Japanese way, and they look on it in the same light as we might raise our hat or give a cheery "good morning" to a passing acquaintance. The reality of our situation is that there's no doubt that the Japanese have the ability to force us to comply with their will and we can either do it willingly, or be compelled to comply through the use of force. We may be imprisoned here for a long time. It will certainly make life easier for us all if we comply. I would therefore strongly recommend that, unpalatable as it may feel, we comply with our captor's requirements with dignity.'

Having spoken, Captain Stratford turned to the three men on the stage and bowed stiffly from the waist, holding the position for several seconds before returning to an upright stance. There was silence, then a pause, then Helen bowed towards the stage. David followed suit, then, slowly at first, the others. David broke into a grin when Roondie, who was standing nearby, murmured 'God Save the King' as he bowed stiffly. There was a short, strangled chortle from Ginger Robson that was totally lost on the Japanese and, in any event, passed unnoticed. The tension was broken and the atmosphere relaxed. Again, they all turned towards the stage.

Chief of Police Nakao Masatake was next to speak. He addressed the prisoners in Japanese in a loud, authoritative voice using short, halting sentences. Midorikawa translated into English as he went:

'Shokun no seifu ga taihen ni warui ga tame ni, wa ga kuni wa taigi o mamoru tame yamunaku senso o shite iru.'

'You have a very bad Government that Japanese Government has been compelled to fight against,' repeated the interpreter.

'Kogun wa osore o shiranai sekai de saikyo no guntai de ari, maketa koto ga nai. Kono senso mo keshite makerukoto sh nai de aro.'

'Japanese soldiers are the bravest and best fighters in the world; they have never been defeated and will not be defeated in this war.'

'Waga kuni wa seisen o goju nen kan tsuzukeru kakugo to junbi o shite iru.'

'Japan is prepared to fight for fifty years.'

'Eikoku oyobi sono domei koku ga, kyo made no senkyo karashite senso ni yabureru koto wa meikade aru. Sono uede, karera no bosei ya don yokusa wa basserareru de aro.'

'Britain and her Allies will be defeated, as progress of the war to this time proves, and furthermore, they shall be punished for their tyranny and greed.'

'Kimiachi no okareta fuko na tachiba wa rikai dekiru ga, keibitaicho ni yori hasserareru kisokuni shitagai, otona shikushite ireba, waga kuni ni no seifu ga yoi taigu o ataete hogomo suri shi, shokun ni wa totemo akarui mirai ga matte iru to iu koto tsuke mo kuwaetai.'

'I am very sorry for your unfortunate position but if you remain good people and obey all the regulations issued by the Commandant, you will receive good treatment and protection from the Japanese Government and you will have a very bright future.' He stepped back.

It was now Commandant Nemoto's turn, again speaking in Japanese with Midorikawa interpreting. He went to great lengths to explain the camp routines and its 173 regulations. The prisoners could not possibly remember a fraction of them. Some of the more extreme or frustrating rules included:

Rule 7.   Must not smile or look sarcastic at roll call

Rule 49.   Must not look over walls

Rule 59.   Men must not wave or smile at women and vice versa

Rule 102.   Must bow to every guard on meeting

Rule 103.   Must not bow with hands in pockets

Rule 105.   A bow must last about 5 seconds

Rule 109. Must refer to the guards as '*Tai yin*', to sergeants as '*bucho*' and to Japanese people as '*Nipponjin*'

Rule 110. *Bucho* must not be referred to as '*bucho*' (a tricky one, that)

Rule 120. Must not be sick without previous permission

Rule 148. Must not be too happy

Rule 154. Must not be unreasonable and ask for more and more.

(For a list of all the Rules, see Appendix 2.)

Breach of any regulation or disobedience of any order issued by a guard, the Commandant explained, would result in beating or removal of privileges or any other punishment deemed appropriate.

The morning dragged on and on. Most of what was said was totally lost on David and the others, who were now tired, hot and hungry. With no seating in the hall and the day now very warm, they began to shuffle restlessly. It was almost 1100 before the performance was completed and the Chief of the Special Branch and Commandant Nemoto departed. This time there was no dissention from the internees to the cry of '*keirei*' from the *bucho* in charge of the guards as the officers exited the hall but, although physically complying with the order, suppressed resentment bubbled just below the surface.

As the officials left, David turned to another prisoner, Fred Garner, who was standing nearby, 'That interpreter chap's a slimy looking character,' he remarked.

Fred grinned, 'Yes,' he said, 'and his nasty little mate has a face just like a fish.'

So 'Slimy' and 'Fishface' they became.

The remainder of that first day was a semi-confused blur of activity and attempted organisation of the prisoners on the part of the Japanese. They were divided into six groups with between twenty to twenty-five internees in each group, which reflected the physical layout of the building and the sleeping and eating arrangements. Indeed, the two small mess rooms on the ground floor could only cater for twenty-five people at a time, necessitating three sittings in each to cope with the total prisoner population. The adult males made up four groups.

By mutual consent, Captain Stratford was appointed spokesperson for the internees and given the title of '*Otokobucho*' (Male Chief). It was his function to convey all orders from the camp authorities to the prisoners and, conversely, to present all requests from the internees to the Japanese authorities for consideration, whether on behalf of an individual or on behalf of the camp as a whole. He was responsible for ensuring that the internees kept their quarters clean and that proper internal discipline was maintained. He was authorised to strike or beat any internee who disobeyed his commands but, needless to say, this 'privilege' was never exercised. Furthermore, what little authority he did hold was always subject to the interference of any guard or official who happened to be present or have interest in any particular issue, at any time.

The women and children made up the other two groups. They occupied both floors of the northern wing of the building. With consent of the Japanese, they also elected their own spokesperson and Mrs Florence Thoms, who had been travelling with her husband to Colombo on the *Nankin*, was selected for this position. Known as the '*Onnabucho*' (Female Chief), Mrs Thoms had similar duties and responsibilities to Captain Stratford, except that she had a particular responsibility for specific women's matters. Stratford retained responsibility for matters that affected the camp as a whole.

For the women and children, access to the outside was via a flight of steps and a small door at the north-western end of the ground floor and another at the north-eastern end, both leading out to the convent gardens. For exercise, they were limited to several narrow concrete paths, from which they were forbidden to deviate. They were kept separated from the men at all times.

Also on the ground floor were the assembly hall, where they had first gathered, the two small mess rooms previously mentioned, a kitchen (spacious but poorly equipped although it did have ample Western-style crockery that had been left by the departing Sisters), pantries and storerooms, as well as the Japanese staff and administration offices. There was a small basement below this level that contained the furnaces and boilers and a small storeroom.

The men's accommodation was contained entirely on the first floor and comprised two large rooms in the southern arm of the building, one occupied by the Greeks and the other by the *Kirkpool* lads, with the remaining men accommodated in small, three-berth, rooms either side of the main north–south corridor. The men were kept separated from the women and children by a fire-proof steel door at the northern end of the corridor, kept locked at all times. The central arm of the first floor also contained the convent chapel, which was generally available to the internees for the conduct of religious services. The men had access to a separate exercise yard via an exit through the shoe room near the assembly hall, on the ground floor. The wearing of outdoor shoes was not permitted inside the building and the shoe room provided storage and a place to change for the very few of those fortunate enough to possess both indoor and outdoor shoes. Of necessity, most of the internees, including the children, went bare-footed indoors.

Access between the two main floors was via two flights of stairs separated by a broad landing, adjacent to the main entrance at the centre of the building. A large bell, which was to dominate their existence, hung in a prominent position on the landing. The internees were forbidden to use these main stairs and instead, to obtain access between the accommodation spaces and the mess rooms, used the internal, back stairs, situated at the rear, at either end of the main building.

David was allocated one of the small, three-berth, rooms that he shared with Fred Garner, a passenger from the *Nankin* who had been travelling to India with his wife to take up a post in the British Consular Service. Fred was a particularly interesting person as he had previously held a position in the British Embassy in Peking (Beijing), where he had learned to speak and read Mandarin. As the written Chinese and Japanese scripts are almost identical, Fred was able to provide very credible translations of written Japanese, although unable to understand the spoken word. He was able to keep this valuable skill secret from the Japanese. The third person with whom they shared was Colin Gray, also a *Nankin* passenger. Colin was a tea planter who had been returning with his wife to their plantation in Ceylon.

The room was approximately 2.5 metres by 4 metres and contained a small table, two wooden chairs and three small built-in cupboards for the stowage of personal items, of which they had precious few.

David emptied the flour sack containing his gear and took stock of his meagre possessions before carefully stowing them away in one of the cupboards. Of the clothes he was wearing at the time of his capture, nothing remained. He had discarded his boots before attempting to shimmy down into the waiting lifeboat, and the other clothing he was wearing at that time was torn to shreds in the explosion and had to be cut from his body by *Thor's* doctors. Since then he had begged, scrounged and stolen from his German captors a number of useful items. Excluding the white shorts and shirt he was wearing, they comprised:

1 pair of lightweight tropical shorts

1 white tropical shirt

1 pair of leather Roman sandals; (the only footwear he possessed)

2 sets of underwear

1 pair pyjama bottoms

1 medium sized towel

1 safety razor and four blades

1 small drinking glass; and

1 toothbrush.

The Japanese provided each prisoner with a straw sleeping mat (*tatami*) measuring 180 cm by 90 cm and about 5 cm thick, a mattress (*mattoresu*) and a Japanese quilt (*futon*), both filled with cotton wadding. A rough woollen blanket (*mōfu*) and one sheet (*shītsu*) completed their issue of bedding.

When the *tatami* mats were laid out for sleeping, space was at a premium, with very little of the floor remaining uncovered. Each room also had a single electric light and a radiator, connected to the central heating system for the whole building. A single window overlooked the entrance courtyard at the front of the building and allowed David and the others to see over the perimeter wall to the paddy fields and the mountains beyond.

They were each allocated a number that was branded into a wooden tag which they wore around their necks at all times, attached by a leather thong. On one side, the number was in English numerals and on the other, the Japanese symbol for that number. Each prisoner was known by his or her number and addressed by the Japanese guards as such. David was prisoner forty-three. His name in Japanese was '*shi-ju-san*', literally, four-ten-three.

Sixteen guards (*Tai yin*) were assigned to the camp, divided into two squads of eight, and two sergeants (*buchos*), one in charge of each squad. Without exception, the guards were young men, none being over the age of twenty five. The period of duty for each squad was 24 hours, with the changeover occurring between 0830 and 0900 daily. It was the guards' duty to keep all internees, both men and women, constantly under surveillance, indoors and out. They patrolled the buildings and inspected prisoners' rooms at frequent intervals, often several times in one day. The guards were drawn from the Special Branch of the Fukushima Police Prefecture and, when not on duty, were accommodated in a separate building outside, but adjacent to, the camp.

Commandant Nemoto Kô was in overall charge. He lived locally and attended every day, wobbling back and forth on his police bicycle, accompanied by his Alsatian dog that followed him everywhere. Nemoto, in turn, reported to the Chief of the Special Branch, Nakao Masatake, in Fukushima city. The internees suspected that Nakao held the real influence in the running of the camp, but he visited only on rare occasions and had little direct involvement in the day-to-day routine.

Midorikawa Kôzô, the interpreter (now known as 'Slimy') had an enormous influence on the internees' daily lives. He and his wife Sue, who could also interpret and arguably had a better command of English than her husband, lived permanently on site, occupying a small room at the northern end of the building on the ground floor, near the main entrance. They took their meals with the remainder of the prison staff. Prisoners and guards alike were totally dependent on his ability as an interpreter, and his integrity in conveying meaning without embellishment or bias. It soon became obvious that he took a sadistic delight in portraying the internees' comments and requests in the worst possible light, often with quite serious consequences.

Meals for prisoners and staff were prepared in the camp kitchen by a solitary male cook, Shonosuki Takahashi, who lived on the premises with his demented, but harmless, bedridden wife. He was assisted by three local women who lived outside the camp. There was also a camp gardener named Suzuki, who had been employed by the convent nuns prior to the war. He was an elderly man and, besides looking after the gardens, he also tended the central heating installation. He also resided outside the camp.

On that first day, everyone was hungry but waited patiently while the cook set about the task of preparing the midday meal. Due to constraints on space, the internees shuffled through the two small mess rooms for meals, group by group, throughout the afternoon and early evening. In each mess room there were two long trestle tables with a backless form bench for seating on either side. Plates, cups and inferior-quality cutlery, but not knives, were provided. It was not permitted to remove these from the mess room. Any losses or breakages were punished by loss of all food for twenty-four hours.

The *Kirkpool* lads were in one of the early groups to be fed, and they enthusiastically seated themselves at the tables, only to be told by an angry and frustrated interpreter that they must form a line and present themselves at the servery counter. The servery had a sliding hatch, but it was firmly closed. After a frustrating wait, the hatch slid back and a small dinner plate was thrust out for the first 'customer'. Anxiously pressing forward, Alfie noticed that the startled recipient was clutching two thin slices of white bread, and a plate containing a few spoonfuls of watery soup. Optimistic as ever, Alfie and the other lads were convinced that this was only the first course and that a generous portion of rice with meat or fish would follow. Reality hit when Alfie, having quickly demolished his 'meal', presented himself back at the servery, and thrust his plate forward for more food. Although bellowed in Japanese, it was quite clear to Alfie that, from the cook's language and antics, more food would not be forthcoming. He made a strategic withdrawal.

Fifteen minutes was the time allowed for each meal and talking was not permitted.

As Alfie and his group made their way back to their quarters they met David, in the next group, heading for the mess room. Recognising Alfie, David asked as they passed, 'What did you get to eat Roondie?'

'Nowt,' replied Alfie – with feeling.

The women and children fared a little better, particularly the children. It seemed part of the Japanese psyche that they have a great empathy for children, and, except on rare occasions, the children were well treated and generally better fed. Michael, who, like Howard, was initially accommodated with his mother in the women's section of the convent, remembers their first meal as *two pieces of bread with a beautiful stew.*

The evening meal was no better than lunch and comprised a few ounces of white bread, a tiny portion of steamed fish, a piece of raw pumpkin, and a cup of weak tea, without milk or sugar. However, with an air of totally unjustified optimism, some of the internees suggested that as it was the first day, the staff were probably disorganised and the situation would improve – how quickly that idea was dispelled.

The final event on that long, hot day was *'tenko'* (roll call). Firstly the men were accounted for, then the women, and finally the children. The event was a total shambles. Everyone, including the guards, was hot and tired. Despite the efforts of the interpreter, it was almost impossible to understand what was required, and tempers were short. The guards rushed around, shouting, pushing and prodding, hopelessly attempting to get the men into some sort of line.

Tenko was held daily at 0605 and 2100 marking the beginning and end of each day. In the mornings, a first 'wake up' was sounded at 0600 by the ringing of the bell. This was the signal for the prisoners to roll up their bedding and stow it against the wall in each room. On the second bell, at 0605, the men formed a single line in the corridor outside their rooms, in the order of their prisoner numbers, from one *(ichi)* to ninety-one *(ku-ju-ichi)*. When they were assembled the *bucho* called *'Tuski!'* (come to attention) then *'Meni neri!'* which was the order for each prisoner to put his right hand on his hip, turn his head and eyes to the right, then shuffle until the *bucho* was satisfied that the line was straight. The next command was *'Lourie!'* at which the prisoners came back to the position of attention with arms by their sides and head and eyes facing the front. *'Bango!'* (number) was the command for the men to start counting, with each prisoner, in turn, calling out his number in Japanese: *'ichi, ni, san, shi … hachi-ju-ku, ku-ju,'* and finally *'ku-ju-ichi.'*

If for any reason the sergeant was not satisfied with the count, the numbering would start again, and again, and again, until such time as he *was* satisfied. For some inexplicable reason of culture or background, it was particularly difficult for the black British Africans, who found it almost impossible to pronounce Japanese words. Invariably the count halted when it came to them but, try as they might, they could not call their numbers. And so, back to the start. The problem was only solved when the resourceful inmates resorted to a little deception. The man standing next to the unfortunate fellow having difficulty, after calling out his own number, would then alter his voice and also call out the next number in the sequence. The grateful African would simply open his mouth in a soundless mime and the count would continue. It seemed to work.

The next command was '*keirei,*' the order to bow to 45 degrees from the waist while the sergeant saluted in return, all the time glancing left and right to ensure the internees were conforming in the appropriate, respectful manner. If not, the order to '*keirei*' was repeated, again and again, until such time as the *bucho was* satisfied or, depending on his mood, an on-the-spot beating or a period of standing rigidly to attention under the bell might take place. Finally the order '*oouse,*' was given, sounding similar to a relieved hiss, something like air escaping from a balloon. This was the order for the men to dismiss and return to their rooms. The whole procedure was then repeated in the women's section. However, on that first night, after half an hour of shouting, pushing and threatening, the *bucho* settled for his own head count and warned, through the interpreter, that on the following morning, *tenko* would continue until they had it right.

It was 2130 when David and the others collapsed on their *tatami* mats exhausted, very hot and still hungry. Despite their tiredness there was little rest. The night brought no respite from the oppressive heat and, as darkness fell, the plague of flies that had harassed them throughout the day was replaced by the torment brought on by a hoard of attacking mosquitoes. Frogs in the adjacent paddy fields set up an incessant croaking. The temperature that day peaked at 34.4 degrees, the highest July temperature in Fukushima since records had been kept. On its own, the heat was just bearable but the oppressive humidity drained their energy. Wearing only a pair of shorts, sweat trickling between his shoulder-blades and under the persistent attack from buzzing mosquitoes, David reflected on the remarkable events that had brought him to this place, and the extraordinary events of the day. *What would happen to them? How long would they be here? Did Muriel know he was alive?* He tossed restlessly, bathed in sweat.

Sleep was a long time coming.

FUKUSHIMA

Sunday 12 July 1942 – The Second Day

It was 0600 and the ringing of the bell brought David from a fitful sleep to startled consciousness. It took a moment to adjust to the unfamiliar surroundings and to remember where he was. His body ached from the unaccustomed hardness of the *tatami* mat and the small brick-like pillow; then the events of the previous day came flooding back. David and his two room-mates, Fred Garner and Colin Gray, rose with difficulty, rolled up their bedding and stowed it against the wall. At 0605 the second bell sounded and the men began to tumble out of their rooms into the corridor, some still only half awake.

Any illusion that their stay in the convent was to be a mild inconvenience, or a not-too-unpleasant interlude, while they waited for repatriation, was quickly dispelled. The guards stamped noisily up and down the passageway, pounding the walls with the hilts of their swords shouting, '*Tenko, tenko, tenko,*' as they tried to form the men into some semblance of a line, forcibly shoving those who were a little slow. '*Tuski,*' yelled the *bucho* when they were all outside, and so the performance of roll call began. On completion, they began their daily routine, according to the schedule set out by the Japanese:

0615 – 0700	Wash up and clean rooms
0700 - 0720	Morning worship (for those wishing)
0720 - 0820	Breakfast (covering all three sittings)
0820 - 0900	Exercise period
0900 - 1200	Work (although there was seldom work to be done and that, generally voluntary)
1200 - 1300	Lunch (again in three sittings)
1300 - 1600	Work
1600 - 1800	Rest
1800 - 1900	Dinner
1900 - 1920	Evening worship
1920 - 2100	Rest
2100	Evening *Tenko*
2115	Bed
2120	Lights out.

Apart from the set times for *tenko* and meals, they were mostly left to their own devices. Boredom was the greatest enemy. So far, they had not been allowed into the convent grounds to exercise and the continuing oppressive heat, coupled with the uncertainty of their situation, made life indoors miserable. Being the only form of exercise available, David and most of the others paced the first floor corridor: from the southern end, where the Greeks and the *Kirkpool* lads were accommodated, to the steel, fireproof door that separated the men's and women's quarters – a distance of sixty-four paces. The women, who had no similar internal space in which to exercise, were worse off.

For countless hours the men paced the corridor like caged animals, heads bowed, unspeaking. So intense and personal were their meditations that any interruption – a bump, someone passing by – made tempers flare.

Men and women were permitted to attend worship in the chapel between 1900 and 1920 daily. The religious observances of all internees were respected by the Japanese, but any thought that this would provide an opportunity for husbands and wives to fraternise or exchange greetings was dispelled. Men and women sat on opposite sides of the chapel with no relaxation of this rule allowed. At least one guard was present for every service and the applicable rules were strictly enforced:

Rule 113.	Must look straight ahead in church
Rule 115.	Must not loiter outside church
Rule 116.	Must not peer into church through windows
Rule 117.	Must not wear blanket in church
Rule 118.	Must not watch women going to church
Rule 119.	Must not cross knees, put hands in pockets or fidget in church.

David was not a religious man in the accepted sense of the word, probably a reaction to his strict Presbyterian upbringing, and he therefore chose not to attend church. He did, however, have his own very strong sense of moral values and of what was right and wrong. He was generally well liked by the other internees who often sought him out when they needed advice or a sympathetic ear.

The organisation and categorisation of the internees continued. Each of the six groups elected a group leader whose primary function was to act as the conduit between the members of the group and the *Otokobucho* (Captain Stratford) or the *Onnabucho* (Florence Thoms), as appropriate. David was a group leader and had responsibility for the twenty-three ex-crew members of the *Kirkpool* and the *Wellpark*.

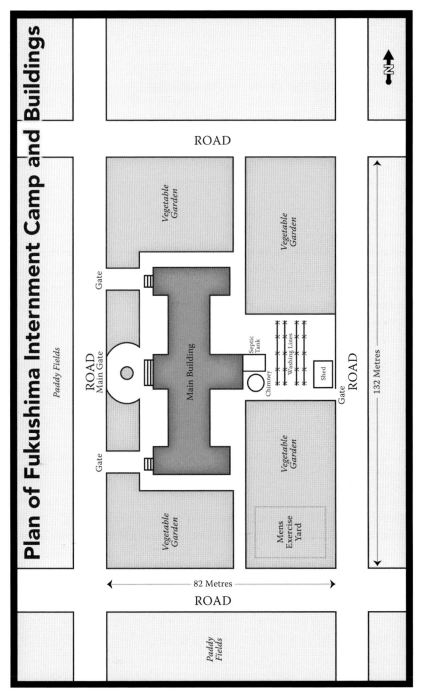

Plan of Fukushima Camp and Buildings.

An unwanted complication was that, with the exception of their captain, John Piangus, the Greeks were all staunch communists. The only common ground they shared with the other prisoners was an intense hatred of the Germans. Consequently the Greeks kept largely to themselves and contributed little to the overall smooth running of the camp. One member of the crew of the Greek ship was a Dutch woman, a stewardess named Caroline Dimitrakopouloy, married to the ship's radio officer. She was billeted in the women's section of the camp.

The detailed documentation of the internees also began. The initial records, provided by the Germans, were checked and cross-checked. Identities, nationalities, circumstances of capture and myriad other details, mostly useless, were slowly drawn out in a series of individual interviews over a period of several weeks. The process was complicated by the variety of nationalities and languages involved. For example, a Greek sailor who spoke passable English translated from Greek to English which was, in turn, translated into Japanese by the interpreter. The process was slow and there were many inaccuracies. Justification provided by the Japanese was that the information was required to enable them to notify the neutral powers, and through them their families, that they were being held in protective custody in Japan. However, there was no evidence that the information was ever passed on.

A cursory medical examination was conducted by Dr Ginyo Hakozaki from the Fukushima Prefectural Health Department, who took charge of the prisoners' health throughout their period in captivity. Wearing spectacles with lenses as thick as pebbles, her examination was no more than a prolonged stare into each prisoner's eyes. It took just under an hour for her to examine ninety-one male prisoners, whose view from a distance of three or four inches of the highly magnified eyes of a middle-aged Japanese woman was disturbing, if not comical.

Meals on the second day were no better than on the first, and set the pattern for the months ahead. There was no serious shortage of food in Japan at this time so it was concluded that there was a deliberate policy by the Japanese to restrict food to that required for subsistence. At this time the daily ration comprised:

Morning meal:	5 ounces of white bread
	1 teaspoon of thin jam
	1/3 pint of weak tea without milk or sugar
Midday meal:	5 ounces of white bread
	1 ounce of meat or fish
	2 ounces of vegetables, generally raw
Evening meal:	As for midday meal

Shonosuki Takahashi, the camp cook, purchased the food twice weekly at the local markets. It was supplemented, very occasionally, with fruit and vegetables grown in the convent gardens. The food was paid for by the German Embassy in Tokyo, which, under the terms of the Geneva Convention, retained the responsibilities of the 'Arresting Power', and therefore ultimate responsibility for the prisoners' wellbeing. The internees believed that some of the money provided by the Germans under this arrangement was not used to purchase food, but was diverted to line the pockets of senior Japanese police officials. Also, several of the prison guards stole food from the kitchen to feed their own families. Other food, which had been allowed to go bad in the storeroom, was thrown out. The overall result was that meat, butter, eggs, bread, fruit and pumpkins, paid for by the Germans in good faith, never reached the intended recipients.

When it became known at the markets that food was being purchased for enemy civilians, the local population and merchants became resentful and uncooperative. As a consequence, Shonosuki was frequently abused, overcharged or sold inferior quality produce, which should have been fed to the animals, or thrown out, days before.

From the internees' viewpoint, the best that could be said of Shonosuki was that he had no real malice towards the prisoners and was simply doing a job, although badly, and with a complete lack of enthusiasm or any real compassion. In the end it could probably be said that he did what he could with what he had.

In any event, it was the internees who suffered.

~

The women and children were processed in the same pattern as the men. They were given numbers, underwent the same cursory medical examination, were allocated rooms and mustered for routine *tenkos*. Helen and Howard were accommodated together in a room that they shared with Mrs Evelyn Gray, whose husband Colin, was in David's room in the men's section. Their room was adjacent to the steel door that separated the men's and women's quarters. It was quickly established that, if a lookout was placed at the top of the stairs in the men's quarters, whispered conversations between the women and their husbands could be held, generally after lights out, until late at night. This was a little unfair on Howard and others near the dividing door, as they were kept awake into the night. There followed some heated discussions between those who wanted contact with their husbands and those nearby who were constantly disturbed by the arrangement. Eventually, compromise was reached and a regular roster of those wishing to communicate was established. This system of communication between the male and female prisoners was known as the *phone* and individuals would often make comment that, 'I spoke to so-and-so on the *phone* today.'

Michael was with his mother in a room they shared with Mrs Phyllis Hercombe who, like Helen, had escaped from Singapore ahead of the advancing Japanese, but had finished up in Darwin, before booking passage on the *Nankin* in the belief that Australia was in danger of invasion.

~

It became clear very early that the guards had been ordered to adopt an overly aggressive attitude towards the internees. Initially, this took the form of pushing, shouting, stamping and waving arms; however, it was not long before more severe punishments began.

YOKOHAMA

Saturday 18 July 1942

Having completed an uneventful passage from the Indian Ocean, where she had parted company with the *Thor* and the *Regensburg* on 28 May, the SS *Nankin* slipped into Yokohama Harbour and dropped anchor. By design or chance, four of the five ships that had played such a prominent role in David's life since the sinking of the *Willesden* were now together. The *Ramses, Dresden* and *Regensburg* were joined by the *Nankin*. The only ship not present was Gumprich's *Thor*.

FUKUSHIMA INTERNMENT CAMP

July–October 1942

The internees cleaned their own quarters, the corridors, the wash-rooms and the lavatories. They were also forced to work in the grounds and gardens. Additionally, Commandant Nemoto sought volunteers for work parties to carry out other tasks within the camp and grounds. No one was compelled to join these groups but it was a way to overcome boredom. Generally, those regarded as having officer status did not carry out manual labour but undertook, or were allocated, other tasks such as group leaders, camp committees, and teaching or running educational programs for children and adults.

The Japanese chose four men and one woman to work in the kitchen, preparing food, cleaning and washing up. They were changed at irregular intervals and were recompensed by having access to some additional scraps of food or a few cigarettes.

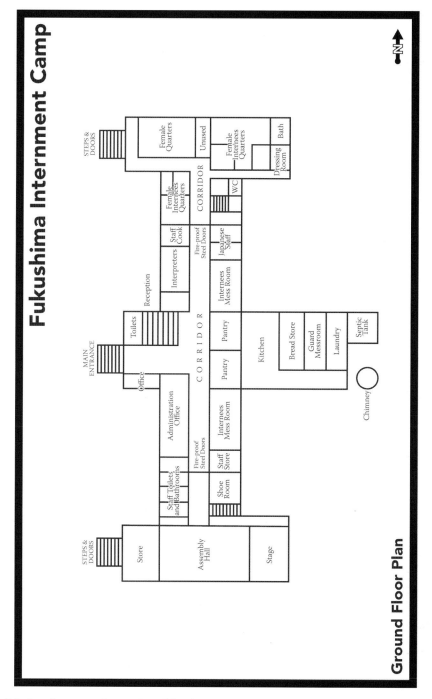

Fukushima Internment Camp – Ground floor layout.

Another six men, also chosen by the Japanese and changed at intervals, were employed as sweepers whose task was to clean and tidy the two mess rooms and those areas of the camp, including offices and the Guard Room, occupied by the Japanese.

Finally, six or eight of the men voluntarily formed a gardening squad and worked in the convent gardens, weeding and carrying out other tasks. They were also paid in cigarettes. The soil was rich and the gardens were well established and tended when the nuns had been in residence. Under the care of old Suzuki, the camp gardener, and with the labour provided by the internees, they were able to grow onions, spinach, asparagus, peas, radishes and an ample supply of potatoes but, apart from a few radish tops, none of these were given to the prisoners. It was only by guile and cunning, when away from Suzuki's watchful eye, or that of the patrolling guards, and under threat of severe punishment, that the occasional vegetable or piece of fruit was secreted away and smuggled back indoors to supplement the food ration.

Shortly after their arrival, Captain Stratford, in his capacity as *Otokobucho*, approached Nemoto and complained about the quality and quantity of the food. Cases of severe diarrhoea and acute constipation had begun to appear. Amongst the women, menstruation became very irregular and, in many cases, stopped altogether. All this was put down to the inadequate food, and Stratford was concerned that the low grumblings, already evident, would develop into outright rebellion if nothing was done.

There was no doubt that the quantities were insufficient, inexcusable at a time when there was no widespread shortage in Japan and the convent garden was producing abundant crops. The Japanese did, however, attempt to make some allowance for Western dietary differences. For example, the cook attempted to bake European-style bread, but the results were disastrous. It was extremely 'doughy', insufficiently baked, and almost inedible. Also, the few vegetables that *were* provided were presented raw. Although, from a nutritional point-of-view, this was probably no bad thing, to the Geordie lads from the *Kirkpool*, brought up at sea on a diet of sausages, eggs and chips, the food provided in the camp was considered repugnant.

Stratford approached Nemoto's office with some trepidation, due to his understanding of the Japanese psyche and, this being his first such visit, he was unsure of the reception he might receive.

The Captain knocked and waited. The door was opened by Midorikawa who gestured him to come inside. There was no chair so Captain Stratford stood. Nemoto was at his desk, head down, apparently absorbed in some administrative task. After several moments he looked up and Stratford bowed. There was a rapid exchange between interpreter and Commandant, who had clearly been warned of the purpose of the visit, and was not pleased. Midorikawa said, 'The Commandant wishes to know why you are here wasting his valuable time on small matters that are of no importance?'

'My people are becoming ill,' Stratford responded, 'there's not enough food, and what there is, many of them cannot eat. Some of our people arrived here with wounds, still not healed from the time of their capture, and they need more and better food and urgent medical treatment.'

'Slimy' raised his voice, almost to the point of hysteria, and responded without reference to Nemoto, who was observing the proceedings thoughtfully. 'I must remind you,' Slimy shouted, 'that you are a defeated people and must not ask for more and more. Your women behave in arrogant manner towards Japanese. If Japanese women behave in such a way they would be beaten by their husbands. The Commandant says you are only being held here because the Germans have asked, and that if you behave well you will soon be released in exchange for Japanese prisoners. In the meantime the food you have is same as Japanese family and you must be grateful for what you have.'

'Please tell the Commandant,' Stratford responded, quietly but firmly, 'that we appreciate the efforts of the Japanese authorities to obtain our release but we must have more food and better medical treatment or we will all become ill and perhaps die.' Being aware that Germany still held responsibility for their wellbeing, he went on, 'Please allow me to write to the German Embassy in Tokyo to seek their help in providing more food.'

Midorikawa spoke to Nemoto before responding angrily, 'There will be no letter and no more food. This meeting is now ended.' Nemoto dropped his head and returned to the papers on his desk.

Having no option, Stratford bowed to Nemoto, then returned to the men's quarters to break the gloomy news. He was upset because he believed this first meeting had set the pattern for future lack of sympathy or cooperation by the Japanese. He was, however, encouraged by Nemoto's comments about the ongoing negotiations for repatriation. Perhaps they would all be home for Christmas after all!

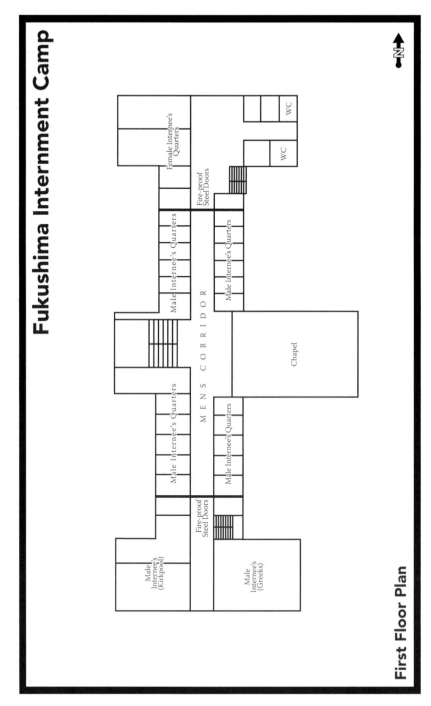

Fukushima Internment Camp – First Floor layout.

By the end of July the medical situation was becoming serious. Finally, after further representations by Captain Stratford, Dr Hakozaki, the same Japanese doctor who had examined them on arrival, accompanied by a single nurse, arrived at the camp. Elizabeth Scott, a passenger on the *Nankin* and a State Registered Nurse, attended throughout the visit.

Mr Arthur Daniels, manager of a branch of the Chartered Bank, suffering from a boil on his buttock, was examined first, followed by several young men with shrapnel wounds on the arms and legs. Through the interpreter and amid much laughing and joking, the doctor asked each in turn if they were suffering from venereal disease.

There were two pots of zinc ointment left behind by the convent sisters. One was fresh, the other hard and stiff. Dr Hakozaki looked at both, laughed and instructed Elizabeth to apply zinc ointment dressings to the shrapnel wounds, handing her the stale jar and pocketing the other. The zinc was so stiff, it was almost impossible to apply. They ignored Elizabeth's protests. No dressings or bandages were supplied. Un-sterile rags were used instead.

Another man, a Greek, was suffering from diabetes and had been on insulin for about three years. He asked the doctor for a further supply. After much laughing and talking between the doctor, nurse and Slimy, they told him that he was too fat and 'did not need anything like that.' Whether or not it was due to the starvation diet provided in the camp, together with its complete lack of fat, will never be known; however, the unfortunate gentleman *did* survive the war.

Most of the women were suffering from acute diarrhoea or constipation due to lack of food and the unaccustomed diet. Dr Hakozaki told them not to eat too much. No further advice was given and no medicine or special diet was ordered.

Hakozaki and the nurse left the camp after a little over an hour.

To the shame of the camp authorities, it was one of the women who was first to be beaten by the Japanese. The incident was sparked by yet another complaint about the quality of the food. On 1 August, not long after Captain Stratford's first unsuccessful confrontation with Nemoto, Florence Thoms, as *Onnabucho*, was asked by the other women to go to the office, also to complain about the food. Although they were aware of the previous failed attempt by Captain Stratford, it was thought that a direct appeal by the women on behalf of the children might have a better chance of success. Florence was accompanied by several other women to provide moral support, but they were roughly turned back by the *bucho* on duty, before they reached the Administration Room, where official meetings with the Japanese were generally held. Florence went on alone. She took with her a piece of the bread which she showed to Nemoto and explained, through Midorikawa, that it was unwholesome and making the children sick. 'Would it be possible,' she asked politely, 'to provide more bread and of a better quality, especially for the children?'

Firstly, Midorikawa went purple in the face then, shaking with rage and ranting unintelligibly, he stepped forward and slashed Florence across the face with his open hand; twice. Such was the force of the blows that Florence's head snapped back and she reeled backwards, almost losing her balance. Her hands went up to her face where red welts appeared and, although clearly in a state of shock, she attempted to regain her composure and dignity, staring directly into the interpreter's eyes.

'I demand to see a representative of the German Embassy,' she said in a firm voice, but with jaw trembling from shock and anger.

Midorikawa grabbed Florence by the throat with both hands and, shaking her violently, pushed her back against the wall 'You demand! You demand!' he screamed, 'You demand nothing unless Japanese say so.'

Nemoto and the *bucho*, who were also present, made no attempt to interfere or assist but simply looked on dispassionately, despite Florence's plea for help and clear distress. Midorikawa finally gained control of his rage and released her. Florence staggered to the door and returned to the women's quarters, one hand on the wall for support, the other to her face, sobbing in distress and disbelief.

The following day the camp received a visit from Nakao Masatake (Fishface), Chief of the Special Branch of Police from Fukushima, the same officer who had addressed them on the day of their arrival. There had been an urgent communication from Nemoto as a result of the food complaints and it was decided to reinforce the rules before matters got out of hand. Again the whole camp was mustered in the assembly hall and addressed through the interpreter, who showed not the slightest remorse or outward sign of concern following the previous day's violent outburst.

'It has been decided that all prisoners must sign paper to say they will obey rules,' he said, translating Fishface's words. 'Again, I must remind you that you are losing the war and the food you are getting here is better than people receive in the defeated countries of England and Australia. You should be thankful that

Japanese provide you with what you need. If you wait for the pleasure of the Japanese and not ask for more and more you will receive many good things like more food and clothing or cigarettes and soap and towels. If you ask for more you will receive nothing.

'Japanese does not fight war against women and children and authorities in Tokyo still try to arrange your release but bad Americans sink mercy ships that would take you home. Even so, if you behave well and not ask for more, you will soon return to your own country.'

The message was clear enough.

Next day the food ration for all children was reduced, because five-year-old Miguel Fernandes had seen his father, British subject and company secretary Leopoldo Fernandes, exercising in the men's yard, and ran across from the women's area to greet him, breaking the rule that the women and children should be strictly segregated from the men at all times. Any thoughts that there might be any future reasonable negotiation or dialogue between prisoners and the camp authorities, on conditions in the camp, were dispelled.

The punishment arbitrarily meted out to Florence Thoms, and that imposed on the children as a result of the Fernandes incident, set the pattern for the first months in captivity. The breach, or supposed breach, of any of Nemoto's 173 regulations, or disobedience, or slightest hesitation in obeying the order of any one of the guards, resulted in swift retribution, more often than not totally disproportionate to the seriousness of the alleged offence.

So severe were the punishments and so universally applied, that it became very clear that it was a deliberate policy imposed by Nemoto himself and designed to break the spirit of these overly proud, arrogant foreigners. Punishments for men and women alike, and sometimes even the children, included:

- a reprimand by Nemoto
- slapping on the face or head, either on the spot by the guard concerned or in the administrative office if the incident was serious enough to be brought before the Commandant
- standing to attention or kneeling in the sun or cold for hours on end, with beatings if the offender moved
- prohibition on going outdoors

- confiscation of outdoor footwear
- stoppage of all meals for a designated period
- stoppage of cigarette ration or prohibition on smoking
- standing to attention holding a bucket of water in each hand
- punching or beating with a stick or baton about the head and body

It was also common practice to punish the whole camp for a breach of regulations by a few or even a single internee. The object was to create dissension amongst the prisoners and bring pressure to bear on any one of them who might be tempted to disregard the regulations.

⌒‿

Alfie kept a secret diary meticulously throughout his time in captivity, aware that discovery by the Japanese would bring rapid retribution. Recurring themes were the quantity and quality of the food, the crimes and punishments meted out by the camp authorities, communication with family and friends, and the prospect of repatriation, reflecting the issues that dominated the thoughts and daily lives of all.

Initially Alfie used writing materials that he had scrounged from the German crews of the *Regensburg* and *Dresden* and what he was able to trade with the *Nankin* passengers, who had been able to recover writing materials from that ship. When these sources were exhausted he improvised.

Alfie quickly realised that the toilet paper provided by the Japanese was almost identical to that provided in the British Public Service throughout the British Empire since time immemorial: rough on one side and glossy on the other. The glossy side took ink remarkably well, and from that time Alfie and others in the camp had no shortage of writing paper, despite the ban on its use for this purpose under Rule 125. For some reason, the Japanese never queried the amount of toilet paper consumed in the camp. Perhaps they just put it down to yet another incomprehensible custom of these very strange Europeans?

Ink was another issue. Late in their first summer of captivity, Alfie was walking in the exercise yard with Tom Oon, a young British Chinese clerk who had been a passenger on the *Nankin*. Alfie remarked on the beauty of the brilliant red poppies that adorned the convent gardens.

'Yes, they *are* beautiful, aren't they,' Tom responded, 'and useful too. I remember as a boy we used to crush the petals to make ink and it worked very well.'

'Let's try it,' said Alfie and together, away from the eyes of the ever-watchful gardener and camp guards, they gathered and secreted about their persons sufficient petals to make a useful supply of ink. It worked a treat. Ink problem solved.

On Saturday 15 August, 'Old Hemy' died. Vincent Hemy was the 4th Engineer on the *Kirkpool.* Due to his weather-beaten face, and partially balding grey hair, he was known affectionately by Alfie and the *Kirkpool* lads as 'Old Hemy' although, at fifty-five, he was still a relatively young man. Hemy had complained of stomach pains on the previous day and the doctor had been summoned. After a cursory examination she diagnosed the complaint as a stomach ulcer but prescribed no treatment or medicine. On Saturday morning the pain worsened and at 2202 that night, he died. There was no autopsy, but Elizabeth Scott believed the most likely cause of death to be acute peritonitis, brought on by stress, inadequate and inappropriate food, and the general harsh conditions of imprisonment.

Alfie and Ginger were given the task of laying out the body in the most dignified way they were able and attaching the lid to the rough wooden coffin provided by the camp authorities. With several others of the *Kirkpool* lads, and supervised by the Japanese, they carried Old Hemy to the Mount Shinobu cemetery, just outside the camp, and buried him on a slight rise, in the Catholic corner, with a plain white cross to mark the spot. Henry Osborne, a Catholic Missionary and a passenger from the *Nankin,* carried out the simple ceremony. Captain Stratford also attended.

On 18 August, Mrs Rosalind Bok gave birth to a female child, Susan Ann. Rosalind was a British Chinese citizen travelling to Ceylon on the *Nankin* with her husband, Bok Sye Foo, who was to take up a position with a British airline. Florence Thoms arranged a suitable room in the women's quarters to be set aside for the birth and a Japanese midwife and a nurse were in attendance. After the birth, the midwife attended daily for a period of ten days.

In addition to the camp ration, Mrs Bok was given extra soup, rice and jam but she was unable to provide breast milk for the baby. Accompanied by Florence, Rosalind went to the administration office and asked for milk. The *bucho* on duty forced her to bare her breast, which he roughly squeezed. Having satisfied himself that Rosalind was indeed speaking the truth, he approached another British

Chinese, Maria Mok, who had three children under four, and demanded she give up part of her milk ration to feed Rosalind's baby. She did so.

No clothing was provided for the baby, but the women rallied round and improvised, as best as they were able, from the materials available.

Alfie, Ginger and a couple of the other lads from the *Kirkpool* were in the initial group of 'sweepers', responsible for cleaning up, among other areas, the Japanese guards' mess room near the kitchen on the ground floor. Besides taking their meals there, the room was used by the guards as a staff room where they were allocated lockers to keep personal items of clothing or equipment. Each morning they gathered there between 0830 and 0900 for the change of shift, to eat breakfast, discuss the events of the day or take a cup of tea and read the newspapers.

Shortly before 0900 each morning the outgoing shift departed and the new shift proceeded to the administration office to be briefed by Commandant Nemoto, and for the allocation of the day's duties. This daily briefing session never took more than thirty minutes or less than twenty. The twenty-minute period between 0900 and 0920 was, therefore, the only time during the day when it could be guaranteed that every guard was fully preoccupied with matters other than supervision of the prisoners. It was also the only period when the guards' mess room could be guaranteed to be empty, giving Alfie and his band of sweepers the opportunity to clean and tidy up.

Part of the task was to gather and fold the Japanese newspapers, spread around where the guards had left them. Alfie and his team had no knowledge of Japanese writing so, to them, the newspapers were simply a meaningless collection of unintelligible characters. The papers were folded and stored without so much as a thought until one day, a month or so after their arrival, Alfie noticed a map in one of the papers, clearly identifiable as the Pacific. There were broad arrows emanating from Japan, indicating some sort of outwards progression. The arrows swept down from Japan through the Philippines to the Dutch East Indies (Indonesia) and New Guinea, south-west through the Caroline Islands to the New Hebrides, eastwards to Midway Island, north-east to the Aleutians and westward and south-westward through China to Burma, Siam (Thailand) and Malaya. Alfie assumed, quite correctly as it turned out, that the arrows represented the major advances by the Japanese since their attack on Pearl Harbor. Later that morning, Alfie passed this information on to David, his group leader. 'Pity we can't read Japanese,' Alfie reflected, 'then we would really know what was going on.'

'Ah! Perhaps we can,' David responded, his voice trembling a little with excitement. 'Roondie, not a word of this to anyone until I get back to you,' he said, before hurrying off to find Fred Garner and Harold Stratford.

He found them in the men's exercise yard where he broke the news. They excitedly discussed the possibilities and implications of receiving daily news bulletins, and how they might achieve this. They decided it would be too dangerous for Fred to go to the guards' mess room to read the papers because, although the guards were out of the way between 0900 and 0920, there were too many of the other staff working in the vicinity and Fred's presence and interest in the papers would be difficult to explain. They thought it best if Roondie, or one of the other sweepers, could pass the newspaper to another internee who would conceal it about his clothing and carry it to some secure spot where Fred would be waiting to examine it at length. It would have to be somewhere where interruption was unlikely, even by the other prisoners. They ruled out all of the ground floor as there were too many people about and there was no secluded spot where Fred's presence could be explained. David and Fred's room on the first floor was an option but on reflection they decided that the male internees' toilets on that floor fitted the bill almost perfectly.

That afternoon they had a dry run. Malcolm Scott, second radio officer from the *Kirkpool,* was to be the 'runner', so they brought him into the plan. The route from the guard's mess room to the men's toilets was complex and involved first going through the kitchen and pantry into the main, ground-floor, north–south corridor. Then there was a choice: Malcolm could either go straight across the corridor to the main staircase (which the internees were forbidden to use) that emerged on the first floor, adjacent to the toilet block, or use the approved back stairs at the southern end of the building. This latter course would, however, involve passing the administration office where Nemoto was holding his morning briefing. As all the guards would be *at* the briefing, they decided that the main stairs was the best option. To be *absolutely* safe it was decided that there should be no longer than 15 minutes from the time Alfie passed the newspaper to Malcolm until the time it was returned. The practice run went without problems.

Timing was critical. As soon as the guards left for their morning briefing, just before 0900, Alfie and his boys entered the mess room with buckets and mops, ready to begin work. Alfie took the newspaper, secreted it in his shirt and walked casually through the kitchen and pantry. Meanwhile, Malcolm, who was returning from the exercise yard through the shoe room, met Alfie in the main corridor. Checking all was clear, Alfie quickly passed the newspaper to Malcolm who then headed for the main staircase. Reaching the men's toilets on the first floor, he observed with satisfaction that, as arranged, one of the toilets was 'in use'. Malcolm took up the adjacent cubicle and passed the papers under the dividing screen to where Fred was waiting. It was 0902. At 0913 precisely, the papers reappeared. Malcolm concealed them in his shirt, flushed the toilet, then set off for the return journey. The newspaper was passed back to Alfie who was hovering in the vicinity of the ground floor pantry then it was returned to the neat pile in the guard's mess room. The time was exactly 0915. Later, group leaders were briefed by Fred on the contents of the papers and they, in turn, passed the news on to the members of their group. The women were kept up to date by whispered messages passed by *phone*.

This procedure was performed almost daily for the three years of their internment and, although the Japanese had a strong suspicion that outside news was somehow reaching the internees and conducted frequent searches as a consequence, they never once suspected how it was done. To say that these daily news bulletins had a positive effect on camp morale would be an understatement. From that time on, not only were they aware of the Allies' progress across the Pacific towards Japan, they also gained great satisfaction from the knowledge that they were able to deceive the Japanese.

Audrey Jeffrey's Willcox & Gibbs portable sewing machine.

Audrey Jeffery's sewing machine, recovered from the *Nankin*, achieved something close to iconic status in the camp due to its incredible usefulness and as a tangible demonstration to the Japanese that, despite the hardships and deprivations, the internees could, and would, retain their dignity by always wearing clean, well-maintained clothing. Audrey had been aboard the *Nankin* taking passage to India to take up a position with the Lutheran Church Mission. A competent seamstress, she had picked up the machine on a whim, from a small second-hand shop in Melbourne, just prior to departure. It was a Willcox & Gibbs Portable, operated by turning the small handle attached to a fly-wheel on the right-hand side of the machine. It fitted neatly into its laminated plywood carrying case, and its fold-down, suitcase-style carrying handle made it very easy to transport. When the *Nankin* passengers had returned to the ship to recover personal items, shortly after capture, Audrey made sure that the precious sewing machine and a handy supply of cotton were the first items collected.

The ex-*Nankin* passengers and crew were relatively well off for clothing and other personal items due to the generosity and consideration of the Germans at the time of their capture, although most were lacking any form of heavier, winter garments. The seamen from the three British tramps and the Greek ship *Pagasitikos* were, like David, less fortunate and had only the clothes they wore when captured plus what they had been able to scrounge or steal from the Germans. Repair and maintenance of what little clothing they had, therefore, assumed major importance.

Audrey's imagination and ability to improvise were extraordinary. She made shirts and shorts for the men out of discarded women's clothes, sheets, pillowcases and any other material that could be found. When the supply of cotton for her sewing machine ran out she obtained more by unpicking bandages, old clothes and socks. She even knitted booties for the babies using wool obtained by unpicking the sleeve from her sweater and using knitting needles crudely fashioned from split bamboo. However, while there was no difficulty in providing sewing services for the women by these means, the banning of all communication between the sexes made it difficult to provide similar services for the men. The women passed the problem to the men's section on the *phone* and it was not long before they arrived at a solution. They developed a scheme that became known as the *Indian rope trick*.

The men's bathrooms on the first floor were almost directly above one of the women's toilets on the ground floor. The men unpicked an old coir floor mat, found discarded in the boot room, and made a very serviceable, light weight rope to which they attached a small basket. After evening roll call, which tended to be the time of least activity by the guards, they placed articles for exchange in the basket and lowered it to the floor below. The basket was swung gently and retrieved, as prearranged by *phone*, by the waiting women below. On receipt of a whistled signal from the women, the basket was recovered, complete with its contents of inward goods. In this way, not only items of clothing for repair, but additional small items of food for the children, written messages and other articles were passed between the men's and women's sections in relative safety.

The two boys, Michael and Howard, adapted quickly to life in captivity, as one would expect from children of their age. Throughout their time in the camp, despite the hardships and deprivations, there always seemed to be a little extra for the children. Sometimes it would be extra food put aside by their mothers from their own meagre portions or provided by the men's section via the *Indian rope trick*. In either case the adults survived on less to ensure the children had enough.

Also, the Japanese as a people had, and continue to have, a great love of children and although some of the crueller guards were capable of, and sometimes guilty of, inflicting the harshest corporal punishment on the boys for seemingly minor misdemeanours, others were relatively kind and entered into many of their games and provided the occasional item of fruit or other food.

On 21 July, less than two weeks after their arrival in Fukushima, Howard celebrated his 7th birthday. Birthday cards from Michael, David and one or two of the others were improvised from the available materials, and somehow Helen miraculously produced a 'cake' made of stale breadcrumbs and compressed boiled rice. They made candles from wooden toothpicks, threaded through coloured beads. A few bright flowers, stolen from the garden, provided added decoration. Although the accompanying rendition of 'Happy Birthday dear Howard' will not go down in the annals as one of the great musical events of the time, it was the occasion of much merriment and did much to relieve the general depression brought on by the circumstances of their captivity.

For Michael and Howard, boredom was the biggest problem. With no school to attend, and no toys or playthings, a very restricted outdoor playing area and only the women for company, each day dragged endlessly. Mealtimes were the only relief from the drudgery of the daily routine. Things did improve with time, but only slowly and due largely to the remarkable ability of children to use their imagination and to improvise.

One day, while playing one of their endless games of hide-and-seek in that part of the grounds allocated to the women and children for exercise, Howard came across an unusually shaped stick. It was about 15 inches (38 cm) long and perhaps 1½ inches (4 cm) thick with a pronounced bend half-way along its length. By some quirk of nature it was flattened on one side and it vaguely reminded Howard of the Aboriginal boomerangs that he had seen when attending school at Dural. He picked it up and examined it closely before holding it by one end and giving it a tentative throw. He was delighted with the result and gave a small yell of triumph as the stick, spinning as it went, soared across the vegetable patch in a graceful curve, before coming to rest near a small patch of asparagus. 'Michael. Michael. Come and see this!' Howard called, 'come and see what I've found.'

Michael appeared from behind an azalea bush where he had been hiding, wondering what all the excitement was about.

'Give me a shot,' he said, after listening to Howard's excited explanation, and taking the stick in his right hand, hurled it into the air with an equally pleasing result. The 'throwing stick' became a treasured toy and provided the boys with endless hours of fun. They had competitions to find out how far it could be thrown and how high, how far apart you could catch it when standing face to face and how close you could get it when throwing it towards some pre-determined target. Occasionally, one of the friendlier guards would join them in these games, with much laughter and merriment all round. At the time, however, neither of the boys imagined the part that Howard's treasured throwing stick would play in improving the conditions for all of the internees at the camp.

The question of the boys' education again became an issue and Madeline and Helen took the matter up with Subasini Biswas, the teacher who had organised their classes on the *Regensburg* and the *Dresden*. Another of the ladies, a stout middle-aged woman named Annie Law, who wore her hair in a tight bun and had been travelling to India on the *Nankin* to take up a position in a missionary school there, also agreed to help. Due to the difference in their ages, separate lessons were organised for each of the boys. Other women in the camp also helped. It was not long before Howard was attending regular classes in spelling, reading and arithmetic and Michael was receiving tuition in such diverse subjects as Latin, Mathematics, English, History and Geography. The classes did much to occupy the boys and provided a welcome diversion, and considerable satisfaction, for their tutors. The biggest drawback was the shortage of paper and pencils, books and other teaching aids, but they managed well with the resources available.

Throughout the whole of that first August and September, the weather remained unbearably hot and humid. On one occasion the temperature reached 39.1 degrees, the hottest ever recorded in Fukushima: a record that still stands. Water restrictions were introduced and residents were asked to cut their daily consumption by 30%. For the internees, this meant the existing inadequate water supply was reduced to a trickle. There was no way to reduce the oppressive heat, nor was there sufficient water to wash sweat-soaked clothing and sheets. Prickly heat and heat sores were commonplace, but there was no effective treatment. The children and infants suffered most.

The situation was made worse in that the internees did not understand that water restrictions were in place throughout the district. They believed, quite incorrectly, that their Japanese guards were just being bloody minded and had cut water supplies solely to impose further unnecessary hardship.

One warm night, early in September, David awoke from a recurring nightmare. He was back on the *Willesden*, under attack from diving aircraft. Apart from himself, everyone on board was dead, and he ran from body to body trying to shake them into life, but with no success. He shook harder and harder. Surely someone must be alive! Suddenly, he was awake. The whole building was shaking and for a moment he didn't remember where he was. Colin Gray was trying to get to his feet when Fred Garner called out from his sleeping mat: 'What the bloody hell's happening?'

David came rapidly to his senses. 'I think it's an earthquake,' he shouted, and the three of them, still barely awake, stumbled into the corridor to be greeted by the other prisoners pouring from their rooms, all equally frightened and confused. Children screaming and sounds of panic from the women's quarters added to the confusion. People staggered around in the dark, not knowing what to do.

Within 30 seconds or so the tremors ceased and some sort of order returned. The guards and the interpreters came running at the commotion, trying to restore calm but even after the shocks subsided the children continued sobbing, not convinced that the danger was past.

From that time and throughout their period of captivity, earthquakes were a feature of their lives and, although never quite comfortable, they did accept them as part of the burden of life in this strange land.

Despite the unbearable conditions, some of the men were forced to continue working under the relentless midday sun. On 11 September, Nichol McIntyre, the sixty-four-year-old kindly Chief Steward from the *Nankin,* who had welcomed Helen and Howard aboard in Fremantle seemingly a lifetime ago, fainted while weeding the vegetable garden. The guards prevented other men working nearby from assisting him into the shade and McIntyre was forced back to work by an angry guard wielding an evil-looking bamboo baton. He collapsed again at tea that afternoon and, later the same evening, without regaining consciousness, died.

YOKOHAMA

Thursday 1 October 1942

On the early morning tide, the German supply ship *Ramses,* on which David and the other internees had been imprisoned in Yokohama Harbour back in July, slipped its moorings and headed south through the Oraga-suido narrows, guarding the approaches to Yokohama, and headed for the open sea. On board were ten Norwegian seamen, including Captain Christoffer Tuften, Commanding Officer of the *Aust,* captured and sunk by the *Thor* on 3 April, and two of his officers.

Ramses was carrying a cargo of whale oil, fish oil, lard, coconut oil and tea, all badly needed in Germany. She was also carrying a mixed assortment of building materials to be unloaded en-route to support the Japanese occupation of Borneo. After languishing in the Far East since the beginning of the war with Germany, the ship was, at last, bound for Europe and home.

The German and Japanese authorities had even greater difficulty knowing what to do with Norwegian prisoners than they did with the British merchant seamen and the civilians captured from the *Nankin.* Invaded and occupied by Germany in 1940, Norway and Germany were, technically, no longer at war. Furthermore, Japan had never declared war on Norway and therefore refused to accept any responsibility for Norwegian nationals. This left the unfortunate crew of the *Aust,* and other Norwegian flag vessels captured by the *Thor* and other German raiders, in something of a hiatus. For the Germans, the solution was to ship all Norwegians back to Europe, on any vessel available, with a view to their ultimate repatriation to Norway. A number found themselves aboard the *Dresden* which had departed Yokohama on 15 August, and eventually succeeded in running the Allied blockade, reaching Wilhelmshaven in December 1942. Others, less fortunate, departed Yokohama on 5 September aboard the *Regensburg* but she was torpedoed and sunk in the Sunda Straits on 11 October by an American submarine.

Captain Tuften and his fellow officers had been with David and the others as prisoners aboard the *Thor* and were transferred with them to the *Regensburg* on 4 May. Tuften well remembered the arrival of the crew and passengers from the *Nankin*, captured by the *Thor* on 10 May. When David and the others were transferred at sea to the *Dresden* on 31 May, Tuften and other crew members from the *Aust* remained on board the *Regensburg*. When she arrived in Yokohama on 7 July the Norwegians were separated from the other prisoners and confined aboard the *Nankin*, then undergoing maintenance in Yokohama. Captain Tuften was therefore very much aware of the general circumstances of the capture of the *Nankin* and the fate of its passengers and crew. From later information gained from the Germans in Yokohama, they were also aware that the passengers and some of the crew of the *Nankin* had been interned in a Japanese camp, 'somewhere to the north of Tokyo.'

GERMAN RAIDER THOR – OFF YOKOHAMA

Friday 9 October 1942

Günther Gumprich was well pleased when *Thor*, showing the effects of her long period of duty at sea, slid past the island of O-Shima and entered the Oraga-suido narrows. He expected to berth in Yokohama within the hour. His crew had worked tirelessly and under great hardship since departing Kiel a little over 10 months previously. The men had not set foot ashore in the intervening period and the prospect of drinking themselves into oblivion in one of the numerous local bars and/or pursuing the cooperative bar girls to the extent their sobriety would allow, was a very welcoming prospect.

Gumprich's record of sinkings was impressive and gave good cause for satisfaction. It comprised:

Pagasitikos	3490 tons	23 March 1942
Wellpark	4650 tons	30 March 1942

Willesden	4563 tons	1 April 1942
Aust	5630 tons	3 April 1942
Kirkpool	4842 tons	10 April 1942
Nankin	7131 tons	10 May 1942
Olivia	6307 tons	16 June 1942
Herborg	7892 tons	19 June 1942
Madrono	5894 tons	4 July 1942
Indus	5187 tons	20 July 1942.

This made a total in excess of 50,000 tons of Allied shipping sunk or captured in a period of only four months.

Gumprich's latest orders from the German High Command were to refit *Thor* in Yokohama before sailing, as soon as possible, to conduct further operations in the Pacific–Far East area. The intention was that *Nankin*, now renamed *Leuthen*, and also undergoing refit in Yokohama while doubling as a prison ship, would act as support vessel.

Three days earlier *Thor* had exchanged greetings with the *Ramses*, heading south for Borneo, Batavia and home. Gumprich had bid them luck and good sailing, and wished that he too was returning home.

As *Thor* approached her berth, Gumprich could see the figures of Admiral Wenneker and Captain Sauerland waiting on the quay to greet them. He was looking forward to letters from home and latest news of the war. 'Slow ahead,' Gumprich ordered, then 'Stop main engine,' followed by 'Half astern, starboard 30!'

Weighted heaving lines curved gracefully out from the ship and were gathered in quickly by the sailors on the dock, hand over hand, bringing in the heavier manila lines to secure the ship in its allotted berth.

Gumprich gave the final orders: 'Stop main engine, finished with main engine, double up all lines and secure,' before leaving the bridge to greet his guests.

FUKUSHIMA INTERNMENT CAMP

October–November 1942

Throughout October the last of summer's blistering heat eased but the comfortable autumn climate that followed passed too quickly. From the first-floor windows of their prison, David could see the distant peaks of the Azuma Mountains with their first frosting of winter snow. On 26 October, snow fell in the convent grounds but didn't settle. With no winter clothing to keep out the biting cold, the internees took to wearing blankets around their shoulders throughout the day, whether indoors or out.

Captain Stratford repeatedly requested an issue of winter clothing for everyone, particularly warm underwear, but all such requests were refused. Although warm clothing appeared to be reaching the camp, it was only issued to the Japanese guards. It was only in cases of extreme emergency, or to preserve decency, that any warm underwear or other garments were issued to the internees.

As a concession to the prisoners at this time, or perhaps as a cruel, deliberate hoax, Commandant Nemoto authorised twelve internees, selected at random, to write letters to their next-of-kin advising them they were alive and well and interned in Japan. The letters were written, but not one reached its intended destination. There is no evidence that a single letter left the camp.

On 1 November there was a severe frost and by this time the trees had shed their autumn leaves. On 9 November the snow arrived in earnest and remained until the following March.

Michael and Howard built a snowman.

Fukushima Internment Camp – Front of building – 2002. (Courtesy of Chris Best)

YOKOHAMA HARBOUR

Saturday 21 November 1942

Günther Gumprich and his fellow officers were gathered on *Thor's* bridge watching a 7000-ton oil tanker, flying the German ensign, nudge its way into an adjacent berth with the assistance of two harbour tugs. The new arrival was the supply ship KMS *Uckermark,* which had run the British blockade in Europe in order to support the German commerce raiders operating in the South Atlantic and Indian Oceans.

Uckermark had originally been named KMS *Altmark* but she was renamed after the famous incident in 1939 when she was intercepted in a Norwegian fjord by the British destroyer HMS *Cossack,* and the 299 British Merchant seamen who were imprisoned on the ship were liberated in a daring rescue.

Uckermark had sailed from the German base at La Rochelle, France, in September where she had embarked stores for the raiders, including steaming oil, aviation fuel, ammunition, torpedoes and two replacement Arado seaplanes for the *Thor.* She re-supplied the raiders *Stier* and *Michel* in the South Atlantic before going on to Batavia (Jakarta) then Singapore, where she loaded crude oil and rubber for Japan. Bringing plentiful supplies and, with the latest news of the war at home, Gumprich and his officers were delighted to witness the ship's safe arrival in Yokohama.

FUKUSHIMA INTERNMENT CAMP

Wednesday 25 November 1942

It was early evening, and there was great excitement in the camp. Four new prisoners had arrived, providing a welcome diversion from the monotony of daily camp life. The newcomers were: Mrs Marion Sparke and her ten-year-old son Graham; Pat Radford, a twenty-year-old fair haired lass; and Andrew White, a sixteen-year-old lad. All were British Caucasians and had been travelling from Britain to Cape Town on the passenger–cargo vessel *Gloucester Castle*.

The tragic tale related by Marion Sparke, of their capture and subsequent events, was all too familiar, but none-the-less shocking, as it so closely mirrored the experiences of those already in the camp.

On 15 July, close to the equator in the Gulf of Guinea, night fell quickly. The tropical downpours experienced by the *Gloucester Castle* as she passed through the Intertropical Convergence Zone brought little relief from the oppressive heat of the day. By 1900 it was quite dark and the only sounds were the deep beat of the ship's engines, the hissing of the sea as it foamed along the ship's hull, and the ever-present whirring of the ventilation system.

The evening meal was about to begin, and Marion and Graham were making their way down to the dining room from their small cabin on B-Deck when their world erupted. There was a blinding flash, accompanied by a massive explosion, as a torpedo hit amidships, lifting the ship and breaking its back. Those not killed by the initial blast were hurled off their feet, the lucky ones into the sea and the less so, against items of the ship's superstructure or equipment, battering their bodies to pulp. Then the shelling began. Round after round of high explosive pounded the already doomed vessel. The first shell struck just below the bridge and the second destroyed the dining room, killing the unfortunate passengers who had gathered early for the evening meal. The roar of escaping steam and people screaming filled the air. The ship listed heavily to starboard and settled quickly by the stern. Those on the upper deck who were still alive were hurled or leapt into the sea, already alight from burning oil. Those below decks when the attack began didn't stand a chance – death came quickly.

Four minutes after the first explosion, the ship was gone. Miraculously, a lifeboat was launched and a few lucky souls were dragged on board, some badly wounded.

Fukushima Internment Camp – South Wing – 2002. (Courtesy of Chris Best)

The speed and unexpectedness of the attack was staggering. One moment a proud ship going about its business – next, total destruction. Marion found herself in the water; how she got there, she had no idea. She called out to Graham and relief flooded through her when she heard a response nearby. Luckily they were both competent swimmers as there had been no opportunity to retrieve life jackets from their cabin. They clung to a piece of floating wreckage and by the light of the burning oil they could see others around them, many face-down and clearly dead. Someone coughed nearby. Others called out for help but there *was* none.

After a seeming eternity, and in danger of sliding off her temporary raft due to sheer exhaustion and the need to hold desperately on to Graham, Marion heard what sounded like a small boat's engine, and German voices calling in the darkness. A few minutes later, strong hands plucked them from the sea.

The boat was the motor launch from the KMS *Michel,* a German raider under the command of *Kapitän zur See* Helmuth von Ruckteschell. *Michel* had approached to within two miles of the *Gloucester Castle* under cover of darkness before launching its devastating attack. There was no opportunity given to abandon ship. Destruction was inevitable, rapid and delivered with total German efficiency.

The butcher's bill was horrific. Of the 151 people on board the *Gloucester Castle,* ninety were killed. Many more were badly wounded. Marion, Graham, Pat Radford and Andrew White were the only survivors from the twelve passengers on board. Miraculously, none of them were seriously hurt. Six women passengers and two children had perished. Amongst them were both Pat and Andrew's mothers.

After two weeks aboard the raider, survivors from the *Gloucester Castle* were transferred to the German supply vessel *Charlotte Schlieman* already packed with prisoners, taken from other victims of the *Michel,* for passage to Singapore, where fifty of the fittest were dropped off to act as forced labour before the ship continued on to Japan.

They arrived in Yokohama in mid-September, where they were transferred to the *Nankin,* already holding prisoners from other victims of Germany's raiders.

For David and the others imprisoned in Fukushima, this was the first news they had heard of that ship since it had parted company with the *Regensburg* in the Indian Ocean on 28 May.

After two weeks aboard the *Nankin,* Marion and the three youngsters, over whom she had now assumed the role of surrogate mother, were transferred, firstly to Osaka, then to an internment camp in Kobe. Here they were allowed to visit shops, go for walks and play tennis while enjoying ample food of excellent quality. However, their good fortune was not to last for, after two weeks of this luxury, they were told to bundle up their belongings for yet another transfer, this time to Fukushima.

Marion, Graham and Pat Radford were housed in the women's quarters. Being a year younger than Michael and three years older than Howard, Graham fitted in well, and it was not long before the three of them were doing everything together, including being repeatedly punished and chastised by their Japanese guards for their many misdemeanours.

Andrew White, being alone and a little older, was billeted with the men. Although only sixteen, his body was approaching that of a man. He had been through a horrific experience and was in desperate need of the emotional support that Marion Sparke had provided. Seeing his need, David took it upon himself to act as the boy's mentor and part-time tutor, and they were soon firm friends.

HMAS ADELAIDE – SOUTH INDIAN OCEAN

Saturday 28 November 1942

'Bridge – masthead! Smoke bearing green two five!' It was 1416 when the lookout spotted a wisp of grey smoke on the horizon to the north and called his report down to the Officer-of-the-watch. The officer raised his binoculars and searched the horizon where the lookout had indicated. *Yes, there it is,* he mused. He spoke into the voice-pipe connecting the ship's open bridge to the Captain's day cabin, situated on the deck immediately below. 'Captain, sir! – Officer-of-the-watch,' he called, 'I've got smoke bearing green two five. Estimated range twelve to fourteen miles: closing.'

'Very good,' came the immediate response from Captain Esdaile, *Adelaide's* Commanding Officer, 'I'll be right up.'

The Australian light cruiser *Adelaide* was an improved version of the Royal Navy's 'Chatham' Class. She was laid down during World War I in the Naval Dockyard on Cockatoo Island in Sydney Harbour. She missed the First World War and consequently her construction program was delayed, so she did not enter service until 1922. At 5550 tons' displacement, her Parsons' turbines and twin screws could drive her at a top speed of 24.8 knots, with a clean bottom (i.e. clear of barnacles and other marine growth). She had been modified several times between the wars and in 1942 her armament comprised eight 6-inch guns and three 4-inch anti-aircraft guns, an assortment of smaller weapons, and two depth charge chutes.

From July 1942 *Adelaide* was based in Fremantle, tasked with convoy and escort duties in the Indian Ocean.

On 28 November, the cruiser, together with the Dutch cruiser *Jacob van Heemskerk* and two Australian corvettes, was escorting a small convoy of merchant ships bound for the Persian Gulf. They were approximately 650 nautical miles to the west of Australia's North West Cape and, to this point, the voyage had been without incident.

Captain Esdaile reached the bridge to hear the lookout report that two masts were in sight, then the top of a funnel. He quickly assessed the situation and mentally calculated a course and speed to intercept the oncoming vessel. This done, he turned to the Officer-of-the-watch. 'Come right to a new course 015 degrees and increase speed to 20 knots,' he ordered, before joining the rest of the bridge team in a careful study of the oncoming vessel. It appeared to be a passenger–cargo ship of about 8000 tons and of indeterminate age and nationality. It was certainly worth closer examination. As *Adelaide* leaned gently out of the turn in response to the wheel and the call for increased speed, Esdaile turned to his Chief Yeoman of Signals. 'Chief' he said, 'Signal to *Heemskerk*. "Unidentified vessel closing from the north. Join me."'

As the range closed, the strange ship turned away, and a few minutes later *Adelaide's* wireless office picked up a distress message: 'RRR *Taiyan*. Being followed by suspicious vessel.' There was no ship with that name in any publication *Adelaide* carried on board. The range was closing rapidly. Mindful of the tragic loss of HMAS *Sydney*, with all hands, in her battle with the raider *Kormoran* twelve months previously, in very similar circumstances, Esdaile ordered the ship to Action Stations. All guns were trained on the stranger. A further distress message was received: 'RRR *Taiyang* still being chased.'

It was 1530 when *Adelaide's* Navigating Officer produced a photograph of KMS *Ramses*, from the reference book *German Armed Merchant Vessels*. In all essential details this appeared to be the ship under observation. Captain Esdaile was no longer in doubt. The distance between the ships had closed to 12,000 yards. At 1536 *Ramses* stopped and lowered two boats on her port side. A few minutes later there was an explosion near the ship's stern and a pall of smoke all but enveloped her, leaving only the masts and the top of the funnel visible. Suspecting a trap, *Adelaide* immediately opened fire, as did *Heemskerck*. The lightly armed *Ramses* was no match for the two powerful Allied cruisers. She sank at 1552. The crew had already abandoned ship, leaving only the Captain (Captain Falke), the wireless officer and one other officer to complete the scuttling arrangements and sink the ship. However, *Adelaide* and *Heemskerck* had made this unnecessary.

Captain Esdaile ordered the Dutch cruiser to rejoin the convoy while *Adelaide* picked up survivors: seventy-eight German crew (now prisoners of war), ten Norwegian seamen (now free men once more), a pig and a dog.

How quickly luck can change in war.

GERMAN SUPPLY VESSEL RAMSES – SOUTH INDIAN OCEAN

Saturday 28 November 1942

For Captain Tuften of the *Aust,* and the other nine Norwegian sailors aboard the *Ramses*, the day had begun as any other. Since passing and exchanging greetings with Gumprich's *Thor* on 6 October, they had enjoyed an uneventful voyage. The ship had called at Balikpapen on Borneo's East Coast and unloaded a mixed cargo of building materials, before proceeding on to Batavia to load rubber, desperately needed in Germany to support the war effort, and 1500 cases of quinine. The ship sailed from Batavia on 23 November with the next port-of-call planned to be Bordeaux, France. With luck they might get home for Christmas.

At approximately 1400, a number of ships were sighted to the south. *Ramses* had run into a well-defended, Allied convoy. Captain Falke altered course away, but there was no escape from the two powerful cruisers racing towards his ship. He tried to bluff his way out by hoisting the Norwegian flag and signalling that they were the Norwegian vessel *Taiyang*, but the two cruisers were not fooled. Clearly outnumbered and outgunned, Falke gave the order to scuttle the ship and get away in the boats. Three charges were set and when the first exploded, eight minutes later, the two Allied cruisers opened fire, which they kept up at a steady rate until *Ramses* sank, Norwegian flag still waving. Strangely, no-one in the overcrowded lifeboats was injured, although a number of shells came very close.

Now the roles are reversed, mused Tuften from the lifeboat, *the Germans are prisoners and we Norwegians are free.*

⁓

As soon as they arrived on board, *Adelaide's* Intelligence Officer debriefed the Norwegians on their experiences at the hands of the Germans and Japanese. Captain Tuften reported that while a prisoner on the *Thor* back in May *that* ship had intercepted and captured the Eastern and Australian Shipping Company's vessel *Nankin,* and that the passengers and crew were believed to be safe and were being held in a civilian internment camp north of Tokyo. He also revealed that other prisoners aboard the *Thor* had included seamen from the British tramps *Wellpark, Willesden* and *Kirkpool,* but was regretfully unaware of the names of any of these personnel or their eventual fate.

This news was the first that the Allied Powers had received of the possible fate of the *Nankin,* and her passengers and crew, since the final message received from the ship on 10 May: '*Nankin* abandoning ship Lat. 26° 43' S.; Long. 89° 47' E.' It was also the first news received by the Allies of the possible fates of the *Wellpark, Willesden* and *Kirkpool.*

FUKUSHIMA INTERNMENT CAMP
Saturday 28 November 1942

News of the new arrivals from the *Gloucester Castle* spread quickly through the camp and tales of the comparative luxuries experienced by Marion Sparkes and the others in the Kobe camp grew with every telling. Resentment and even greater hatred of their Japanese captors quickly boiled over, close to open rebellion. Something had to be done but, mindful of his earlier experiences, Captain Stratford realised he would have to be careful about how he approached the unpredictable Commandant.

Over the previous month or two there had been a small but significant increase in the variety and quality of the food provided by the Japanese, but the quantities were still pitifully inadequate. The bread ration had been increased to 7½ ounces per meal and the meat ration was increased at the midday and evening meals. A little liver paste was now provided on occasion, as was a small amount of pumpkin. Sometimes there was weak tea (although not much better than hot water) with a little sugar, but never any milk except that provided for the children

Ushered into Nemoto's presence, Stratford praised the Japanese for their generosity in providing the extra food, but suggested to Nemoto that the internees would think more highly of their captors, whom, he suggested, were not soldiers but simply policemen doing a very difficult task, if the very rigid conditions in the camp were relaxed a little and the women and children, who after all were no threat to the Japanese, were provided with more food and clothing and a little more freedom to mix with the men.

Caught off guard by Stratford's approach, Nemoto was lost for a response but advised, through the interpreter, that such matters were outside his authority and could only be decided by the Interior Ministry in Tokyo – a classic example of the 'I'd like to help, but my hands are tied' approach. Captain Stratford agreed to speak to the new arrivals and order them not to talk to the other internees about conditions outside the camp – a ridiculous instruction that Stratford well knew he would not enforce.

For some reason that remained unclear, Stratford's approach caused embarrassment and confusion in Nemoto's mind for, the following day, and only for the second time since they had been interned, Chief of Special Branch Nakao Masatake (Fishface) arrived from the precinct headquarters. He told Captain Stratford, through the interpreter, that the circumstances at Fukushima were entirely different from that of the British women and children interned at Kobe, as they had been residents in Japan at the outbreak of the war. Indeed, this was why Mrs Sparkes and the others had not been allowed to remain at that camp. He said that, for this reason, Captain Stratford's requests were selfish and unreasonable and any such further requests of a similar nature would be to their disadvantage.

Stratford was dismissed, totally mystified by the unfathomable logic behind Nakao's remarks but having no choice other than to accept the outcome. He was also mystified by the inconsistencies in Nemoto's responses to his requests and stored that information away to use to his advantage later.

Very quickly, the excitement generated by the arrival of Marion and the others died down. Things in the camp returned to normal. Very little changed.

It was about this time that a small incident occurred that had a profound effect on all their lives.

Howard, Michael and Graham Sparke were playing with Howard's precious 'throwing stick' at the front of the convent in that area reserved for exercise by the women and children. They were standing roughly 15 feet (about 4.5 metres) apart in a rough circle and the 'game' was to throw the curved stick to another 'player'

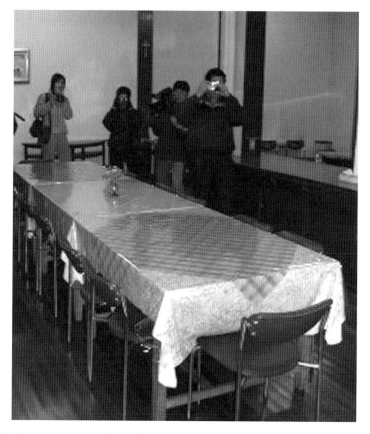

Fukushima Internment Camp – Dining Room – 2002. (Courtesy of Chris Best)

who would attempt to catch it, in much the same way as we do with a frisbee today. A point was awarded every time the stick was dropped and the one with the least points at the end of the game was the winner.

They were being watched by one of the guards whom the boys had nicknamed 'Loopy', due to his simple, but not unkindly, manner.

Graham threw the stick to Howard but it was just out of reach and, as he moved to catch it, he stepped back off the path onto the garden and, losing his balance, fell flat on his back. No damage was done but the whole episode was too much for Loopy who erupted in spasms of raucous laughter, joined by hardly constrained chortles from both Michael and Graham.

Slightly embarrassed, Howard got to his feet and brushed himself down. 'All right,' he said 'if you think that's so funny, see if you can do this?' and he hurled the stick into the air with all the strength his seven-year-old body could muster.

Whether it was the strength of the throw or a fluke of the wind will never be known but the stick sailed in a graceful arc through the air and landed with an audible *clunk* on the convent roof, before sliding down over the terracotta tiles and lodging in the guttering, adjacent to one of the attic dormer windows.

Loopy was beside himself with mirth but seeing the look of dismay on the boys' faces, caused by the loss of their precious throwing stick, he beckoned them over. Using a combination of signs, grunts and pigeon English–Japanese, accompanied by much waving of the arms, he indicated that, if they gained access to the attic, the stick could be retrieved via the adjacent dormer window. With that, he headed off towards the administration office, indicating that the boys should follow.

By the time they reached the office, a small group had gathered, attracted by the mild commotion. As well as Slimy, the interpreter, there was the *bucho*, Mrs Thoms and Madeline Charnaud, wondering if the boys were in some sort of trouble, and several others of the women. After a lengthy explanation of what had happened and what was required, it was agreed by the *bucho* that Loopy and Howard would lead a 'recovery' team, but they were to be accompanied by Madeline and Florence Thoms to ensure there was no danger and that nobody fell off the roof. Loopy lead the way, importantly clutching the attic key in his left hand.

The attic had been permanently out-of-bounds to both male and female prisoners since their arrival. Even the Japanese guards were unsure of what might be up there. The only access was from the first floor landing via a single flight of narrow wooden stairs that terminated in a heavy, locked wooden door.

Such had been the speed of departure of the nuns, there had only been time to gather a few personal items to take with them. Everything else required to run a busy convent, kindergarten and clinic had been hastily boxed and stored in the attic.

While Loopy and Howard struggled with the dormer windows, which were very stiff through lack of use, Madeline and Florence quickly searched the attic for anything of value. They had about two minutes, and what they found was a virtual treasure trove. There was ample plain white paper and other writing materials, books in English for children and adults, children's toys, some disinfectant and cotton wool, linen sheets and a myriad of other useful items that could transform their lives, if they could only remove them from the attic. Running out of time, they grabbed what they could and concealed it about their clothing while trying to make a mental inventory of everything in the attic as a basis for future, better-organised raids.

Howard's throwing stick was recovered, the key duly returned to the office, and Madeline and Florence beat a hasty retreat to the women's quarters to examine their 'loot'. The operation was pronounced an outstanding success. That night there was much excitement as the loot was examined and news of the raid was passed through to the men's quarters on the *phone*.

YOKOHAMA HARBOUR

Monday 30 November 1942

Günther Gumprich was well satisfied but, after seven weeks in Yokohama, he was keen to get back to sea. The refit had gone well. Major maintenance had been completed and *Thor* had been re-stored and re-ammunitioned. She was now almost ready for sea. The crew was well rested, although softened a little by their extended period in port. This did not concern Gumprich; he was confident that after a few days at sea they would again be hardened into an efficient, well-trained fighting force, ready once more to wreak havoc on the enemy's merchant fleet.

Thor was berthed alongside the *Uckermark* to facilitate the transfer of stores, ammunition and fuel. The fuel transfer just completed, a team of Chinese coolies were in *Uckermark's* now empty fuel tanks cleaning them with liquid detergent to remove the highly explosive fuel and oxygen residue. One of the coolies was using a wheel spanner to open a ventilation valve, when it slipped from his grasp. The spanner was rubber coated to prevent creating a spark in just such a situation but, over years of use, much of the rubber had worn away, exposing bare metal. The coolie gaped in dismay as the spanner spiralled out of sight into the empty tank.

It was 1445 and Gumprich had just hosted a very successful lunch on board the *Thor*. It had been attended by dignitaries from the German Embassy in Tokyo as well as officers and officials from the Japanese Navy and War Ministry. A number of German and Japanese reporters had also attended and they were now taking photographs on the ship's focsle. At that moment Gumprich, accompanied by his lunch guests, was in the stern-sheets of *Thor's* motor launch, crossing the basin where the ships were berthed, in order to visit the *Nankin*, now renamed the *Leuthen*, and herself almost ready again for sea.

It was reported later that the explosion rattled the windows in the Argentinean Embassy some 15 miles away and that workers at the Nissan flour mill, 6 miles away, were thrown off their feet and splattered with broken glass.

Gumprich looked on in horror as a second explosion, even more powerful than the first, sent a huge fireball rocketing skywards. He and his guests covered their faces with their arms to protect themselves from the searing heat. Exploding ammunition added to the horror as fuel from the stricken vessels flowed out across the basin and ignited. A third explosion ripped off part of *Uckermark's* superstructure and deposited it neatly on top of *Thor's* bridge.

Gumprich tried to return to his doomed vessel to assist his men, many thrown into the water by the force of the explosions. However, the sea was covered with black, burning oil with the resulting conflagration rapidly spreading across the basin, consuming everything in its path. Try as he might to reach his men, the task was hopeless. Gumprich's launch was driven back by the blistering heat and he could do little but wring his hands in despair as screaming men died in agony, pleading for help that could not be delivered.

Traffic in nearby streets gridlocked as fire engines, ambulances and police converged on the scene, sirens wailing. The fire was unstoppable and the destruction, total. Within minutes *Leuthen* herself was fully ablaze, as was a small Japanese tanker, the only other vessel in the vicinity.

All four ships were reduced to wrecks. Nothing was salvaged.

Thirteen of *Thor's* crew and fifty-three from the *Uckermark* died, as did an untold number of Chinese and Japanese labourers working in the vicinity.

～

The internees at Fukushima learned from the Japanese newspapers that a tragedy of some kind had occurred at Yokohama but reports were heavily censored and little detail was given.

With the loss of the *Thor* and the *Nankin/Leuthen,* Gumprich's fortunes had, indeed, turned.

FUKUSHIMA INTERNMENT CAMP

December 1942

By mid-December, the whole camp was suffering from the constant, bone-chilling cold. The icy winds off the frozen Azuma Mountains seemed to penetrate David's soul. Coal was delivered to the camp in November but it was well into December before Nemoto allowed the convent furnace to be fired. Even then, the heating system was only operated intermittently, and barely took the chill off the freezing air. Men, women and children alike huddled in little groups or were endlessly pacing the corridors, blankets around their shoulders, in a vain attempt to keep out the cold. Even the guards were affected, finding every possible reason to remain indoors. Tempers amongst the internees were short, and David was often guilty of snapping angrily at a fellow prisoner for no other reason than their arms had brushed as they passed.

It was about this time that David came to accept that the war might not end quickly, and talk of repatriation was just that – talk. Constant promises and assurances by the Japanese had come to nothing. David was of the view that it was simply a blackmail tactic used by their captors as a control measure, but many of the internees, more optimistic and less pragmatic than David, did not share his view. They remained convinced that negotiations were progressing and they would soon be released. David did not discourage them in these thoughts or express his own views publicly. If it was hope at the prospect of imminent release that kept them alive and going from one day to the next then who was he to dispel their illusions? It worried him, however, that when the realisation did eventually dawn, as it surely must, the let-down would be all the more severe.

It happened on one of the rare days when a watery sun broke through the freezing overcast and the three boys, Michael, Howard and Graham, were able to go outdoors. They were playing in the snow near the front door of the convent. The door itself was quite substantial, constructed from fine oak. The top half was elaborately inlaid with stained glass. In normal times it was the main entrance to the building and its solid structure and grandeur was in keeping with this function.

The boys were playing with a leather ball that had been 'acquired' during the attic raid. It was similar to an American baseball but a little larger and not quite so hard. Remarkably and quite inexplicably, the sudden arrival of the ball, as well as other items taken from the attic, was never questioned by the Japanese. The boys were having a grand time, playing in the snow and throwing the ball. Michael was standing with his back to the front door and quite close to it when a particularly wild throw from Howard missed its mark and sailed a good two feet over his head into the glass portion of the door. Howard and Graham looked on in horror as the glass shattered. Michael, in a valiant effort to avert the tragedy, lunged after the ball but only succeeded in slashing his arm on the broken glass, causing extensive bleeding.

The boys had no time to recover from their shock, or realise the consequences of what had happened, before one of the nearby guards, unfortunately one with a reputation for unpleasantness, came striding over, waving his arms and shouting. On seeing what had happened he pushed Howard in front of him and grabbed Michael and Graham roughly by the arms and shook them both violently.

'*Ni tassuru ofis,*' (Come to office), he yelled, pushing and dragging the boys towards the administration office. Howard whimpered audibly and Michael, clutching his bleeding arm, left a trail of bright red blood in the pristine snow.

The guard thrust the boys roughly into the office, where the *bucho* and another guard were warming themselves in front of a large charcoal brazier. Alerted by the commotion, Commandant Nemoto emerged from his office and listened in stony silence, all the while tapping his leg with his bamboo cane, as the guard explained what had happened. Nemoto stood before the three boys, glowering at them for what seemed like an eternity. Howard tried hard to control his sobbing but when Nemoto used his bamboo cane to raise his chin and stared directly into his eyes, it all became too much, and a dribble of urine ran down his leg.

Nemoto paced angrily in front of the boys then started to yell at them in a voice verging on hysterical, while prodding them in the ribs and stomach with his cane. Slimy, the interpreter, arrived from his own office nearby, attracted by Nemoto's raised voice. The Commandant ended his tirade and seemed to have reached a decision. He spoke rapidly to Midorikawa and the *bucho*. A guard was dispatched to fetch the boys' mothers, while another thrust two cast-iron pokers into the brazier to heat.

Madeline, Helen and Marion arrived in a rush, not knowing what was happening, but quickly took in the scene and realised the seriousness of the situation from the children's terror. The guards prevented the women from approaching the boys to comfort them. They were pushed roughly to one side to watch – helplessly. Captain Stratford, also alerted to the situation, arrived quickly at the scene.

Nemoto questioned Howard through the interpreter, who was smirking openly and seemed to be taking sadistic delight in the whole proceedings. Questions were fired in quick succession, without waiting for answers: 'Why did you break the window? Who told you to do it? Do you understand you are responsible for this boy's cut arm?' pointing at Michael. 'Do understand that if the cut turns septic it will be your fault? Do you realise you *all* must be punished because of your stupid behaviour?'

Fukushima Internment Camp – Men's Corridor – 2002. (Courtesy of Chris Best)

It went on. Seven-year-old Howard was incapable of response and, head bowed, sobbed uncontrollably.

Nemoto's mood seemed to darken. He broke into a sadistic smirk and spoke quickly to Midorikawa who seemed to share his amusement. Slimy ordered the three boys to lift up their shirts and bare their stomachs. The *bucho* removed the two pokers from the brazier and brandished them menacingly. They were glowing red-hot and the boys felt the heat, even at a distance. Midorikawa took one of the pokers from the *bucho* and thrust it in Helen's face. 'You are to burn the boys' bellies so they will remember not to behave badly again,' he demanded.

Helen reeled backwards, hand up to protect her face from the intense heat. 'Go to hell!' she spat, and attempted to reach Howard, but she was restrained by one of the guards. Marion began to cry and the boys looked around in terror for any sign of escape. There was none. They pleaded with their mothers, 'Please don't let them burn us.'

It was all too much for Madeline. She had clearly had quite enough. She stood directly in front of Nemoto and stared him in the eyes. She spoke firmly but her voice was as cold as ice and as hard as steel. A tigress protecting her cubs could not have shown more determination.

'I'm very sorry that this little accident has taken place,' she said in a deliberate, measured tone, 'but these small children have already undergone the terror of being shelled at sea and surviving in open lifeboats, to be plucked from the ocean and imprisoned in the most trying of circumstances. Whatever the differences between our countries, it is not the fault of the children. To punish children, just because you can, would be regarded as an act of extreme cowardice in my country. This is why Japan can never win this war. If the Japanese were an *honourable* people you would make allowance for such trivial offences committed by children. I demand that you to stop this nonsense before it goes too far. Show the generosity of the Japanese towards women and children by releasing them now.'

Nemoto listened carefully to Midorikawa's translation and was clearly caught off guard and shaken by Madeline's calm manner and determined approach. He had wanted to see them all sobbing in terror and pleading for mercy, but a nagging doubt was rising in his twisted mind, that perhaps he had gone too far? He was now unsure how to react without losing face.

Captain Stratford, who to this point was standing quietly in the background, sensed Nemoto's hesitation and uncertainty and chose the moment to weigh in with his own support, very quietly, but like Madeline, staring Nemoto in the eyes with the same steely determination.

'You must already be aware,' he said, 'that Japan can never win this war. The might of America is such that you will eventually be defeated. When that time comes you and everyone else in authority will be held accountable for your actions.

'I give you my solemn promise,' said Stratford, in a voice so cold and determined that even Slimy was shaken, 'that if any of these children are touched or harmed in any way, both you and Midorikawa will be tracked down at the end of this war and brought to justice, to be punished to the limits allowed by law. The best you could hope for would to be imprisoned for the remainder of your lives, but it is more likely that you would both be hanged as common criminals.'

The atmosphere in the administration office changed, but was still electric and balanced on a knife edge. The earlier, brash, amusing, bully-boy approach by

Nemoto and Midorikawa was replaced by uncertainty and an overriding need to preserve face. Stratford had a moment of concern, wondering if they had pushed Nemoto over the edge, but it was unnecessary. Doubt replaced bravado in the Commandant's thoughts as he desperately tried to extricate himself with honour, but that point was already past.

Nemoto hesitated, then snatched one of the pokers from the *bucho's* hand, approached each of the three boys in turn and burnt off a portion of their hair. The smell of burning hair filled the room. The heat was excruciating and ugly red blisters erupted on the boys' heads where the iron came too close. The women looked on in horror. Helen retched and choked back vomit, but was only partially successful. Captain Stratford held her to prevent her falling.

Deed completed, Nemoto glared defiantly at Stratford and the three women, then returned the still glowing iron to the brazier, before turning on his heel and without another word, stormed from the room.

The sense of relief was colossal, but this was not the end of it. As further punishment, the three boys were forced to stand for an hour on the first floor landing, under the bell, holding a bucket of water between them. A guard stood by to prod and berate them whenever the bucket touched the floor. At the end of an hour, none of the three could walk and they could barely stand. Their still deeply distressed mothers were again summoned, to take them away.

This incident forged a bond of friendship between the three boys that no outsider could possibly comprehend.

It was just two days before Christmas.

~

The spirit of that Christmas, and the indomitable attitude of the internees, remained one of David's most vivid recollections of the winter of 1942-43.

There is some amazing quality in the British psyche that emerges at Christmas, regardless of place or circumstance, and never was it more apparent than at the civilian internment camp in Fukushima at the end of 1942. For weeks beforehand, on both the men's and women's side of the camp, eager volunteers were busy, making toys for the children out of anything that came readily to hand. They made copies of all the well-known Christmas carols and secretly distributed them. After lights out, hearty renditions of *Silent Night, Oh Come all Ye Faithful* and *Good King Wenceslas* were picked up in both women's and men's sections of the camp and rang throughout the corridors.

At first the Japanese were confused and lacked any comprehension of what was happening or why. Then they became angry and Captain Stratford was sent for. All singing was banned because previous permission had not been sought and the prisoners were 'too happy'. Even this did not dispel the spirit of Christmas and on the day itself, Caroline Dimitrakopouloy dressed up as Santa Claus. Using Madeline Charnaud's kitbag as a sack, dolls, toy animals, games such as draughts and dominoes and other small items, all made from available scraps with great ingenuity, were distributed to each of the twelve children in the camp.

Although the men and women were still not allowed to mix, the message to the Japanese was clear: *You can take away our freedom but you can't destroy our spirit.*

FUKUSHIMA INTERNMENT CAMP

January–March 1943

Howard was not well. On Monday 4 January he refused to eat his evening meal and went to bed early, complaining of a headache. Helen was not overly worried until next morning, when he awoke with a temperature and complained of a raging headache and violent stomach pains. Concerned, she sent for Annie Law, who, along with Elizabeth Scott, was a qualified nurse. Annie examined Howard, noting that his temperature had risen to 103 degrees and that he had broken out into a rash of rose-coloured spots.

She turned to Helen, then, moving out of Howard's earshot, said, 'Helen, I believe he is suffering from chicken pox. Normally, that wouldn't be a worry, but, in our circumstances, it *is* cause for some concern, particularly as it will almost certainly spread to the other children. I don't want to worry you unduly, but there's also a very small chance that Howard has typhoid fever – the symptoms are very similar. If that turns out to be the case we have a very serious health problem in the camp. One way or the other, we have to isolate him from the other children, and we must get the doctor here straight away to conduct more tests.'

This was one of the rare occasions that Nemoto did not demur, and Dr Hakozaki arrived the same day, one of the very few occasions that she came as soon as summoned. She took blood samples and, later in the day, confirmed that chicken pox was indeed the cause of Howard's illness. Helen, waiting anxiously for the results, was much relieved.

Despite Howard's isolation, the disease quickly spread through the women's side of the camp. Michael was the next to fall ill and, within days, most of the other children were infected. Under other circumstances the epidemic would be no cause for concern but here the undernourished children's immune systems had no capacity to fight the disease. The Japanese ignored pleas for additional and more nourishing food. There was little that they could do except let the disease run its course. Luckily, this occurred without serious consequences.

An interesting aside to the chicken pox episode was that Howard's 'isolation ward', a small dressing room in the eastern corner of the women's quarters, looked out over the washing lines. On several occasions, he observed one of the women waving her hands in front of her face in a very strange manner. Fascinated, Howard approached the woman when he was well. Audrey Jeffery, owner of the sewing machine, explained what she'd been doing. 'I was using sign language,' she said, laughing. 'It's used to talk to people who are deaf, but I was using it to talk to a friend in the men's section.'

'Can you teach us boys how to do it?' Howard begged excitedly.

'I can teach you some of the simpler signs if you like,' said Audrey, and over the next few weeks she taught Howard, Michael and Graham a number of signs that allowed them to pass simple messages to each other over a considerable distance. From that time the boys took great delight in using their 'secret code' to pass messages under the Japanese noses.

~

On 10 January Tom Melia arrived in the camp, after discharge from hospital in Yokohama, to rejoin his mates from the *Kirkpool*.

Tom lied about his age when he signed on as a galley boy in North Shields, the same day as Alfie Round and Ginger Robson. He was, in fact, only fifteen, but such was the shortage of manpower to crew Britain's merchant ships, the authorities did not enquire too deeply into his past or credentials.

During the engagement with the *Thor*, Tom was badly wounded, losing the whole of his left buttock to a piece of flying shrapnel. *Thor's* doctors, and later those on the *Regensburg*, did everything they could to repair the damage, and Tom underwent several skin graft operations, but the conditions and facilities on board those two ships were such that the wounds were very slow to heal. On arrival in Yokohama, Tom was transferred directly to the local hospital, where he underwent further treatment. Although still not fully recovered, he was well patched up, but his wounds remained a source of further problems and discomfort.

From his hospital bed in Yokohama, Tom could see out over the dock area and witnessed the destruction of the *Thor, Nankin* and *Uckermark* six weeks previously. He brought the first authentic news of the incident to the internees in Fukushima.

By the end of January 1943 they had been incarcerated for a little over six months. While there were many promises of early repatriation, none had amounted to any real prospect of release. All requests by Captain Stratford to contact the German Embassy, or to ascertain whether the International Committee of the Red Cross (ICRC) had been advised of their existence, and their next-of-kin notified of their circumstances, were turned down. Morale was low. Tempers often flared and

Fukushima Internment Camp – Attic – 2002. (Courtesy of Chris Best)

inter-racial bickering was rife. Loud arguments sometimes degenerated into an exchange of blows leaving Captain Stratford to restore calm.

The stress and frustration was even more apparent amongst the women, where they had the additional burden of caring for the children. Madeline Charnaud emerged as a natural leader and the other women respected her wisdom and calm approach to every problem, even in the most difficult circumstances. However, one day towards the end of January, the frustrations boiled over.

Gabby Lyon was an attractive, slightly built woman of twenty-nine who, like Helen and several others in the camp, escaped to Australia from Singapore just

Fukushima Internment Camp – Attic – 2002.

before it fell. She was accompanied by her six-month-old infant son, Clive, having left her army husband, Captain Ian Lyon of the Special Operations Executive and of Operations *Jaywick* and *Rimau* fame, behind. From Perth in Western Australia, Gabby received news that her husband had escaped to India and without further thought or consultation, determined to join him and booked herself and Clive passage on the *Nankin*.

Elizabeth Gleeson was a stewardess aboard the *Nankin*. She was large in stature and, at forty-one, was mature, understanding and had a slow, easy-going manner, typical of many Australian women. Her husband was serving overseas in Australia's armed forces and, having no children, she had seen her present job as a way of contributing to the war effort. Even in captivity, Elizabeth did not relinquish her duty of care to her former passengers and, even more after the tragic death of Chief Steward McIntyre, she had a total commitment to their wellbeing.

Gabby Lyon had great difficulty adjusting to life in captivity and was sometimes morose and withdrawn. Looking after Clive, now a year old, was a burden. She often left him to cry and this was a source of constant irritation to the other women, and sharp words were often exchanged.

On this day, Clive had been crying for some time and although Gabby was nearby she took no notice. In frustration, Elizabeth picked up the baby to comfort him and, at the same time, snapped caustically at Gabby, 'Can't you see the child is distressed? Why don't you do something?'

With a low animal snarl and a speed that caught everyone by surprise, Gabby launched herself at Elizabeth, bringing both her and the baby down in a crashing tackle. With the wind knocked from her by a blow to the midriff, Elizabeth was slow to react and was gasping for breath. Before she recovered, Gabby was astride her on the floor, both hands locked around her neck, shaking her violently and choking the life from her. However, with her superior size and strength Elizabeth loosened the grip on her throat and, before matters could degenerate further, Madeline and several others of the women, attracted by the commotion, were on the scene, dragging the pair apart. Miraculously, the baby was unharmed.

'I never thought I would get away,' Elizabeth said later, 'I really thought she was going to strangle me. It took all my strength to get free.'

The incident was never raised again by Gabby, who carried on next day as though nothing had happened. However, it was a salutary lesson to all that conditions in captivity were such that suppressed anger, despair and frustration were always lurking just below the surface, with the potential to erupt into violence at any time.

MELBOURNE, AUSTRALIA

Thursday 11 February 1943

Mr Thomas Hoey, State Publicity Censor for Victoria, reread the letter from the Australian Department of the Navy. He did not understand why the RAN's Publicity Censorship Office was imposing a total news blackout on any information related to the disappearance of the *Nankin,* or on the fate of her passengers and crew.

The arrival, in Fremantle in early December 1942, of a number of Norwegian officers and sailors from the freighter *Aust,* who had been released when the German blockade runner *Ramses,* on which they were travelling, was intercepted by HMAS *Adelaide,* had caused a mild sensation. The Norwegians reported to the press that they had been imprisoned on the *Nankin* in Yokohama Harbour and were aware that many of the former passengers and crew of that vessel were being held by the Japanese in a camp somewhere to the north of Tokyo. This was the first news of the *Nankin* received by the Allies since her dramatic 'abandoning ship' message of 10 May 1942. Clearly, friends and relatives of the passengers and crew were deeply concerned. However, in accordance with wartime requirements, press reports of the Norwegians' story had been submitted to the Censors, requesting formal clearance prior to publication. The response to this request was the letter, classified 'SECRET', now in Hoey's hand. It read:

'Dear Mr Hoey,

With further reference to your letter SPC/1177 of 15 January 1943, enclosing newspaper submissions on the German ship scuttled in the Indian Ocean, I have been instructed to request that the ban on publication of this material, in whole or in part, be continued indefinitely.

'This matter has been discussed with Allied Headquarters authorities, who were informed that Australian Naval Intelligence was strongly of the opinion that publication of this information should be withheld indefinitely. In putting forward that view, the references to SS *Nankin* were specifically included. A reply has now been received, stating that Allied Headquarters are glad to cooperate with the wishes of Australian

Naval Intelligence in this matter.

'For your information, I quote the following pertinent portion of our letter to GHQ which elicited that agreement:

"It is felt that the public release of any of this material would be most undesirable. No matter what form the stories took, they would indicate to the enemy that personnel ex-*Ramses* had divulged information. Norwegians and similar nationals naturally would be suspect, and this might react unfavourably against persons of those nationalities still in enemy hands. In any case, it would tend to block any source from which information may be emanating in enemy territory.

The enemy will already have assumed that personnel from the scuttled ship have made some disclosures, but the precise extent of those disclosures would not be known to him. As far as the story of *Nankin* herself is concerned, the ship's agents have advised next-of-kin, confidentially, that her personnel are reported to be safe, without disclosing the source of the report. Hence the banning of publication does not withhold the information from the persons most entitled to receive it."

'The press material referred to is returned herewith.

Yours etc.'

The letter was signed by the Assistant Publicity Censorship Liaison Officer at Navy Office, Melbourne, and was dated 9 February 1943. It provided proof, therefore, that Allied authorities were aware, at least from the end of 1942, that personnel from the *Nankin* were alive and were being held captive in Japan. It also shows that the next-of-kin of *Nankin's* passengers and crew were provided with confidential advice as early as January 1943 that their loved ones were alive and being held by the Japanese. Whether or not Allied authorities attempted to ascertain, through the Protecting Power (Switzerland) or the Red Cross, the names of those imprisoned, or attempted to establish contact with them, remains a mystery.

FUKUSHIMA INTERNMENT CAMP

March 1943

It was a blessed relief when the long, bitterly cold winter blossomed into a brilliant spring. The plants and trees in the convent grounds burst into life and the cherry blossoms were magnificent. The snow was gone and for the first time in months the men and women took their morning exercise outside, although still in their segregated areas. The men introduced a daily morning session of callisthenics, for all who were well enough to participate, to maintain health and fitness as well as to demonstrate to the Japanese, their discipline and resolve not to be intimidated or subdued. One of the guards was always present during these exercise periods to ensure, on the insistence of the Commandant, that the time was called in Japanese. '*Ichi, ni, san, shi…,*' the men called, as they performed the star jumps, squats and other exercises, always to immaculate time and always in rigid straight lines. During the winter, these daily sessions had been carried out in the assembly hall but now, with the warmer weather upon them, they used the men's exercise yard in the south-eastern corner of the compound.

The coming of spring also gave birth to a new optimism amongst the internees, although David could find no rational explanation for it other than the slow, but certain, realisation that Japan would ultimately be defeated. There was no improvement in the rations or relaxation of the brutal corporal punishments meted out by the Commandant and guards. Nor was there any evidence that anyone outside the camp was aware of their existence. They had no contact at all with the outside world.

There was, of course, the daily news briefs from Fred Garner and, although heavily censored and very much biased to keep up the morale of the Japanese people, it became evident that all was not going well for the Imperial Nipponese Army. Even if the battles of Coral Sea and Midway could be characterised as drawn matches, they certainly marked a turning point. As a consequence, the magnificent Australian campaign in New Guinea in late 1942 and early 1943, under the most appalling conditions, stopped the Japanese and ultimately pushed them back into the sea. Battles at Kokoda, Milne Bay, Gona, Buna and Sanananda – places previously unheard of – have been added to the annals of Australian military history with such as Gallipoli, Passchendaele and Tobruk. The Australians' New Guinea campaign, together with the retaking of Guadalcanal by the United States Marines in February 1943, prevented the invasion of Australia and marked the limit to Japanese territorial gains in the South Pacific. From this time, America's overwhelming industrial might, ably supported by her Allies, snatched the initiative and rolled back the invader, island by island, to the shores of Japan itself. Although devastating losses were characterised as Japanese 'victories' or, at worst, 'strategic fighting withdrawals', it was impossible to keep the reality of the situation from the Japanese people. Too many young men were departing, never to return. Food shortages and power blackouts became commonplace as the Allies destroyed vital communication lifelines that supplied the essential ingredients to wage war: items such as food, oil and rubber. The Allies were achieving in the Pacific what Doenetz and his U-Boats came so close to achieving in the North Atlantic.

~~~

With the arrival of the warmer weather the boys were able to play outside again and Howard was delighted to discover a small population of frogs inhabiting a pond near the asparagus patch. He advised them, in the strictest confidence, 'If you'll be my friends, I promise not to carry on about your incessant croaking.' Clearly the frogs were in agreement because they became quite tame, allowing Howard to pick them up and carry them about.

Howard and Michael kept David up-to-date on the frogs' progress as well as their other activities, and Helen often spoke to him by *phone* about the boys. With their mutual concern for Howard as the catalyst, the relationship between David and Helen deepened and each began to seek the other's voice.

They began by talking about the boys, but their whispers through the locked steel door went beyond frogs and the boys' misadventures, to what might come in the future. Would they emerge into a new and better world and, if they did, what then?

~~~

The 31st of March was Michael's twelfth birthday, which sparked both a physical and an emotional milestone. Living in close proximity in the female quarters, Michael frequently encountered the women going about their ablutions, and often chanced upon them in various states of undress. Also, a number of the women had remarked to Madeline with a knowing laugh that Michael was certainly 'growing up' as little tufts of hair began sprouting where previously there had been none. Changes were happening to Michael's body and he was experiencing pleasant but confusing emotions. The subtle changes in his body and behaviour did not pass unnoticed by the only female internee who might be expected to show interest, even though a number of years older than Michael: Lavender Yates. Lavender (known as Vanda) was the daughter of Arthur and Susan Yates, tea planters who had been returning to Ceylon on the *Nankin*.

Vanda was very artistic and spent much of her time composing poetry or making sketches using the meagre supply of paper and coloured pencils that had been taken in the attic raid. She was always finding excuses to be near Michael and would sometimes cuddle up to him under his quilt in his room, whenever the opportunity permitted them to be alone. She was soon encouraging Michael to fondle her thighs and breasts while also stimulating *him* with her hands and body. Michael flushed with excitement in anticipation of these playful romps until the inevitable happened and, one day, they were caught.

There followed an almighty row between the two mothers. Madeline was unconcerned, laughing the matter off, regarding it as a normal part of growing up. Susan Yates, a tall and rather gaunt lady, held quite a different view. She was extremely angry, claiming that Michael was now too old to be in the women's section, and demanded to see Captain Stratford with a view to having him transferred to the men's side forthwith! A meeting was arranged and eventually it was agreed that Michael and Graham Sparkes would move to the men's side and share a room with Captain Piangos of the *Pagasitikos*. Commandant Nemoto agreed to the arrangement with the further, and rather surprising, concession that, on account of their age, the boys be allowed to return to the women's side daily, to visit their mothers.

For Michael and Graham, life on the men's side was a complete contrast to the women's. It seemed quieter and more peaceful. The men generally spoke in softer tones, rarely raising their voices, except for the Greeks, who would shout and gesticulate at each other across their large room. When they did have grievances the men tended to deal with them quickly and openly whereas the women would often let resentments bubble below the surface for extended periods. There were also all sorts of activities going on to help pass the time and the two boys were immediately enrolled to commence studies in various subjects.

David again took up the task of teaching mathematics, and he very quickly constructed a comprehensive syllabus in arithmetic and algebra. Daily classes soon commenced, to supplement the lessons they had been receiving when confined to the women's section. The Reverend Charles Boyall, an Australian, took responsibility for English and Mr Gerald Stewart, history. Madeline taught geography during the boys' daily visits to the women's side.

The willingness of the Japanese to allow the two boys to cross over, virtually at will, between the men's and women's sections, was quite extraordinary. It went a long way to resolving the communication problems as the boys were able to convey daily reports on the progress of the war, as gleaned by Fred Garner from his newspaper summaries, as well as other messages. It also facilitated the virtually unhindered transfer of goods and materials between the two sections. Mixing with the men opened a new range of interests for the boys. David and

Michael Charnaud's Report Card 1944.

Alfie, in particular, soon established lasting friendships. The only one to suffer under the new arrangement was Howard, who lost his two mates for a good portion of each day.

BARRY, SOUTH WALES

1 April 1943

Muriel stepped off the bus opposite North Walk on the Colcot Road and with a cheery wave to her travelling companion, Gwyneth Thomas, set off on the hundred yards or so to the family home at number 78. It was almost a year since she had heard that David was missing and with no further news she had almost given up hope. For the first few months, the first words to her mother, Ethel Roscoe, who cared for the children while Muriel was at work, were, 'Is there any news of David?' but as time passed, so did hope, and the inquiries became less and less frequent.

It was a bright afternoon and although the wind was fresh it was not cold. It had been a good day, and Muriel was looking forward to meeting up with Gwyneth later that evening for their regular Thursday night drink at the Colcot Arms and a visit to the local cinema where the latest Clark Gable film was showing. Perhaps they might even meet up again with the two very charming American Marines from the 101st Airborne Division, stationed nearby, who had tried to chat them up the previous week. As she entered the front door she was greeted with squeals of delight from Donald and Andrew, eager to relate the details of the day's activities. Thoughts of David were, at that time, the last thing in her mind. The boys were sitting at the table enjoying their tea of bread, margarine and Nanna Roscoe's homemade jam, made from blackberries gathered in the Porthkerry Woods the previous summer, when Muriel entered.

'Hello boys. Have you had a good day?' she said, giving each of them a hug. 'Tell me what you have been doing.' But before they could reply Nanna Roscoe thrust forward an official-looking white envelope.

'It came today,' she said. 'It's from David's shipping company.'

So unexpected was it, that Muriel was caught completely off guard. The blood drained from her face and adrenaline pumped through her body and she took the proffered envelope with a shaking hand, not knowing what to expect. She tore it open and read quickly:

'Dear Mrs Millar,

We regret we are still without definite news of the personnel of the vessel in which your husband was serving. A year has now passed since we last had news of that vessel. Every possible effort has been made through the Red Cross and other channels to ascertain whether any members of the crew are prisoners of war. We fully realise the anxiety and sorrow which the uncertainty is causing you, but we do not consider that we should yet presume the death of your husband, as there is still a hope, which we regretfully admit is a slender one, that he may have been captured.

Please be assured that we are doing everything possible to obtain news and we will continue to keep you fully advised.

Yours faithfully

Watts, Watts & Co. Ltd.'

Muriel collapsed into a chair and read the letter again. 'We do not consider that we should yet presume death.' What did that mean? 'There is still hope … regretfully slender … may have been captured.' The letter raised more and more questions but provided no answers. David's salary had been stopped some time previously but Muriel could not receive a war widow's pension while there remained some chance that he was still alive. Times were hard but life had to go on.

Muriel chose to remain at home with the boys that night. Her earlier desire for a relaxing night out had evaporated.

FUKUSHIMA INTERNMENT CAMP

April–May 1943

In consultation with the men and with the arrival of more clement weather, it was decided that the time was right for a new, carefully planned and organised assault on the attic. It was agreed that, if it could be arranged, Madeline and Florence Thoms would again accompany one of the boys to the attic with Loopy, the Japanese guard, as they were already familiar with the layout and where the various items of interest were stored. As the attic stairs emerged onto the first floor landing in the men's section, it was arranged that a number of the men form a chain to pass down the items recovered and conceal them about the building. A number of empty cupboards in the chapel were chosen as an initial place of concealment as it was adjacent to the attic stairs and the guards very seldom visited this area outside of regular chapel times. Also, as all of the internees had access to the chapel, it would simplify the later distribution of the material. Further, both men and women were to be posted at various strategic positions inside and outside the building to act as sentries with instructions to create a diversion, should any of the other guards approach or be in danger of interrupting the operation.

Preparations complete, a day was chosen when Loopy was detailed to patrol the women's outdoor exercise area. Howard was given the task of encouraging the guard to play catch with him, as the other boys, Michael and Graham, were, at that time, over in the men's section. Bored by the monotony of his duty, Loopy was only too pleased to participate and entered into the spirit of the game with gusto.

When all was ready Helen, who was loitering nearby, gave the signal for Howard to throw the ball, which he lodged in the roof guttering with commendable skill on the first attempt.

Loopy was rather embarrassed as he felt that he had somehow contributed to the accident and he had no hesitation in indicating to Howard that he would get the attic key to retrieve the ball, as he had done on the previous occasion. The key was fetched and Loopy, with Howard, Madeline and Florence in close attendance, ascended the attic stairs. While Loopy and Howard moved deeper into the interior of the attic, to where they estimated the ball might be, Madeline and Florence began to rapidly fill the bags and pillowslips, which they had concealed about their persons, with all manner of useful things, and pass them back to the eager hands waiting on the stairs.

All was going well, indeed, too well. One of the guards, for some unexplained reason known as 'Titch', entered the front entrance of the building and began to ascend the stairs leading to the first floor landing, where Alfie and Ginger were stationed to run interference, in just such an eventuality. Titch was a particularly unpleasant specimen of humanity, known for his brutality and violent temper. As he approached, Alfie gave Ginger an almighty shove and yelled, 'Why don't you watch where you're going?' Ginger retaliated by launching himself at Alfie screaming a tirade of Geordie abuse, unintelligible to anyone living outside the Newcastle area. Titch was quickly on the scene and began smashing his bamboo baton into any part of Alfie or Ginger's anatomy that he could conveniently reach, all the time screaming at both in Japanese. Still arguing vehemently, Alfie and Ginger were unceremoniously dragged to the administration office, where they received a severe beating. Meanwhile, Howard's ball had been recovered, the loot obtained from the attic had been carefully concealed in the chapel, and the routine of the day restored to normal.

Alfie and Ginger considered their beating a small price to pay and the operation was declared a complete success. Ample supplies of writing materials were obtained as well as several packs of playing cards – much to the delight of the bridge players – books, linen and a host of other useful items.

⁓

It was about this time, through the actions and attitude of the prisoners, that the Japanese became suspicious about the amount of war news that was filtering through to them. It was clear to Nemoto that the internees were getting information from some external source. Unannounced room searches and prolonged questioning of the prisoners, selected at random, were conducted. Suspicion fell on Fred Garner, who was questioned at length, but despite the harsh and threatening nature of the interrogation, he concealed the fact that he was able to read Japanese. He maintained that the only knowledge he possessed of the progress of the war was obtained from Captain Stratford, who, in turn, obtained it from the Commandant himself during the course of their regular meetings on camp matters. Although still not satisfied, Nemoto had no alternative but to let the matter drop. However, as a precaution, the daily newspaper scam was discontinued for several days, until the issue was all but forgotten once more.

LONDON

27 May 1943

The Records Clerk at the Prisoner of War Information Bureau, administered through the War Office off Whitehall, ran his finger quickly down the list of names that had just been received by wireless from the British Section of the Central Tracing Agency of the International Committee of the Red Cross in Geneva. The list, containing 168 names, had been provided to the ICRC by the Japanese, through their Tokyo Information Office for POWs, under an agreement brokered by the ICRC and the Swiss Government, who were acting as the Protecting Power (PP) for all British personnel held in Japan. The clerk observed that all those on the list were British subjects, and were noted as being held at the Kawasaki No. 1 POW Camp near Yokohama.

The thing that struck the Records Clerk as slightly odd was that less than half of those listed held military rank and the rest, judging from such titles as 'Captain', 'First Officer', 'Second Officer', 'Fireman', and the like, were probably in the British Merchant Navy. Curiosity now aroused, the clerk took the list to a nearby office where records were held of British personnel, including merchant seamen, posted as missing at sea.

It was a slow task and took several days, but gradually a pattern emerged. Every name on the list fell into one of several, clearly defined categories; they were either military passengers or crew members from the passenger ship *Nankin*, last heard of in the Indian Ocean on 10 May 1942, or crew members of the British tramp steamers, *Wellpark, Willesden* and *Kirkpool,* ships all listed as 'Missing presumed sunk' for the past twelve months. However, a further cross-check of the crew and passenger lists for these vessels showed that a number of people were still unaccounted for. The greatest probability was that they had been lost at sea or killed in action; but this did not explain the absence of the seventy-five or more civilians, including women and children, listed as passengers on the *Nankin*. It was inconceivable that all of the military passengers on that vessel had survived whereas every one of the civilian passengers had perished. It was clear, therefore, that personnel from these ships had, for some reason that was not yet clear, been separated into two groups some time after their capture. The list received by the Records Clerk from Geneva contained the names of those from only one of these groups. That being the case, *where,* mused the clerk, *were the rest?*

The Records Clerk was persistent and determined to get to the bottom of the mystery. The name *Nankin* was familiar and he recalled some months previously advice received from Australia that a group of Norwegian Merchant Navy officers, freed from a German blockade runner in the Indian Ocean, had advised that a number of *civilian* passengers from the *Nankin* were known to be alive and interned in a camp, somewhere in Japan.

Gradually the pieces fell into place. The clerk concluded, and his superior officer agreed, that the surviving crew and military passengers from the *Nankin*, together with the surviving crew members from the *Wellpark, Willesden* and *Kirkpool*, had somehow finished up in a POW camp at Kawasaki and that the civilian passengers from the *Nankin* had been separately interned in another camp, the name and location of which was presently unknown. The others, comprising the wounded from the crews of the *Nankin, Wellpark, Willesden* and *Kirkpool*, could not be accounted for and were therefore presumed to be dead. [6]

Therefore, on the basis of the available information, next-of-kin were advised, and the Central Tracing Agency of the ICRC were requested to investigate the existence and circumstances of some seventy-five civilian prisoners from the *Nankin*, believed to be held in a civilian internment camp, somewhere to the north of Tokyo.

BARRY, SOUTH WALES

Saturday 5 June 1943

Muriel had Saturday afternoon off and was busying herself about the house when she heard the afternoon post land on the mat just inside the front door.

---

6 Unknown to the authorities at this time, this latter group had been transferred at sea from the Regensburg to the Dresden, on 31 May previously, along with the civilian passengers from the Nankin.

She immediately recognised the now familiar envelope from David's shipping company, and quickly tore it open. The words leapt out of the page, striking like a hammer blow to her heart.

'Dear Mrs Millar,

It is with deep regret that we must advise you that we have received information from the Prisoner of War Information Bureau in London that your husband has been officially categorised 'missing presumed dead', based on information recently received through the International Committee of the Red Cross (ICRC).

'The ICRC was provided, by authorities in Japan, with a list of names of officers and crew of your husband's ship, the SS *Willesden*, who have been captured and imprisoned in a POW camp near Yokohama, Japan. No other information was provided.

'We regret to advise you that your husband's name was not on that list, leading to the conclusion that he was killed, or was wounded and later died, in the action that resulted in the capture of the remaining crew members.

'Without wishing to provide false hope, there is the smallest possibility that your husband's name was omitted from the list in error or there is some other explanation for its absence. This possibility is, however, deemed extremely unlikely.

'When you feel able, you should contact this office to make arrangements in relation to outstanding monies and any pension that may be owing to you.

'The Chairman and Directors of the Company join me in expressing their heartfelt sympathy at your tragic loss.

Yours sincerely
For Watts, Watts & Co. Ltd."

MELBOURNE, AUSTRALIA

Monday 21 June 1943

Mr Hoey was justly pleased. Following an article by Ramon Lavalle, First Secretary to the Argentine Legation in Tokyo, in the May 1943 edition of *The American*, that contained some detail of the loss of the *Nankin* and other vessels in Yokohama Harbour on 30 November 1942, he had again written to the Department of the Navy, enclosing draft articles submitted by a number of Australian newspapers.

Hoey was seeking a review of the earlier decision to censor all stories related to this matter. His argument was that Lavalle's article put the loss of the *Nankin* in the public domain and therefore there was no security compromise in Australian newspapers publishing similar material relating to the ship's loss. Indeed, *any* information on the loss of the *Nankin* was very much in the public interest.

Hoey read the letter from Navy Office, classified 'SECRET', one more time:

'Dear Mr Hoey,

With reference to your letter of 14 June, returned herewith are the proposed *Sydney Morning Herald, Daily Telegraph* and *Sydney Sun* stories on the SS *Nankin*.

2. As there are several problems connected with this matter, I have not commented specifically on this material. Instead, I am enclosing what may be termed a "specimen story" to illustrate the type of material to which Navy would have no objection. Naturally, this is not a "handout," official or otherwise. Navy is not making any statement on the matter, and no published material should convey that impression. The "specimen" is forwarded only as a method which (possibly) will assist Censorship in guiding the Press as to the nature of the stories to be submitted to Censorship by the Press.

3. It will be noticed that <u>no reference</u> is made to the following:
The name of the scuttled German ship
The nationality of the persons who told the first story of the *Nankin*
None of the alleged details of methods used in her capture
None of the information given on any other subjects by any persons from the scuttled German ship

4. Although the following points are not included in the "specimen", there is no objection to their use by the Press:

a. The names of such of the ship's officers as are included in the stories returned herewith (provided the Press have checked these with the ship's agents)

b. The name of the Line to which the *Nankin* belonged, or the nature of her work before the war

4. There is no objection to the <u>broadcasting</u> (on radio) of the story, subject to the same conditions as for the Press.

5. The points mentioned in Paragraph 3 above are particularly

important. It will be recalled that, when the survivors from the scuttled German ship were landed in Australia, some of them gave to the Press information which, at the time, Navy was most anxious should not be published. That anxiety still exists, for, assuming that the enemy is by now aware of the identity of the scuttled ship, he still will not be certain what information the passengers (or even the crew) gleaned in Japan, or how much of that information is such that its publication would give the enemy a valuable indication of the extent of our knowledge on certain matters; it might also suggest to the enemy that we have permitted publication of some of the information and deliberately withheld publication of kindred information.

Yours faithfully

Etc

Publicity Censorship Liaison Officer.'

As a consequence of this advice, the following article appeared in *The Daily News* and a number of like articles appeared in other Australian newspapers, on Wednesday 23 June 1943, under the headline **'SHIP MYSTERY SOLVED'**.

'News brought to Australia some months ago by seamen rescued from a Nazi blockade runner, that the crew and passengers of the passenger liner *Nankin* were safe, was officially confirmed today.

'The announcement ends months of anxiety for relatives. The passengers included a number of women and children proceeding to India to rejoin husbands and fathers.

'*Nankin*, an Eastern and Australian liner of 7131 tons, had disappeared mysteriously.

'Today's official advice stated that the ship was captured and taken to Japan with her 112 passengers unhurt. She was attacked in the Indian Ocean while on her way from Sydney to India.

'Details of the capture have still to be made known, but the *Nankin*, with her big passenger role, was in no position to fight. The crew comprised 150, most of the officers being Australians, with coloured seamen, firemen and stewards.

'Captain H.G. Stratford of Sydney, who is well known in the Eastern trade with Australia before the war, was in command.

'For months the only information received in Sydney was that the *Nankin* had been able to transmit one brief message: "Abandoning ship."

'When Allied warships intercepted a blockade-running merchantman in the Indian Ocean towards the end of last year they rescued a number of seamen who had been held captive by the Japanese for some months. These men had been taken capture in the South Atlantic.

'They were the first to bring to Australia the news of the fate of the *Nankin* and her passengers and crew.

'They got their information in Yokohama. Along with other prisoners they had been finally taken to Japan and while in Yokohama harbour were confined in holds of captured ships.

'Their theory was that, after capture, the *Nankin* was sailed to Japan by a prize crew. It was while they were at Yokohama that they received what was considered to be reliable information to the effect that the *Nankin* passengers and crew were safe and well.

'Intervention by the Allied warships saved these seamen from being taken back to Germany.

'The blockade runner was scuttled by her crew, all of whom were landed at an Australian port.

'When the *Nankin* disappeared, next-of-kin were informed that it was feared she had been lost through enemy action.'

FUKUSHIMA

July–December 1943.

The internees in Fukushima were unaware of any efforts by the ICRC, the Protecting Power (PP) or any other agency to establish the fact of their existence, wellbeing or whereabouts. As far as they were aware, rightly as it turned out, no information related to their internment had been passed on by the Germans or the Japanese. Meanwhile, the struggle in the camp to live out each day without descending into despair went on.

Tuesday 13 July turned out to be an important day on the internees' calendar. The previous Sunday had marked the completion of one year of internment, still with no prospect of repatriation despite promises and rhetoric. On this particular Tuesday there was an air of cautious expectation evident amongst the guards, heightened by the arrival of Fishface from Fukushima. Nakao was accompanied by another officer, not previously seen, itself an indication that something important was about to happen. Captain Stratford was sent for –

the others waited. A little while later, Stratford returned and announced that Nemoto was to be replaced and, from that day, a new Commandant, Captain Mitsuhashi Yosio, would be in command.

Mitsuhashi was short, even for a Japanese, but sturdy in frame and a little overweight. He wore rimless glasses, had close cropped hair and a pencil moustache. He had the habit, when in the presence of any of the internees, of standing with feet slightly apart, clutching a black bamboo cane, with which he constantly tapped his right leg.

The arrival of Mitsuhashi, soon nicknamed the 'Pumpkin Controller' due to his personal, almost obsessive, interest in the issue (or more frequently, non-issue) of pumpkins from the prison gardens, heralded the introduction of a stricter, even harsher, regime of discipline and punishment than that presided over by Commandant Nemoto. However, he did impose a greater measure of control over the guards than Nemoto had done, and was more predictable in his behaviour. Captain Stratford found that, with the right approach, Mitsuhashi could be persuaded to agree to simple requests that improved the lot of the detainees. For example, so disastrous and lacking in any culinary merit were the efforts of the Japanese cook that the Pumpkin Controller agreed to the Greek contingent taking over the preparation and cooking of all meals, although still under the supervision of Shonosuki. The improvement in the quality of the food, although not the quantity, was immediate, and morale throughout the camp improved markedly. However, Mitsuhashi also instituted a deliberate, much harsher, policy of physical violence, particularly in regard to the men, as a means of enforcing his authority.

On the afternoon of 18 August, an incident occurred that was typical of the mindless punishments inflicted on the internees during Mitsuhashi's tenure as Commandant. It involved Arthur Daniels and Douglas Scott, both merchant bankers, who were passengers on the *Nankin* and were to have taken up financial positions in India.

The two men were carrying out their normal daily ablutions when Mitsuhashi and Midorikawa appeared unexpectedly on the scene and demanded that both present themselves at the office. The two were accused of pouring water over their bodies in contravention of Rule 12: 'Must not pour jugs of water over oneself in washrooms.' Douglas was using a face towel to wipe himself down at the time and Arthur had not yet begun to wash, so both denied the accusations vehemently. Their protestations of innocence were ignored. Mitsuhashi ordered the pair to kneel by the bell with hands clear of the floor. Due to a previous injury, Douglas found the position impossibly painful and complained to Fishface, who spat in his face, then stood over him while four of the guards battered him about the head and body with bamboo batons. For some unfathomable reason Arthur was released, but Douglas was kept kneeling until 0900 that evening.

The following day, still having difficulty walking, Douglas was called back to the office and made to sit under the bell for a further 10 hours, until he was prepared to admit that he *had* poured water over himself while washing. Seeing such an admission as the only way to end the farce, he capitulated, and was immediately released. During this episode, Douglas received nothing to eat or drink.

The Pumpkin Controller was totally devoid of courtesy and displayed a particular offensive and morbid interest in the sex life of the women, encouraging similar behaviour from the guards. The women were prevented from locking toilet or bathroom doors and suffered the humiliation of guards bursting in, often performing obscene gestures accompanied by sickening laughter. So offensive was the behaviour of both Commandant and guards during this time that the internees, particularly the women, came almost to view Nemoto's period in office as one of benevolence!

On one occasion 'Vanda' Yates, Michael's friend, suffered a particularly unpleasant experience. She was sitting in the garden a little apart from the other women, reading a book, when one of the guards came up and attempted to draw her into conversation. He came unpleasantly close and with a lecherous look, accompanied by suggestive and vulgar gestures, said, 'You sleep with me? I give you two bars of soap.'

Vanda jumped up in alarm and hastily backed away, book clasped to her chest. 'Go away. Please go away,' she pleaded. Grinning lewdly, the guard came on. He exposed his penis and urinated a few feet in front of the now terrified Vanda, while simulating masturbation.

Vanda screamed, 'Get away. Get away!' and frantically pushed past him, fleeing into the building, sobbing uncontrollably.

Phyllis Hercombe was another of the women caught up in Mitsuhashi's obsession. Called to the office, she was accused of 'looking at the men from a window in the women's quarters' then underwent an insulting and humiliating interrogation on all manner of sexual matters, while Mitsuhashi and Midorikawa performed obscene gestures in front of her.

It was also about this time that another extraordinary episode occurred. Florence Thoms, in her capacity as Headwoman, was called to the Office and with only the Commandant and Slimy present, was asked which of the married women wanted children, and which could not have children for any reason, and whether the women understood the use of contraceptives? Then, for a period of several weeks, four out of the fifteen married couples at the camp were closeted in a small room, which was locked from the outside, and 'left to their own devices' for precisely half an hour without interruption. The couples in question were further ordered to keep their 'meetings' secret from the remainder of the internees. Then, quite suddenly, and without further explanation, the practice was discontinued. However, Florence was later interrogated as to which women had subsequently menstruated.

Then again without explanation, after fifteen months in captivity with almost fanatical adherence to a policy of the strictest separation, all families were permitted to assemble together for a period of two hours. Wives sobbed with joy as they held their husbands, and fathers choked back emotion as they hugged their children for the first time in so long. Those without families formed little groups and chatted about the things that were important to them. David sought out Helen and Madeline. They talked about the progress of the boys' studies, conditions within the camp and the progress of the war, and what might become of them all when it was over.

From this time, reunions were permitted at roughly monthly intervals, lasting for periods of between thirty minutes and two hours.

$$\sim$$

Life in the camp ground on through the summer of '43 with a return to the oppressive heat and climatic conditions they had suffered the previous year. The internees worked hard to break the mind-numbing monotony by occupying themselves with school lessons for the children, lectures on a wide range of subjects for those adults who were interested, card games, chess from pieces painstakingly carved from scraps of wood and the manufacture of clothing and cleverly constructed household items from all manner of materials that came to hand. However, the brutal and seemingly mindless and degrading treatment of the internees continued.

$$\sim$$

Towards the end of 1943 the white bread, baked by the Greeks in the camp kitchen, was replaced by small bread rolls that were easier to manage and apportion. They weighed between 6 and 7 ounces each and sometimes contained potato or other vegetables. Initially, three rolls were issued daily to each internee. They were nutritious, and would have formed a good staple had it not been for the reduction of other food items in their diet. Jam, butter and liver paste were eliminated and meals without meat or fish were common. On other occasions there were no vegetables and the issue of fruit became infrequent.

～

Summer merged seamlessly into an autumn that was all too short, and before long they were looking at the approach of a second bitter winter. Christmas 1943 was celebrated in much the same way as the previous year, with toys for the younger children and the traditional round of carol singing, but feelings throughout the camp were mixed. Some still looked forward optimistically to the prospect of repatriation while others had no horizon on which to focus and saw their incarceration stretching endlessly into the future.

For David, as for most of the others, time passed slowly. It was only a self-imposed mental toughness, driving him to keep as busy and mentally active as possible, that made things bearable. At those times that he felt unwell, and when the thought of yet another day of imprisonment brought him close to despair, he forced his thoughts to focus on home and family and happier times. It was those who lost an emotional connection with the outside world, who withdrew into themselves and spent endless hours in the seclusion of their rooms that suffered most.

The New Year came and went, and 1944 was ushered in without ceremony or fanfare.

TOKYO

Thursday 2 March 1944

Mr M. H. C. Angst, Delegate in Japan to the International Committee of the Red Cross (ICRC), had every reason to feel satisfied. He had just returned from the office of Interior Minister Shigemitsu who had sent for him to advise of the existence of a previously undisclosed facility on the outskirts of Fukushima, that was holding a number of foreign nationals.

Since receiving notification from the ICRC's Central Tracing Agency in Geneva of the suspected existence of such a facility, back in July 1943, Angst had been pressing the Minister to confirm its existence and to provide a list of names of those being held there. He was, however, rather surprised, and more than a little bemused, at the explanation given by the Minister as to why previous advice concerning the facility had not been forthcoming, despite repeated requests.

'The foreign nationals at this facility were not, until yesterday, the responsibility of the Japanese Government,' explained the Minister. 'They were simply being held in "protective custody," on a temporary basis, at the request of the German Government. *Germany* had final responsibility for their custody and wellbeing while negotiations for repatriation were being arranged. However, due to unreasonable demands by the Allied Powers,' he went on, 'repatriation is no longer an option. Therefore, I must now formally advise you that, as of yesterday, 1 March, Japan has assumed responsibility for their custody and welfare. The foreign nationals will continue to be held, for their own protection, in pleasant surroundings in Fukushima, until the war ends.

'To assure you that this is the case and to confirm they are being well cared for, arrangements have been made for you to visit the facility on the 24th of this month.

'This morning, I conveyed this same information to the Ambassador for Switzerland as the Protecting Power. Switzerland will therefore represent the interests of the foreign nationals from now on. A representative of the Swiss Ambassador will also visit the facility in due course,' he concluded.

'Thank you for your courtesy in providing this information,' Angst responded, then, 'As you know Minister, the ICRC has a responsibility to distribute food and other parcels to Prisoners of War and, as you are aware, a shipment of such parcels has recently been received via the mercy ships *Gripsholm* and *Teia Maru*. With your permission, I would like to arrange an immediate distribution of food parcels to the foreign civilians being held at Fukushima.'

'Of course such action is not necessary,' the Minister replied, 'as these people are well fed and cared for, as you will see yourself during your visit. However, the Japanese Government does not persecute innocent women and children and if you consider that Red Cross parcels will help, then the necessary arrangements will be made to permit their delivery.'

FUKUSHIMA

Tuesday 14 March 1944

It was mid-morning when the rather battered truck shuddered to a dusty halt outside the convent's main entrance. The Isuzu, 4-wheeled truck, was widely used throughout Japan and the occupied territories as the main utility workhorse for the Japanese army. Commercial versions of the vehicle were a common sight around Fukushima, and David noticed them passing by on numerous occasions as they went about their business. Such vehicles were also used for deliveries to the convent itself and were not, therefore, normally cause for comment. What drew the attention of David and the others to this particular vehicle was the large red cross painted on the canvas canopy. Word flashed quickly through the camp. The excitement was electric.

Commandant Mitsuhashi, who had been forewarned of the vehicle's arrival, was quickly on the scene. He examined the documents presented by the driver, a representative of the ICRC, then summoned Captain Stratford and Florence Thoms. 'I am to advise you,' he said through the interpreter, 'that parcels have arrived from the Red Cross. You will please arrange for them to be distributed to your people.' With that, he turned on his heel and retreated to his office leaving the *bucho* and the two camp leaders in charge. Clearly Mitsuhashi was not pleased by the arrival of the parcels but he had received his instructions from the Prefecture Office and there was little he could do.

Captain Stratford organised an efficient system of distribution, and as goods were handed out, recipients were required to sign a receipt: 'I have received today one food package from the AMERICAN NATIONAL RED CROSS through the International Red Cross Committee.'

Parcels were handed down from the back of the truck, with women and children receiving theirs first. Alfie and Ginger ensured receipts were signed and ready for return to the Red Cross, a procedure that ensured parcels arrived at their intended destination intact. Each parcel contained:

3 x 12-oz tins of pressed meat

1 x 1-lb tin of whole powdered milk

1 x 8-oz tin of salmon

1 x 6-oz tin of jam

1 x 4-oz tin of coffee

3 x 4-oz packets of butter

½ lb of cheese

1 lb of dried fruit

8 oz chocolate

2 small cakes of soap

5 packets of cigarettes (20s)

1 x 6-oz tin of pâté

Overwhelming joy filled the convent as the parcels were handed out and unpacked. The squeals of delight as each item was revealed brought tears of gratitude and no child exploring the wonders of their Christmas stocking could ever have experienced so much joy. If those who had packed the parcels could have witnessed the scene, they would have been deeply moved and amply rewarded for their efforts.

To say that the arrival of the Red Cross parcels lifted morale would be a gross understatement. Not only did they provide an essential supplement to their subsistence diet but it demonstrated, for the first time in twenty months, that there were people outside the camp who were aware of their existence and were able to help. Furthermore, the tins, packets and other containers provided a source of raw materials that were ingeniously converted to all manner of useful items, making life in captivity just that little bit easier.

The Red Cross parcels arrived just in time to avert a major crisis in the health and wellbeing of the internees. For several months now there had been a gradual but steady reduction in the amount of food available for daily consumption. The Greek seamen did their best to prepare the pitiful rations that Shonosuki was able to purchase in the markets, but it was increasingly clear that Japan was running out of food. Strict rationing had already been introduced for the general populace.

Shonosuki was now well known in the markets, and vendors were even more reluctant than previously to provide food.

There were in the garden, cultivated by the internees' own labour, onions, spinach, peas and a kind of large white radish. However, only the radish tops were given to the internees, and those at infrequent intervals. The greater part of the garden had been sown with potatoes but, although yielding a harvest estimated at three to four tons, the prisoners received nothing. Had they not received the food parcels, it would have been difficult for most to have survived the winter without serious consequences. Captain Stratford, on many occasions, made representations to the camp authorities about the inadequacy of rations. The Pumpkin Controller's response was that, in other camps, only one roll and one plate of stew was issued to each prisoner daily, a claim hard to believe.

Although the content of each food parcel was nutritious and very much welcomed, the ICRC was only able to provide one parcel to each internee approximately every three months. It was found that if the contents were used sparingly, each parcel could, with difficulty, be made to stretch out for a period of roughly three weeks!

FUKUSHIMA

Friday 24 March 1944

It was evident that something most unusual was afoot when the morning *tenko* was cut short. The prisoners were ordered to dress in their best clothes: men and women were allowed to mix freely, and a team of well-equipped cinematographers suddenly appeared and commenced filming.

When the Red Cross delegate arrived, at precisely 1030, he was presented with the spectacle of a church service in progress, families chatting in casual groups, and some of the men doing physical exercises in the yard. He was shown a well-stocked and equipped convent dispensary and he noted the two pristine Japanese nurses in attendance. The main hall had been miraculously converted to a reading room-cum-library, well furnished with tables and chairs and an impressive array of well-stocked bookcases. English language newspapers were liberally spread about and several vases of flowers added the finishing touch.

However, none of the internees were permitted to speak to, or even approach, Mr Angst and his team with the exception of Captain Stratford, and this only in the strictly controlled environment of the office and in the presence of the Commandant and interpreter. Stratford was, however, able to convey some of their major grievances, but only in the broadest terms. He was also able to express his heartfelt thanks for the Red Cross parcels that had arrived ten days previously. Angst did, however, promise to ensure that the names of those held at the camp would be forwarded to the appropriate authorities, and he also agreed to look into the matter of the sending and receipt of mail.

The Delegate and his team left the convent at 1330, having witnessed the internees partake of a plain but nourishing lunch. By 1430, all the trappings had been removed and the normal rules and oppressive routines firmly re-established.

The following day, as promised, Angst transmitted the list of names of those being held at Fukushima to his headquarters in Geneva. He added that, in his view, they were being held 'in pleasant surroundings and were adequately fed and cared for.'

Several days later the list was received at the Prisoner of War Information Bureau in London. David's name was on it, along with Alfie Round, his mate Ginger Robson, and the other wounded seamen from the *Wellpark, Willesden* and *Kirkpool*. It took authorities some time to recognise the association and rationalise the 'Fukushima List' with the 'Kawasaki No. 1 List', received almost twelve months previously, that contained the names of the other prisoners captured by the *Thor*.

However, after receipt of information from Australia, authorities in London were able to identify which prisoners now held in Fukushima were passengers or crew from the *Nankin* and which were from other ships captured by the *Thor*.

The wheels of bureaucracy move slowly, even in wartime, and it was mid-August 1944 before the Prisoner of War Information Bureau in London was able to positively identify the name and origin of all those on Angst's Fukushima List.

Meanwhile, in Fukushima, the Angst visit heralded some rapid and remarkable changes in the lives of the internees. In addition to the first Red Cross food parcels, that had arrived on 14 March, other parcels containing First Aid Kits, bulk medicines, clothing and blankets, toilet requisites and US Army boots also began arriving, although very slowly at first and never in sufficient quantities. Other items received included books, socks, thread, toothpowder and toothbrushes, gramophone records (but no gramophone) and nail-files. Newspapers, both English and Japanese, were also provided from this time, although often on an irregular basis. As a consequence, Fred Garner and his team were able to discontinue the very risky newspaper scam, except on those occasions when newspapers were not forthcoming. At the end of March the first letters from the outside world were received although, initially, only for a very few. Neither David nor Alfie were among the lucky ones.

There was also new hope that letters written by the internees themselves might at last reach families at home. After nearly two years of isolation it seemed that the edge of the curtain had begun to lift – just a little.

During the visit of the Red Cross Delegate, Harold Stratford had been advised that the Swiss Ambassador to Japan was looking after British interests and that Switzerland had undertaken the duties of their Protecting Power. He was also advised that a visit by a delegate from the PP would take place shortly, on a date yet to be arranged.

This latter visit occurred on 26 April and it was during this visit that the Delegate broke the devastating news that, for reasons unknown to him, all negotiations relating to possible repatriation had been broken off.

FUKUSHIMA

Saturday 29 April 1944

David was worried that Michael was unwell. It was several days after the visit by the Swiss Delegate and he was showing no interest in his lessons. He was very lethargic and, at times, seemed close to tears, without apparent reason.

'What's wrong,' David prompted gently, 'aren't you feeling well?'

'It's not me,' Michael responded, 'it's mother. Since we were told that we're not going to be exchanged she has been crying a lot and she hardly ever seems to eat. She just wants to stay in bed and it seems almost as though she's given up hope of ever going home. She tries to hide it during my visits but I know she's terribly unhappy, and I'm so worried. I don't know what to do.'

David put his arm around Michael and gave him a hug. 'Right,' he said, 'we'd better do something about that right away. Let's forget lessons for today and go for a walk in the yard instead.'

Madeline Charnaud's reaction to the news that all negotiations for repatriation had ceased was exactly what David had long feared. Until now, she had been so resolute and determined that the other women looked to her for strength and guidance. Whenever any of the others were low or depressed, Madeline was always there to help and support, but she had always been driven by the thought that it was only for a few more months at the most, then they would all be returned to their homes and loved ones. Madeline's state of mind was not helped by a body weakened through lack of food for, like most of the mothers in the camp, she had, every day, put aside one-third of her daily ration to provide a little extra for Michael. After two years in captivity something had to give, and when the PP delegate shattered her belief in the prospect of repatriation, the thought of ever returning home seemed to fade, and the prospect of continued hardship and imprisonment for the indefinite future was more than Madeline could cope with. It was more than any reasonable person could be expected to cope with.

$\sim$

David and Michael walked the men's exercise yard together, David with his head bowed in thought. He seemed to reach a decision, stopped walking, and turned to Michael. 'I think I need to write her a letter,' he said, 'to tell her what a grand job she's done and how much all of us here on the men's side admire her strength and courage. Yes, that's what I must do, and I'll do it right away so you can take it with you when you visit her tomorrow. Now that that's settled,' he added, 'you must stop worrying. Scamper away and find Graham and I'll see you again tomorrow.'

David wrote the letter that evening and Michael delivered it to his mother next day. She opened it and began to read, at first with little interest but as she read on, her eyes sparked into life. Soon she was sitting upright, absorbing every word:

'Dear Mrs Charnaud,

'I hope that you won't think it presumptuous on my part in writing you this chit and it's just possible that it may help you a little. I know perfectly well that when I am feeling low and depressed I find nothing so stimulating as the knowledge that I have friends, people who think about me and care about me; it gives one such a grand feeling, particularly when we are stuck here, a small community on our own in this far off corner of the world. I shall never forget the day when the Red Cross parcels arrived here and the reaction I felt, joy, relief and gratitude, those emotions were singing up inside me and almost choking me, not for the material comforts which they brought, but for the message of hope and encouragement which they brought from the outside world and the certain knowledge that we had not been forgotten, and what a grand feeling it was to know that we had been remembered and that people outside were thinking about us and trying to help us. I guess most of us felt like that when the Red Cross Representative arrived here in person. That was better still and confirmed the knowledge which the parcels had given us. Only on two previous occasions have I felt similar emotions; the first was after waiting for what seemed a lifetime, the nurse came and informed me that a son had been born to me. I wonder if that makes you smile? I was quite a youngster then, only twenty-four and it made a tremendous impression on me. He is a fine healthy boy of seven now, and the second occasion was when my ship was sunk by the German Raider in the South Atlantic and I was picked up badly wounded from an over-pivoted and sinking lifeboat when we thought all hope was gone. We certainly have all of us had some experiences crowded into the past two years, haven't we, but I would like you to know Mrs Charnaud how tremendously I have admired the splendid spirit and the splendid courage which you women have shown throughout all our misfortunes; you've set such a grand example to us men and I feel quite sure it has done more than anything to imbue us too with some of that splendid spirit which will enable us to carry on until the final chapter.

This latest news which we have just had from the Representative of the Protector Power representing our interests in Japan seems to have caused some of you ladies great distress. After what you have been through it is not un-natural as it takes very little these days to affect us one way or the other, but surely things are not as black as all that. The majority of chaps over here are quite bucked about it all, but a lot depends on the mental attitude one has adopted towards this question of exchange and, even though negotiations are not in progress at present, I see no reason why they should not be resumed at any time, particularly as there appears to be quite a number of women and children from other camps too to be repatriated and I feel pretty sure that should an exchange be arranged the women and children from this camp will be included. For my own part, while always retaining a slight hope that an exchange might take place before the end of the war, for a long time now I have had no concrete hopes in that direction and I have adopted a mental attitude accordingly and as far as I can see the end of the war is in sight, so "what the hell boys" – excuse my French!

I know it's frightfully hard, particularly for you women who are unattached and have children. The children themselves are such a serious problem, but it is not a bit of use worrying and making oneself ill. Women at home and all the world over are playing their part in this war, playing it nobly and splendidly so don't you think it is up to us to play our part too? You've done it so well up until now, don't give in, let's continue to play it. We can't do very much I admit, but we can keep cheery in spite of the odds and help ourselves by helping each other and show these people here that we can take it with a grin, don't you agree? If that is the part that we're fated to play, let's play it well. I *too* have a wife and two kiddies at home in England but I can't do them a bit of good by worrying about them and making myself ill, and don't forget they are everything in the world to me, but I can help them far more by doing my best to help others and by forgetting my own cares and worries. Life is a funny business but it seems to work out right in the long run.

When I was Chief Officer on the East Coast of England in 1941 I was running between Hartlepool and London; it was just one continual nightmare at sea and in port and at that time it was the most dangerous stretch of coast in the world. Air raids in Hartlepool, our minds in London, mines, torpedoes and air bombing at sea, home for a few days with my wife and kiddies in South Wales, more air raids and bombs.

Very often when I came home in the middle of one I would find the two babes tucked away under the staircase sleeping soundly. We had no air raid shelter, guns would be blazing away, planes circling overhead, bombs dropping, searchlights and flares lighting up the sky, things were pretty grim in those days. I was lucky to keep afloat for a good spell, until one night my ship caught one too. It was bound to get it sooner or later, law of averages; I was the only surviving officer, jolly lucky to be picked up on a pitch black night in the winter in the North Sea. I had a spell in hospital then home for a while and then back to sea again. It was hell for my wife, poor kid, and I guess she's been through a pretty tough time these past two years. For them and all our folks we have to keep smiling; the end's in sight now and all this bloody courage will soon be over and so Mrs Charnaud it's up to us to do our bit and keep smiling. The folks at home will do theirs and now I'm afraid I must leave you with my apologies for this rather long rambling letter and sincerely hope you will be your old cheery self again soon.

Yours very sincerely,

David Millar'

Madeline read the letter twice; then she cried. She had just taken the first step on the way to regaining her old cheery self.

FUKUSHIMA

June–August 1944

Some time in June, the Chief of the Special Branch of Police in Fukushima, Nakao Masatake (Fishface), was replaced. The new Chief was the much more benevolent, understanding and capable Inspector Tari Kyûshi, who quickly recognised the major deficiencies in the administration of the camp. As a consequence, he had Captain Mitsuhashi Yosio, the 'Pumpkin Controller' and sexual deviant, replaced. The new Commandant was Captain Yabe Shichirô, an altogether more reasonable and compassionate man than either of his two predecessors. Under Yabe's leadership, all ad-hoc punishments and bullying by individual guards ceased.

The guards themselves, who had been sixteen in number at the outset, had gradually been reduced to five as the war went against Japan and their services were more urgently required elsewhere. However, five was an adequate number for camp administration purposes, and their duties kept them sufficiently busy not to have time to harass the internees to any significant extent. Under Yabe's administration, families were allowed to meet regularly for two hours a week and, towards year's end, daily meetings of an hour a day were permitted. A further concession was that the two State Registered Nurses, Annie Law and Elizabeth Scott, were allowed to visit the men's side daily, to tend to the sick. Although being able to provide very little in the way of medicines, the psychological effect of these visits was enormous.

Commandant Yabe was able to maintain good discipline over his staff while always behaving with consideration and understanding towards the internees, particularly the women, children and the sick. Indeed, apart from the woeful shortage of food and lack of even the most basic medical facilities, which were also issues suffered by the general population throughout Japan, conditions within the camp during the tenure of the third Commandant were quite tolerable.

Throughout 1944, with better access to newspapers and Fred Garner's newspaper scam as back-up when required, it became increasingly obvious that the Axis Powers were rapidly losing ground on every front and that victory for the Allies was only a question of time.

Although the news was still heavily censored, it was impossible for the Japanese to conceal the reality of the situation on the ground. The internees noted, with great satisfaction, the Allied advances through Italy and its ultimate collapse, the D-Day landings in Normandy on 6 June, and the liberation of Paris in August. In the Pacific they noted the ever-greater successes as the Allies leap-frogged through the island chains from New Guinea, almost to the shores of Japan itself. Places never previously heard of dominated the daily discussions of the latest news: Guadalcanal, Wake, Kwajalein, Truck, Guam, Leyte, Okinawa and Iwo Jima were the cause of excited speculation as they fell like dominoes to America's industrial and military might. Fingers stabbed excitedly at maps, carefully traced on any paper available, showing the extent of the Allied advances.

Surely, David mused, *next Christmas must be our last in captivity.*

⌒‿

Towards the middle of July another parcel of letters arrived at the camp, courtesy of the International Red Cross. For some it was their first confirmation that family and friends were aware of their capture and circumstances but, for the second time, neither David nor Alfie were among the lucky recipients. However, there was *one* letter, in a rather ominous and official-looking envelope, addressed to Helen Guy.

Howard, now nine, was sitting in the first-floor corridor when he heard his mother sobbing. Not knowing what to do and being too frightened to enter her room, he was on the verge of panic when he was approached by Evelyn Gray, whose husband was billeted with David, emerging from Helen's room. 'Your mother has received some bad news,' she said, taking Howard's hand, 'You need to be very brave and comfort her.'

Feeling very scared, Howard entered the room. Helen was holding the letter in her hand and, without words, passed it to Howard to read. It said that his step-father, John Guy, had been lost at sea. The ship he was on had been sunk and all hands were presumed dead. Howard went to his mother's arms but could not control his grief and began sobbing on her shoulder. *What an awful world*, he thought.

That evening Helen and Howard, together, passed the news on to David via the *phone* and, from that time, on those occasions when the men and women were allowed to mix, David sought them out and provided what little comfort and understanding he could.[7]

BARRY, SOUTH WALES
Saturday 19 August 1944

Muriel was mildly surprised when she answered a knock on the front door, to be confronted by the telegram boy, arm extended. 'Telegram for Mrs Millar,' he said.

For Muriel, the day had started as any other Saturday, with work at the uniform factory in the morning and a planned shopping expedition after lunch, before getting on with the weekly round of domestic chores. It was fourteen months since David had been posted 'missing presumed dead' and although she still thought of him often, and missed him dreadfully, the deep pain of her loss had faded. In her mind, David was dead and she now had the responsibility of bringing up the two boys as best as she could with the resources she had available. She was receiving a modest 'war widows' pension and although life in wartime

---

7   Ironically, amongst John Guy's few possessions that were returned to Helen after the war, was a letter that had never been posted. It was dated 11 February 1943 and expressed sorrow at Helen and Howard's capture and relief in the knowledge that they were still alive, even though they were prisoners in Japan. The existence of this letter proves that, although the Australian censors banned publication of material relating to the loss of the Nankin in December 1942, next-of-kin were informed.

Britain was still harsh, they would get by. The Allies were pushing forward on all fronts and the end of the war seemed only a matter of time.

The telegram was from the War Office. Muriel tore the envelope open and read quickly:

'WE ARE PLEASED TO ADVISE THAT INFORMATION HAS BEEN RECEIVED THROUGH THE INTERNATIONAL RED CROSS THAT YOUR HUSBAND, DAVID MILLAR, IS ALIVE AND IS BEING HELD PRISONER OF WAR IN JAPAN.

THE POW INFORMATION BUREAU IN LONDON WILL CONTACT YOU WITH FURTHER ADVICE AS IT BECOMES AVAILABLE AND ON PROCEDURES FOR THE EXCHANGE OF MAIL WITH YOUR HUSBAND AND OTHER MATTERS.'

The blood drained from Muriel's face and she immediately went into shock. Her legs would no longer support her – she sank to the floor clutching the telegram to her breast, sobbing uncontrollably.

Donald, now seven and playing nearby, ran to his mother, ' Mummy, mummy, what's wrong?' he called in anguish.

Muriel reached out and pulled Donald to her, 'Daddy's alive' she sobbed.

FUKUSHIMA

September–December 1944

Some time very early in September, late in the forenoon, David was occupied with a particularly intense game of chess with his friend and room-mate, Fred Garner. The chess set had been painstakingly carved from maplewood, obtained from a tree growing in the grounds, and the 'black' pieces were coloured using polish acquired during the last attic raid. The board was drawn on a removable shelf from the closet in their room. The game was at a particularly critical stage, and David was concentrating on his next move, when his train of thought was interrupted by a polite cough at the door. It was Alfie's mate Ginger. He spoke to David, 'Excuse me, Mr Millar, but you're wanted down at the office right away. Roondie is in some sort of trouble and he wants you to speak on his behalf.'

'We'll finish the game later,' David said to Fred, and hurried after Ginger, puzzled by the strange request. Although he was the elected representative of the Seaman's Group, of which Alfie was part, he had never previously been called to represent any of them in any disciplinary matter. Indeed, if any such representation was required, and it seldom was, it was a task that would normally be undertaken by Captain Stratford. However, under the new Commandant, there had been many changes to the organisation in the camp and David assumed that this was simply a further example of such a change.

Already present in the office when David arrived was Alfie, looking rather sheepish, Commandant Yabe, Shonosuki the camp cook, and a young Japanese woman, probably in her mid twenties, whom David had not previously seen. Notably absent was Slimy Midorikawa, the interpreter. Even more surprising, it was the young woman who spoke first, in very good English, and with a pronounced British public school accent. 'My name is Yasuko Kokubun,' she said, 'my sister Masako and I are the new interpreters. Mr Midorikawa and his wife have left.'

So impressed was David with Yasuko's command of the language and pleasant, helpful demeanour that he almost forgot the reason for his being there. It seemed that Shonosuki was accusing Alfie of stealing potatoes from the kitchen and Alfie, while not denying the accusation, claimed that he was simply trying to provide something extra for another of the *Kirkpool* lads, John Owsten, who had been taken ill. David spoke on Alfie's behalf, pointing out that the crime was motivated purely by concern for his friend and not for personal gain. Yabe appeared to take this into consideration in pronouncing judgment. Alfie was to stand to attention under the bell for two hours and his bread ration was reduced for three days. Roondie shrugged his shoulders and accepted the punishment as a fair cop.

The whole procedure was civilised and well conducted – a far cry from the previous rantings and totally disproportionate punishments that much lesser crimes had attracted during the tenures of Midorikawa and the first two Commandants. Also, for the first time since the start of their internment, David had a sense that the translations were accurate, fair and unencumbered by personal bias or hatred. He was impressed, and quickly passed on the good news to Harold Stratford and the others.

⌒～

Throughout 1944 the food situation in Japan progressively worsened and by year's end the general population were on strict rationing. This had a direct effect on those imprisoned at Fukushima. They were still receiving one roll each, three times a day, but by October meat, fish or vegetables were only issued at one meal. Occasionally, a thin watery soup was served with the morning meal. From

November, weak tea without milk or sugar was restricted to three cups a day and there was up to three weeks between the issue of any vegetables. Meat and fish then disappeared from the menu entirely.

Food became a consuming passion. It was not uncommon for internees to eat weeds gathered from the gardens to supplement the little they had.

~~

Towards the end of 1944, air raid precautions emerged as an issue. The matter was brought up at one of the regular internees' committee meetings and discussed at some length. Although there had been no air attacks on the Japanese homeland, apart from the Doolittle Raid on Tokyo in April 1942, the committee agreed that it was now only a matter of time before Japan came under threat from US long-range B-29s based on recently captured territories, and from US carrier-based aircraft operating to the east of the main island of Honshu. The precautions enforced by the camp authorities up to this time were quite cursory and inadequate. When the alarm sounded the internees were to 'Black out all lights and stand by for instructions.'

A number of open trenches were dug in the grounds but they were never used and were generally full of water. No useful air-raid drills were ever conducted. Clearly, the camp authorities saw bombing of the Japanese homeland to be such a remote possibility as not to be taken seriously. Therefore, in the absence of any other guidance or interest, and believing that air raids would soon be a reality, the internees' committee developed their own plan. It covered the unlocking of the internal fire doors, evacuation of women and children to the basement storeroom and men to the boiler room, fire watching and fighting arrangements and casualty evacuation and treatment. Group leaders, on both the men's and women's sides, were tasked with ensuring that every member of their group was assisted and accounted for as circumstances dictated. The completed plan was submitted to Commandant Yabe but, initially, he refused to even consider it. Despite his rejection, the internees implemented the plan, as far as they were able, of their own volition.[8]

~~

Christmas 1944, their third in captivity, was a special event. Commandant Yabe actively encouraged the internees to hold a Christmas concert, and they entered into the organisation with enthusiasm. The programme comprised twenty events,

---

8   In mid 1945, after many, many alarms, the Japanese belatedly decided to adopt the committee's plan: in toto.

including singing, comedy acts, and individual national performances, reflecting the multicultural composition of the camp's inmates. Irish and Russian dances were performed with great skill and vigour, and the costumes, largely produced by Audrey and her sewing machine, were a credit to the resourcefulness and ingenuity of all involved. The new Chief of the Special Branch, Tari Kyushi, and a number of his senior staff, were invited to attend and occupied the front row. On the night, the assembly hall echoed to peals of laughter, happy voices and resounding applause and despite the rather risky anti-Japanese slant to many of the jokes, and the somewhat obvious nature of some of the caricatures, the Japanese officials seemed not to notice and enthusiastically joined the applause. Men and women were allowed to mix freely throughout the concert and for the rest of the day, including dining together for a special Christmas meal, rather more nourishing than the regular fare. Furthermore, despite the privations now being suffered by the general Japanese populace, as a special concession, the convent heating system was turned on for the whole day.

As New Year 1944–45 approached, David and the others were filled with a new confidence and a sense that the climax of their ordeal could surely not be far away.

FUKUSHIMA

1 January 1945–16 August 1945

In a desperate attempt to raise money for the war effort, the Japanese demanded that the prisoners hand over all items of personal jewellery. If proof were needed that the war was going very badly for Japan, this was it. Wedding and engagement rings were the main items still in their possession. Captain Stratford argued for their retention, but without success.

⁓

The meteorological records for the Fukushima Prefecture show that the winter of 1944–45 was *not* the coldest on record but there were few amongst the 141 internees at the Convent of the Congregation of Notre Dame, that terrible winter, who would believe it. The convent grounds were blanketed in snow and the trees and bushes were snap frozen into magnificent displays of sparkling frost. Icicles hung from the eaves and windowsills. In any other circumstances they would have been admired for their beauty; however, the internees were in no physical or mental state to appreciate the beauty of their surroundings. The biting cold seemed to penetrate their souls. The meagre supply of coal that had barely sustained the central heating system during the first two winters was almost gone, and in the first three months of winter, during the most bitter cold, the building was only partially heated, and then for less than twenty days.

By February, the last of the Red Cross parcels, received the previous November, had been consumed. The shortage of food was critical. Weak tea and dry bread was all that was available for two meals a day, with a few spoonfuls of watery vegetable stew for the third. The fact that no one died during that terrible winter was remarkable, and due largely to the leadership and organisation of Harold Stratford and the camp committee, who martialled what few resources they had to help those in greatest need and ensured that the weakest amongst them were supported by the strongest.

During February, Audrey Jeffrey and Michael were both struck down with life-threatening illnesses.

Audrey had pleurisy, on top of a severe bout of pneumonia. With no medication available, it was a credit to the two nurses, and the other women who cared for her, that she survived.

Michael, still only thirteen, fared better, but his suffering was compounded by the physical separation from his mother, who could do little but fret and pass on encouragement and the few additional scraps of food she was able to scrounge. Suffering from a raging fever, one of the nurses visited him daily, but could do no more than monitor his progress and provide general advice on his care. During this period, a Canadian, Carl Drennen, took it upon himself to provide Michael with twenty-four-hour care. The Geordie seamen were also marvellous, and gave up generous portions of their Red Cross parcels to ensure Michael had sufficient food. Madeline also sent food across, to the extent that her own health was seriously jeopardised.

Eventually, the long, hard winter blossomed into the new life of spring, bringing renewed confidence and hope, but also certainty in the fact that, without additional food and medical supplies, they would never survive another winter. Red Cross parcels arrived in late March and brought much-needed relief, although only temporary. But news from the war was all good. McArthur had invaded the Philippines, making good his 'I will return' promise and, on 3 March, Manila was liberated. On 1 April the US 10th Army invaded Okinawa and massive B-29 raids on Tokyo, Nagoya, Kobe and other major industrial cities became almost a daily occurrence. In Fukushima, the first air-raid warnings sounded, and increased in frequency throughout March and April. However, apart from one isolated incident, no bombs were dropped on Fukushima itself. In Europe, the news was even better. By the end of April, Adolf Hitler was dead by his own hand and on 7 May all German forces surrendered unconditionally. The war in Europe was over.

For David and the others, the end seemed to be in sight. *Surely it was now just a matter of hanging on?*

On Tuesday 21 March, Captain Stratford was summoned to the office to be informed that a fourth Commandant, Captain Ariga Atsushi, was to replace the firm but benevolent Captain Yabe Shichirô forthwith.

Ariga was a man of little education, and quite incapable of maintaining any sense of control or discipline over any of the guards. Under Ariga, the harsh, punitive regime that had characterised the tenure of the first two Commandants was re-established. Slapping and beatings again became commonplace, meetings between families were all but eliminated, and the provision of newspapers ceased. To add further anxiety and tension to an already explosive situation, rumours spread through the camp that, should Japan be invaded or lose the war, all foreign prisoners would be executed. The source of these rumours was never traced.

Conditions in the camp, which were already harsh, became almost intolerable. Arguments amongst the various ethnic groups erupted into violent outbursts on several occasions. It was only through the powerful presence and leadership exercised by Harold Stratford, supported by the camp committee, that order was maintained and a total breakdown of discipline prevented.

Air-raid warnings were now a daily occurrence, and from time to time, white condensation trails were observed in the distance, as high-flying, B-29s went about their business. It was amusing to observe the behaviour of the Japanese guards on these occasions. When the warning was given that Allied planes were coming over, the guards, ably led by Commandant Ariga, dropped everything they were doing and ran helter-skelter to their own shelter at the front of the building, leaving the internees to their own devices. They did not re-emerge until the 'all clear' was sounded. Had they such a course of action in mind, the internees could have walked out of the front gate without hindrance; however, there was little point.

Occasionally, on a still day, the dull *crump* of explosions could be heard as American warplanes and offshore warships bombed and shelled the city of Sendai, thirty miles to the north.

❧

On 7 April, Elizabeth Gleeson died. She had been ill for several months. The cause of death was recorded as an obstruction of the intestines. The previous September she had developed an infected middle finger that had turned gangrenous and was eventually amputated under local anaesthetic by the visiting doctor. No drugs, except aspirin, were given to relieve the pain and her arm became inflamed and swollen to the shoulder. For several months Elizabeth improved slowly, but was never quite the same. Although there was no apparent connection between her finger infection and the cause of her death, the episode weakened her body and affected her mental state. Towards the end, the Japanese *did* make an effort to help her, providing her with a separate room, additional food and injections to relieve the pain, but she was not moved to a hospital, where better care may have been available.

The women were much saddened by Elizabeth's death. She had never fully relinquished her responsibility as stewardess to the *Nankin's* passengers, and had worked tirelessly in the camp to help all who needed her. She was buried in the Mount Shinobu cemetery, close to Vincent Hemy and Nichol McIntyre.

❧

In June, roughly a month after the German surrender in Europe, Madeline Charnaud was approached by one of the guards and told to report to the office. A little apprehensive, and wondering what she might have done wrong, she hurried off to find out what it was all about. To her surprise, she was presented with a registered parcel, for which she had to sign. On return to her room she opened the package to find a short note from the German Naval Attaché in Tokyo, Captain Sauerland, explaining that, as Germany and Britain were no longer at war, he was returning the jewellery that she had entrusted to his care on 12 July 1942, the first day of their internment.

❧

Joy of joys! On Saturday 11 August, mail arrived for those wounded seamen who had been crew members on the three British tramp steamers. It was their first contact with families and loved ones in over three years. There were letters for Alfie and Ginger, and three letters for David, dated between August and December 1944. Where the letters had been in the meantime was impossible to tell. Although wartime requirements restricted each letter to one hundred words, David's letters contained everything he needed to know. Muriel was overjoyed to find out he was alive after not hearing from him for almost 3 years and believing him lost at sea. The boys were both well and growing fast. Donald was now eight and doing well at school, and Andrew, about to turn five, was looking forward to starting school in September. Rationing was not too bad and they all had enough to eat. They were desperately looking forward to the end of the war, when they would all be reunited.

It is impossible to imagine the overwhelming joy that a simple letter can bring. David sought out a remote corner of the camp grounds, where he sat alone and read them over and over again.

FUKUSHIMA INTERNMENT CAMP

Thursday 16 August 1945

The day began as any other. They were wakened by the bell at 0600 with the guard and interpreter present for morning *tenko*, just as they had been for the last three years: 'Attention, hands on hips, eyes right!' shuffle into line, then, 'Eyes front, number!'

Then, from the men, *'Ichi, ni, san, shi …'* and so on down the line, as the performance of *tenko* progressed.

But something strange was happening. The guards were sullen and unusually restrained. There had been talk in the newspapers and amongst the staff of 'super bombs' that could flatten whole cities. Breakfast proceeded as normal, then it was announced that lunch would be brought forward half an hour. This had never happened before. Rumours were rife. Some said there was to be an announcement. Perhaps the invasion of Japan had begun?

At midday, the Japanese staff gathered in the office and Commandant Ariga switched on the radio. Internees nearby reported that they heard martial music followed by a sombre speech given in Japanese. Someone thought it might be the Prime Minister or the Emperor speaking. Shortly after, Chief of Special Branch Tari arrived from Fukushima and the prisoners were instructed to gather in the assembly hall, much as they had on the day of their arrival. This time, men and women were allowed to mix.

The five guards on duty were spaced around the perimeter of the hall, heads down, clearly upset and distressed. There was excited chatter amongst the prisoners, that faded to an expectant silence as Ariga, accompanied by Tari Kyûshi and Yasuko Kokubun, the interpreter, entered the hall. They mounted the stage and turned towards the assembled company. The five guards bowed, in acknowledgement of the presence of the senior police officer.

The internees, as always in such situations, looked to Captain Stratford for leadership. Acting entirely on a hunch, Stratford moved through the group to the front of the hall, speaking softly as he went, 'Nobody bow or move unless I say so.' He took up a position directly in front of the Japanese officials, penetrating eyes staring directly at the Chief of Special Branch and waited.

The tension was electric. It seemed like time was suspended, but, in reality, it was probably less than fifteen seconds before Tari Kyûshi looked down, breaking eye contact with Stratford. Then, he bowed stiffly from the waist, holding the position for several seconds before returning upright. Those close to the front might have observed a tear. At that precise moment, they realised that the war was over.

Captain Stratford had no wish to humiliate the Japanese, and so gave a brief nod in acknowledgement of Tari's bow. The tension was broken. There was an audible hiss of expelling air as everyone began breathing again.

Tari Kyûshi stepped forward and, in an emotional voice, began to speak. Yasuko Kokubun interpreted. 'Yesterday all the countries have come to an agreement and the war has come to an end, so you are all free and no longer internees, but no orders have come yet. It is natural that you all want to go about freely as you like and go into the streets, but the people outside are still excited and so it is best for you all to remain inside here.

'You are going to live here for the time being and the Commandant would like to make the life here as pleasant as possible and wants Captain Stratford to represent you and say what you want. The Commandant will try his best to get what you want but he cannot promise everything.

'At present, there are many police officers here on duty as the people outside are very excited and there might be some stupid people outside to make trouble.

'You will go home bye and bye, but the Commandant cannot say when.

'One word of warning: all this excitement might lead to much noise, singing and music and the people outside might get annoyed, so you must be careful.

'Some time ago, your diamonds and jewellery were handed over. The

Commandant has communicated with Tokyo to return the things taken.

'In the near future you will go back, so if anyone has not got clothing, let them come forward now and the Commandant will try and get something for them.

'You have been here three years and must have felt the inconvenience, especially about food, but it is the same in all countries. The Commandant has been trying his best to get something more but it is still a difficult problem.

'Unfortunately, three people died but the rest of you have come through and the Commandant wishes all to come through for the few more months until the time you return home.

'The camp routine has been changed to make things as pleasant as possible but, with so many people living together, there must be a few regulations.

'There are still some Red Cross boxes left over from the time of the previous Commandant and anyone can have them to pack their things in. Let them give their names to Captain Stratford.

'You are still not to make too much noise. You must be careful not to stir up the people outside. The police officers are here to look after you and so you must listen to what they say for your own benefit.

'There are only a few weeks to go now, so be careful about your health,' he concluded.

'And Amen to that,' muttered Alfie in a quite audible stage whisper that sent Ginger, and others nearby, into uncontrollable giggles.

They were staggered by how quickly and unexpectedly the end had come. The war with Japan was over. There was much hugging, laughing and many, many tears.

PART IV

HOMEWARD BOUND

16 August 1945–5 December 1945

FUKUSHIMA INTERNMENT CAMP

Tuesday 11 September 1945

David boarded the last of the five buses that had arrived twenty minutes earlier. He did not feel sad or elated; there was simply a dull fog in his head, coupled with a gnawing in his gut and a desire to be as far away from this place as possible.

The twenty-six days since they had learned that the war with Japan was over had been full of emotion: laughter, celebration, frustration, impatience and further tragedy.

Immediately following the dramatic announcement that Japan had surrendered, Captain Stratford called a meeting of the camp committee to decide how the camp was to be organised, until such time as arrangements could be made for repatriation. They decided that the total management of the camp should be through the committee, under the leadership of Harold Stratford. From now on, Ariga would take his orders directly from him.

There followed, almost immediately, the most astonishing reversal of conditions in the camp that it was possible to imagine. The attitude of the Japanese towards the internees, in less than twenty-four hours, changed from brutal incivility to an obscene anxiety to please. The only curtailment of complete liberty was a request not to go outside the camp, except in parties and with a police escort.

The men and women mingled freely, and several rooms on the ground floor, previously reserved for use by the Japanese staff, were made available for internees' quarters, relieving the congestion. Husbands and wives, and their children, could, if they chose, share a room. The internees themselves, through the camp committee, now controlled *all* internal camp matters.

Rations were immediately increased and were reasonably plentiful (giving rise to the question of how real the shortages had been prior to this time). The Chief of the Special Branch, who now visited the camp daily, explained that Military control of supplies was withdrawn at the end of hostilities so he was able to obtain more for the camp. The bread ration was raised to four and a half rolls a day; potatoes and leeks from the garden, and other vegetables, were issued liberally. Fresh butter, apples, sugar, oil and meat were also supplied.

A marked improvement in health quickly became evident. The doctor and a dentist visited the camp on the afternoon of 16 August and thereafter, came promptly when requested. Mrs Bok Sye Foo and Mr Ben Johnson, who were both suffering from serious complaints, were removed to a local hospital. One woman, who had tried unsuccessfully for eighteen months to get her dentures repaired, had them put right and returned to her within twenty-four hours.

A supply of clothing to meet their immediate requirements was provided and tradesmen were allowed into the camp to sell Japanese novelties. A typewriter and paper were also supplied at the committee's request. A plentiful supply of soap was issued and most remarkably, the women's longstanding hygienic needs were met by the Japanese without their being asked.

Fukushima Camp showing identification letters for relief supply drop - 25 August 1945. (American Naval Archives)

Despite the sudden reversal in circumstances, the camp guards did not give up *all* their authority without one final gesture. On the morning of 17 August, following celebrations that went well into the previous night, the 0600 wake-up bell sounded as usual. Some of the men, either out of habit or still half asleep, folded their bedding and paraded for *tenko*. Others simply pulled their blankets over their heads, ignoring the bell, and yet others shouted abuse at the Japanese guards gathered in the main corridor.

Captain Stratford was quickly on the scene. He sent for Captain Ariga who appeared, out-of-breath and somewhat flustered, and explained to him, in very direct terms, that from now on, there would be no more bell ringing and no more *tenko*'s. 'Indeed, the sole purpose of your presence,' he made clear, 'is to provide security from any kind of threat posed by the local population. Apart from that, you and your staff are to take no part in the organisation or running of the camp. Is that quite clear?'

It was.

~

On the second day after cessation of hostilities, Captain Stratford received a phone call from the American occupation authorities in Tokyo, advising that it could be up to a month before arrangements could be made for them to leave the camp, but to be assured that everything possible was being done to expedite their evacuation. The US Army colonel to whom he was speaking advised that they were in the process of organising relief air drops of food and clothing but *that* would not happen for a few days.

~

For Alfie and Ginger, being confined within the camp perimeter was altogether too much of a restriction and the desire to wander further afield too much a temptation. It was not long, therefore, before they broke out to explore the nearby town and countryside. Contrary to all advice, they were not threatened by any of the local population, who treated them more as objects of curiosity. On their return to the camp, they reported that it seemed the threat of violence was overstated. It was not long, therefore, before groups of all types and sizes, including some of the older children, were taking daily excursions into the surrounding countryside. Some had police escorts provided by the ex-guards; others chose to go unaccompanied.

One of the guards, Toshio Okita, known to the internees as the 'English Speaking Sergeant' or sometimes 'The Good Sergeant' due to his grasp of the English language and his genuine attempt to treat the internees fairly and with courtesy, invited David to visit the Japanese house of a friend in the town. Toshio had only served at the camp for a few months but during that time had made every effort to ensure, at least on his watch, that the prisoners were well treated. David accepted the invitation in the generous spirit it was made and asked Helen if she and Howard would like to accompany him. Eager to see something of the town beyond the boundaries of the camp, they agreed, and so together one morning they set off.

Fukushima Camp Inmates (1) - August 1945. (Courtesy of Malcolm Ingleby Scott)

To Howard, the walk into town was a strange adventure. Members of the local population stared openly, some showing fear, others greeting them in the traditional way, bowing from the waist with hands clasped in front. A few came up and stroked Howard's head which caused him concern, until David explained that blond hair was unknown in Japan and the people were simply curious. When they arrived at the house they sat on low stools and were addressed by an old man in broken English, coupled with hand signs and some Japanese. Howard found it easy to understand what he was trying to say and acted as the group interpreter.

The old man welcomed them to his house, expressing hope that they had not been too badly treated. He said that the townsfolk had not known that they were interned at the convent and explained, by way of apology, that the whole country was suffering from lack of food and heating fuel.

Tea was served in small cups without handles.

The old man was very proud of his garden and led his visitors outside to show them. It was a small wonderland of flowers, miniature rivulets and waterfalls, very much in the Japanese style.

All three were moved by the gentle kindness of the old man as they said their goodbyes and started back to the camp.

About a week after the cessation of hostilities, advice was received that food, clothing and medicine drops were about to commence. The letters 'PW' were displayed in the convent yard to identify the drop zone. On the morning of 25 August, a flight of Grumman Avengers from the carrier USS *Lexington* flew low over the convent and a shower of leaflets floated down. Quite a number landed in the grounds itself. David picked one up. It was addressed to 'ALL ALLIED PRISONERS' and read:

> 'The Japanese Government has surrendered. You will be evacuated by ALLIED NATIONS forces as soon as possible.
>
> Until that time your present supplies will be augmented by air-drop of US food, clothing and medicines. The first drop of these items will arrive within one or two hours.
>
> DO NOT OVEREAT OR OVER MEDICATE.'

Excitement and the sense of anticipation amongst the internees soared. People formed into little groups and chatted excitedly, reluctant to go indoors lest they miss something. Later in the day, four more aircraft came in, flying very low. They circled the convent once before coming in to parachute supplies into the neighbouring paddy fields. One of the crew members stood by an open door and waved a greeting, giving the thumbs up as the plane passed over. Some of the relief supplies were packed in cardboard cartons and some in what appeared to be canvas kitbags. Work parties were quickly organised to retrieve the packages and bring them within the convent walls. A small handcart, previously used by the gardener, was utilised for the purpose and it was not long before the packages were retrieved, opened and sorted, amidst great excitement by children and adults alike. It was just like Christmas – only better.

Food and clothing drops now occurred almost every day. On the second day, the parachutes were dispensed with and the packages were simply pushed out as aircraft passed over at low altitude. Many of the packages burst open on impact, spraying the contents across the paddy fields. The kitbags fared slightly better than the cartons but became deadly missiles and a real danger to anyone in the vicinity. Sadly, there was a great deal of wastage. Within a few hours, the situation had changed from near starvation to an embarrassment of riches. Matters were in danger of getting out of hand until, once again, the leadership and discipline imposed by Captain Stratford restored sense and order. He directed that all packages be taken to the ground floor storerooms, where they were opened and the contents sorted. Times were arranged for distribution of food and clothing and the medical supplies were handed over to Elizabeth Scott and Annie Law, for their management and use.

Fukushima Camp Inmates (2) - August 1945. (Courtesy of Malcolm Ingleby Scott)

It quickly became clear that the relief supplies provided by the overgenerous Americans were far in excess of what could be sensibly utilised by the internees. Some of the surplus was therefore distributed to the convent's Japanese staff and some to the local peasant farmers, also existing in near starvation conditions. The remainder was stored in the convent to be used by the nuns, whenever they should eventually return.

On Monday 27 August a representative of the Protecting Power arrived from Tokyo and advised that arrangements were progressing and they could expect to leave the convent in about two weeks' time and be taken to Manila, where further arrangements would be made for their onward passage.

Late on the afternoon of Tuesday 28 August, tragedy struck. Air-dropping supplies close to the convent required very accurate flying at very low altitude, coupled with precise timing. Inevitably, errors occurred and on occasions, some of the packages fell within the convent walls. One kitbag, containing tinned fruit and other bulky items, hit the perimeter wall making a hole large enough for a person to pass through. Another package passed directly through the roof of the women's quarters, narrowly missing one of the women. There were several other near misses before the inevitable occurred. Caroline Dimitrakopouloy, Dutch wife of the *Pagasitikos'* radio officer, was standing with her husband near an apricot tree at the north-western corner of the building watching proceedings. Without warning, she was struck by one of the packages. The impact flung her against the convent wall, crushing her skull. Despite immediate first-aid treatment by Elizabeth Scott, who was nearby, and being rushed by car to the Prefectural Women's Hospital, only a short distance away, there was nothing that could be done to save her. She died later that day without regaining consciousness.

All in the camp were stunned by the unnecessary nature of the tragedy. Having survived three years of starvation and privation, it was just too cruel to be struck down so close to returning home. *This* was the Caroline, just thirty-one years old when she died, who had dressed up as Father Christmas to distribute gifts to the children that first terrible winter in captivity, who was so kind and supportive to the other women and who played such a big part in the Christmas concert of 1944. Her husband, Schiriyanous, was inconsolable and wept for hours, before withdrawing into himself and refusing to eat or communicate with any of his Greek shipmates.

Harold Stratford immediately contacted the US authorities in Tokyo and from that time all supplies were dropped in the fields some distance away and recovered using the cart. This did little, however, to lift the dark blanket of gloom that replaced the elation and excitement that had prevailed throughout the camp since the cessation of hostilities.

Caroline was buried in the cemetery on Mt Shinobu, near the others.

On the day she died she had written in a friend's autograph book; 'Ah, a wonderful life starts today.'

~

The end of their time at the convent came quite suddenly. It was 1100 when the black bakelite phone in the office rang. The same US Army colonel who had made the initial contact with the camp four weeks previously asked for Captain Stratford. 'Buses have been arranged to take you to the railway station at Fukushima,' he said, 'you are to be ready to go at 1300 hours. You'll go by train to Shiogama where you'll be looked after by the POW repatriation authorities. I can't tell you much more than that except that they'll be expecting you. Any baggage you have will go separately by truck. You should have it ready to be picked up by 1230. Now, is there anything else you need to know?'

Somewhat taken back by the speed of events, Captain Stratford could do little else but acknowledge the instructions. He quickly called the others together and passed on the news. It was then a frantic effort to gather their few belongings together, ready for departure.

Howard, now ten and remembering very little other than life in the camp, barely had time to say goodbye to his friends. Firstly, he told the frogs what was happening. 'Goodbye,' he said, 'and thank you for being my friends,' then, as an afterthought, 'I do hope you won't be eaten!'

Next, it was the turn of his pet spider. It lived over the window in the boiler house and Howard fed it flies as often as he could. Saying goodbye was harder than he thought.

The trucks arrived on time at 1230 and took the baggage; a few minutes later, the buses arrived. A US Army warrant officer and two sergeants were on hand to assist and act as escorts.

David climbed aboard the last bus and took the seat next to Alfie. 'Well Roondie,' he said, with masterly British understatement, 'it's been an interesting few years but I, for one, could well have done without it.'

'And I'll drink to that,' said Alfie, with feeling.

The buses moved off. Neither David nor Alfie looked back.

The Kirkpool Lads - August 1945. (Courtesy of Malcolm Ingleby Scott)

The journey to the station took only ten minutes. Memories of their arrival at this same station, three years and two months earlier, came flooding back.

They boarded a special train on the main Touhoku line that terminated at Shiogama, the port for the nearby industrial city of Sendai. On the train, in addition to their American escorts, were a Japanese doctor and nurse, Yasuko Kokubun, the camp interpreter, and ex-Commandant Ariga, although the purpose of the latter's presence was not clear.

The train rumbled north through a picturesque countryside of paddy fields, mountains and green valleys until, about 1630, it passed through the city of Sendai. David and the others were staggered by the extent of the destruction caused by Allied bombing and shelling by ships offshore. There was hardly a building left standing. The railway line had been cleared but the train still slowed almost to a walk as it picked its way through the rubble before eventually stopping a few miles further on at the port of Shiogama. Here they were met by special arrival teams from the hospital ship USS *Rescue*, anchored a short distance offshore. They were escorted the few hundred yards to a landing craft, waiting at the beach with front ramp down. Once aboard, they were whisked out to the *Rescue* where they gave up the clothes they were wearing and after a shower, issue of new clothes and a meal, they bunked down in comfortable beds with crisp, white sheets. Everyone was tired after the excitement of the day and most turned in early. David drifted off into an untroubled sleep, looking forward, for the first time in over three years, to what the following day might bring.

HMS RULER – AT SEA

Wednesday 26 September 1945

So much had happened in the fifteen days since leaving Fukushima it was hard to believe that, very soon, they would be stepping ashore on Australian soil and, indeed, for many of the ex-passengers and crew of the *Nankin*, it would be a return home.

The morning after their arrival on board the USS *Rescue* in Shiogama harbour they had been awakened very early and given an ample American breakfast of ham, eggs over easy and hash browns, before being told to gather their belongings once more, for immediate transfer to an Australian destroyer, the HMAS *Warramunga*, which had berthed alongside *Rescue* during the night. *Warramunga* was operating as part of an Allied Task Group, which had been given the job of assisting with the evacuation of Allied POWs from Japan.

It was still only 0600 when the destroyer cast off the lines securing it to the hospital ship and, once clear, *Warramunga's* captain, Commander M.J. Clark DSC RAN, rang down for full power, and the ship's 40,000 shaft horsepower, Parsons' geared turbines soon had her slicing through the water at 30 knots. David, standing on the upper deck, could feel the power of the engines pulsing through his feet as he watched the wake boiling up from the destroyer's stern, stretching back, arrow straight, into the distance.

A little before 1600 a change in engine beat alerted David to the fact that the destroyer was slowing. She entered Tokyo Bay and the approaches to Yokohama, having completed the 300 nautical miles from Shiogama in only ten hours.

David and the others gathered at every vantage point to view the incredible scene as Commander Clark skilfully piloted *Warramunga* through the grey, all powerful and threatening armada of warships anchored in the bay. American, British and Commonwealth warships, ranging from the mighty battleships USS

Missouri and HMS *King George V,* to aircraft carriers, cruisers, and destroyers almost without number; down to the myriad of small landing craft, fussing about the harbour on a plethora of tasks, left *Warramunga* barely enough room to pick her way between them. As she approached her berth the total devastation wreaked on Yokohama and the surrounding district by the massive Allied bombardment came clearly into focus. Hardly a building was still standing.

POW's onHMS Ruler in Manos, Admiralty Is September1945. I am there somewhere!

HMS Ruler - Manus Island - 21 September 1945.

With barely time to thank Commander Clark and his ship's company for their hospitality and the exciting high speed dash down the Japanese coast, they were told that, as there was insufficient overnight accommodation aboard the *Warramunga,* they would spend the night on another American hospital ship, the USS *Monitor,* presently at anchor in the bay. The following morning, 13 September, they were advised of a change of plans. Instead of proceeding to Manila they were now to embark on the British carrier HMS *Ruler* for passage to Sydney.

They joined *Ruler,* also anchored in Yokohama Bay, during the forenoon of the same day. The officers and crew could not have been more helpful and welcoming. The sleeping, eating and recreational arrangements were quickly organised, before the inevitable round of medical checks began once more. For most, long neglected dental work was a high priority and the ship's two dentists were kept busy.

The ship remained at anchor off Yokohama for another two days while more POWs arrived from other camps until, at last, on 15 September, with a total of 445 passengers having joined the ship's crew of 600, they were ready to depart.

HMS *Ruler*, built in the United States and commissioned into service on 22 December 1943, began life as the USS *St Joseph* but was transferred to Britain before completion, under the wartime lend/lease scheme. At 14,000 tons displacement and a maximum speed of 18 knots, she was not the fastest, nor indeed the most glamorous ship in the fleet; however, to those ex-POWs and internees fortunate enough to have secured a passage in her to Australia, she was their ticket home.

For passengers and crew alike the passage to Australia was much akin to a holiday cruise. Sunbaking on the flight deck under the warm tropical sun, reading the first British newspapers they had seen in three and a half years, taking part in the many games and deck sports organised by the crew and community singing in the tropical evenings, were all favourite pastimes.

On 21 September they arrived at Manus, in the Admiralty Islands, to take on fuel and fresh provisions for the final leg to Sydney. The following evening a ship's concert was held, with both crew and passengers taking part. The night was balmy and the sea calm. The stars were brilliant, with the Southern Cross dominating the night sky in a moving welcome to southern latitudes. The singing and laughter went well into the night and there was more than one wet eye as the concert concluded with close to a thousand voices singing '*Now is the Hour*' to the accompaniment of the ship's Royal Marine Band. Suddenly, they were hit with the realisation that those who had hung together and suffered so much for so long would soon be parted.

David stood on *Ruler's* flight deck, staring into the distance, eyes shielded from the sun's glare by his cupped right hand. He had been taking his usual morning walk, on this occasion in company with Helen and Howard, when Howard had suddenly stopped and pointed. 'What's that?' indicating a grey smudge low in the distance.

David studied the horizon carefully for some time, then turned to Howard and broke into an enormous grin, 'If I'm not mistaken,' he responded, 'we're looking at Australia.'

Children onboard HMS Ruler September 1945. Howard Gunstone on far left.

On the morning of Thursday 27 September, a little after 0715 and with the New South Wales coast now close by on the starboard beam, *Ruler's* Navigating Officer turned the ship to bring her on to the leading marks on Middle Head, taking her safely through the massive rock bastions that formed the entrance to Sydney Harbour. As she made her way majestically past Bradley's Head, at a sedate 10 knots, the magnificent Sydney Harbour Bridge came into full view. With the great span of 'their' bridge dominating the near horizon, those Australians from the *Nankin* and the ex–POWs embarked in Yokohama, let out a mighty cheer. They were truly home.

To David, the remainder of that great day was a blur. An armada of pleasure boats, alerted by the press, were on hand to greet them and escort *Ruler* as she covered the last few miles, passing beneath the span of the great bridge, to her berth at Pyrmont No 9. Harbour ferries from Manly, Kirribilli and Watsons Bay, resplendent in their British racing green livery, and with early morning commuters lining their rails, hooted and tooted in a welcome none would forget.

The Australian residents were met on the quay by family and friends but had to be temporarily satisfied with waves and shouts as immigration and defence officials processed them. For David, and the others for whom Australia was not home, emotions were mixed; feelings of great joy for the Australians were tinged with a little sadness that those bonded by the circumstances of a terrible war would soon be parted.

~

Bill and Madge Nichols were there to greet Helen and Howard and whisk them away to their property at Dural. Bill invited David to come with them and stay as long as he wished but not knowing what arrangements might be made for onward passage to the UK, David preferred, for the time being, to remain in Sydney. He thanked Bill for his kind offer and promised to visit over a weekend as soon as that was practical. Meanwhile, along with the other unattached males, who had no one to meet them or anywhere to go, he was transferred to temporary accommodation at Victoria Barracks, near Moore Park, close to the city centre. The married couples, and those with children, were transferred to a variety of transit houses across the central area of the city. Madeline and Michael were allocated a small house near the Randwick Racecourse.

Quite suddenly it seemed, after almost three and a half long years of never being more than a hundred or so yards apart, the internees from Fukushima separated, to take up and renew lives that had been suspended by war. Some were to remain close and maintain contact through the years ahead, while others parted, never to see or hear of each other again. However, they all remained joined by an unbreakable bond, forged by common circumstances, which could only be shared and understood by those who had been there and knew.

DURAL – NEW SOUTH WALES

Sunday 28 October 1945

David and Helen strolled together in silence between the rows of orange trees. There was little still to be said. A week previously, David had been notified, along with others of the Fukushima internees waiting to return home to Britain, that he had been granted passage to the UK on His Majesty's Troopship *Andes*, departing Sydney on 30 October, in two days' time.

With the loss of her husband John, Helen had no immediate reason to return to the UK and therefore decided to stay on in Australia, where the climate was warm and the people friendly, until such time as she determined what direction the future might take her. Howard had settled back into the Dural Public School where he was welcomed as a returning hero. Helen hoped that, surrounded by normal people in normal circumstances, some sense of stability might return to both their lives. They were not yet ready to move on.

As he had done twice before, David had come up from Sydney to spend the weekend with Helen and Howard, and their hosts Bill and Madge Nichols, but this time he had come to say goodbye.

As the time to leave came nearer and Bill readied the ute for the return journey to the city, David and Helen found themselves wandering away from the house to be alone. Both knew that in other circumstances their relationship would develop into something further, but Muriel and the boys were waiting back home and anything beyond friendship could not be contemplated by either of them.

Howard hovered near the ute, eager to be off. Bill and Madge watched as David gave Helen one last hug, a chaste kiss on the cheek, and all were conscious of the words that ached to be whispered, but could never be said. David tried to stretch the moment. 'Take care and keep in touch,' he said, holding Helen close.

'Mind you look after them both now,' he said to Madge as he slid along the seat next to Howard and Bill. A toot on the horn and they were gone.

It would be 30 years before Helen and David met again.

ENGLISH CHANNEL

Monday 3 December 1945

It was 0700 and David, with fellow internee Malcolm Scott, leant on the rail on *Andes* B-Deck, lost in thought and watching in silence as the Isle of Wight slipped by to port and the ship entered the Solent before beginning the final run up Southampton Water to her berth at Britain's greatest marine passenger terminal. They had made landfall on the Lizard Point at 2200 the previous evening and made good time on their passage up the Channel.

David and Malcolm were two of only six merchant navy officers who had been incarcerated at Fukushima, and were returning to the UK on the *Andes*. Like

David, Malcolm had been one of the group leaders in the camp and it was he who had played such an important role in the newspaper scam that had brought them news of the war.

The passage from Sydney had been pleasant and given David a chance to relax and prepare for the resumption of a normal life.

Prior to their arrival at Southampton they had been advised that, before going on leave and reuniting with their families, they would spend two or three days at a reception camp, run by the Ministry of War Transport, with the purpose of providing Merchant Navy ex-prisoners of war, arriving in the UK from the Far East, with the information and support needed to readapt to, and resume, a normal life. Further medical checks would be conducted and officers from the Ministry would be in attendance to assist with applications for pay, allowances and pensions, issue of civilian clothing, food and clothing coupons and a myriad of other bureaucratic requirements deemed to be important.

For David, the most pressing issue was to be reunited with Muriel and the boys and it was therefore with great joy, once all the forms were filled in and the processes complete, that he received the government railway travel warrant that would finally bring him home.

Coming ashore at Sydney. Fred & Muriel Garner and G.P. Stewart

Fred & Muriel Garner and G P Stewart disembark from HMS Ruler in Sydney 27 September 1945.

BARRY – SOUTH WALES

Wednesday 5 December 1945

The 2.34, Great Western branch train from Cardiff, was due in a few minutes. Muriel, bare-headed, was wearing a royal blue dress with white polka dots and an imitation fox fur jacket to keep out the December cold. She licked the fingers of her right hand nervously and smoothed the boys' hair for the umpteenth time. Donald, now nine, remembered his father but Andrew, now six and only two at the time of his departure, remembered him not at all. The boys were dressed in their Sunday best: smart grey suits, short trousers, and shiny black shoes with grey knee-length socks with blue striped tops. White, button-up, shirts and merchant navy ties completed their outfits.

There were quite a number of people waiting on the platform. Donald was full of questions. 'What will he look like? Will he remember us? Will he be staying long?' Andrew was fidgeting and said he wanted to go to the toilet, then seemed more interested in the powerful locomotive, shunting and hissing at another platform nearby.

At last the train arrived. At first they couldn't see him, then he was there, pushing through the crush of people towards them. Muriel started to move towards him but was prevented by Andrew clinging to her leg. She stumbled and almost fell but recovered quickly. Then they were in each other's arms. He was home.

David's war was over.

AFTERMATH

After the war, David found it very difficult to settle. The UK Government, the climate, the strict rationing – all of it made him irritable and short-tempered. Today it would be called post traumatic stress syndrome, and every counselling and support service would be at his disposal. However, in post-war Britain in 1946 it was different. David received nothing and, like many thousands of others suffering from the effects of the war, was expected to pull himself together and get on with it.

From left; Don Millar, David Millar, Margaret Millar and the author at our mother's funeral, Keri Keri New Zealand 3 September 2003.

By the time his two months' leave had expired he was very unhappy. No one seemed to understand what was tormenting him and his relationship with Muriel was in danger of breaking down. He flew into a temper at the slightest provocation and was desperate to get back to sea. The final insult was when he was informed by the Examiner of Masters and Mates at the British Board of Trade that he was required to resit the full examination for Master, Foreign Going, as his time as a POW in Japan constituted a break in service beyond that allowed by the regulations.

On 9 February 1946, he signed as First Mate on the MV *Bidor*, sailing out of Grangemouth, but, at the same time, made arrangements for Muriel and us boys to emigrate to New Zealand where David had family; there, he thought, they might all start again and enjoy a better life. On 11 September 1946, Muriel, Donald and I departed the UK on the New Zealand Shipping Company's vessel TSS *Rangitata* and, on arrival, took up residence at Port Chalmers, on New Zealand's South Island. David then gained employment at sea with the Straits Steamship Company, whose headquarters were in Singapore and from where he made periodic visits to New Zealand when on leave.

In 1950, David retired from the sea and joined Muriel and us boys in New Zealand where he took up a position as an Observer with the New Zealand Meteorological Service. Now ten years old, I had great difficulty adjusting to the presence of this virtual stranger who had come to live with us. The family moved to Invercargill in New Zealand's deep south, the town of David's initial posting. Donald and I received our secondary education at Invercargill's Southland Boys' High School. In 1953, our mother Muriel gave birth to a daughter, Margaret.

David was subsequently posted to the New Zealand meteorological office in Fiji, where he, Muriel and Margaret spent four years (we boys stayed on in NZ) before returning to New Plymouth on New Zealand's North Island. His next appointment was Port Meteorological Officer in Auckland where he served out the remainder of his working life until retirement, in 1971, aged sixty.

With us boys and Margaret now grown up and gone, David and Muriel moved into a small unit at Orewa, a holiday resort just north of Auckland, where they lived for a number of years before moving into a retirement village at Keri Keri in New Zealand's far north, to see out their final years.

David was never to meet Madeline, Michael or Alfie Round again. However, he did briefly meet up with Helen and Howard during a visit to the UK with Muriel in 1973. He also maintained regular correspondence with Helen, until her death in 1983, and subsequently with Howard until David's own death in 2003.

David always stood by us as a family but I often wonder whether this was out of a sense of duty. Would he, deep down, have rather spent his life with Helen – we will never know.

Muriel died at Keri Keri on 31 August 2003 and David, just three months later, on 4 December.

Helen Guy – Circa 1954.

Helen and Howard stayed on in Australia for six or seven months before receiving word that Howard's grandfather in England was quite ill. Helen quickly arranged passage and they arrived back in the UK in the late Spring of 1946.

Howard resumed his interrupted education as a boarder at Elsmere College before winning a prestigious Joseph Lucas apprenticeship at Lucas Automotive, the famous British manufacturer of automotive parts. He was allowed time off to study at Birmingham University where he obtained a degree in mechanical engineering. After thirteen years with Lucas he moved to British Gas where he spent twenty-seven years in various management roles, before retiring in 1993.

Howard married Barbara Tetther in 1965 and they have one daughter, married and living in Brussels. Barbara works as a lecturer in Physical Education at the University of Central England. Howard and Barbara now live in Solihull in the West Midlands.

Helen never remarried, perhaps due to the pain of losing two husbands or perhaps because of David and the remarkable experiences they had shared.

She lived out the remainder of her life in Torquay, South Devon, where she died in 1983. I suspect that David was not far from her thoughts in her final days.

The author with Alfie Round at Murrumburra NSW – 2004.

Despite the chaos in post-war Sydney, Madeline Charnaud was able to arrange passage to India for herself and Michael on the Orient Liner *Oronto*, which sailed on 11 October. After another series of adventures they were finally reunited with Michael's father on his tea plantation in Ceylon (Sri Lanka). Madeline and Michael spent six months relaxing and recuperating before it was time for Michael to resume his schooling in the UK. After the confinement in Fukushima, Michael decided he would take up a career in agriculture and studied at Reading University where he met his future wife, Jill Colledge.

In 1953 Michael returned to Ceylon to make a career on his father's plantation. He was joined by Jill a year later and they were married in a tiny local church at Regalla on 5 January 1955. For the next ten years Michael and Jill enjoyed a life as close to Paradise as one could find on this earth and during this time their marriage was blessed by the arrival of three children. However, the good times did not last and in the mid '60s, the political situation in Sri Lanka was such that they were forced to abandon the plantation and return to England where Michael started his own business.

Now in retirement, Michael and Jill live in their home in Surrey, purchased in 1965. It has a beautiful garden, transformed by Michael into a sea of tranquillity, where they now enjoy their advancing years.

Madeline remained a towering character in Michael's life with her iron strength of will coupled with great tenderness. She passed away in England in 1986 at the grand age of eighty-nine.

Howard Gunstone 2005.

Alfred Round, like David and many thousands of others, had great difficulty adjusting to normal life after the war and chose to stay on in Australia, returning to sea on the Australian coastal trade. He married an Australian girl but the marriage was short lived, largely as a result of torment born of his time in Fukushima and the extended periods he was now spending at sea. Alfie married for a second time and bore a total of four offspring; Stuart, Janet, David and Lindsay. He returned to the UK for a period, but Australia's climate and laid-back lifestyle tempted Alfie to return. Employed in a number of jobs, he eventually settled and ultimately retired in Murrumburrah, a New South Wales country town with only a couple of thousand residents.

It was here that I met Alfie in 2004, while doing research for this book. He provided enormous assistance in reviewing the first two sections, as well as providing a mountain of information, documents and photographs.

Alfie became a committed Christian while in Fukushima and stayed true to his faith for the remainder of his life.

'Roondie' passed away in August 2006, aged eighty-four.

Kapitän Günther Gumprich was awarded the Knight's Cross of the Iron Cross on 31 December 1942. Having commanded the *Thor* with such great success, he was devastated by the loss of his ship and so many of his officers and men in the tragic explosion that shook Yokohama on 30 November 1942. However, he remained on in

Japan and on 21 March 1943 was posted in command of another German Commerce Raider, *Schiff 28*, the *Michel*, at that time refitting in Mitsubishi's shipyard in Kobe. It was the *Michel*, then under the command of Captain Helmuth von Ruckteschell, that sank the *Gloucester Castle*, in July 1942 and on which Marion and Graham Sparke, Pat Radford and Andrew White had all been passengers. It will be recalled that these four were also interned in Fukushima, arriving in November 1942.

On completion of the refit, Gumprich took *Michel* to sea and conducted another successful cruise in the Indian Ocean and his old hunting ground, off the west coast of Australia. Returning to Yokohama in October 1943, while only sixty miles off that great port, *Michel* was intercepted and sunk by an American submarine USS *Tarpon*.

Günther Gumprich went down with his ship.

⌒～

Of those Japanese associated with the running and management of the camp, five were investigated for war crimes. They were:

> Nakao Masatake (Fishface), the Chief of Special Police at the commencement of the internment
>
> Tari Kyûshi, the second Chief of Special Police (from January 1944)
>
> Nemoto Kô, the first Commandant
>
> Mitsuhashi Yosio, the second Commandant (the Pumpkin Controller) and
>
> Midorikawa Kôzô (Slimy), the first interpreter.

Of these, the prosecutions of Tari and Midorikawa did not proceed due to lack of documentary evidence (destroyed by the Japanese authorities at the end of the war).

Nakao, Nemoto and Mitsuhashi were sent to Tokyo at the end of November 1945 and held in custody at Tokyo's Sugamo Prison, awaiting trial, which did not commence until 22 September 1947, nearly two years later. The proceedings were part of what became known as 'The Yokohama Trials'. On 7 October, four days before the scheduled end of his trial, Nakao was released, again due to lack of documentary evidence. Nemoto and Mitsuhashi were both found guilty of war crimes and sentenced to five years' hard labour; however, they were only imprisoned for a further three years and four months, allowing for time already served.

Michael and Jill Charnaud 2000.

As for the convent itself, in mid-September 1945, only a few days after David and the others had departed, the Sisters returned. The local authorities were quick to carry out long neglected maintenance on the building and this, together with much hard work by the Sisters themselves, soon restored the convent to its original pristine state. The clinic was reopened and the Sisters turned to looking after war orphans and ministering to the local populace. The clinic was closed in 1949 but the building itself remained in use for a further 62 years, with very little to indicate that it was once a prison.[9]

A small cluster of white crosses, in a secluded corner of the nearby cemetery on Mount Shinobu, also remain as a reminder of times past. They are engraved with the names of the four who died in captivity:

HEMY Vincent M	Merchant Navy Engineer	Died 15.8.1942	Aged 55
McINTYRE Nichol	Chief Steward SS *Nankin*	Died 13.9.1942	Aged 64
GLEESON Elizabeth	Stewardess SS *Nankin*	Died 7.4.1945	Aged 44
DIMITRAKOPOULOY Caroline	Stewardess SS *Pagasitikos*	Died 28.8.1945	Aged 31

---

9   Sadly, the earthquake and Tsanami that devastated the Fukushima prefecture and surrounding area in March 2011 caused irreparable damage to the convent which is now to be demolished, closing a small, but important chapter in the history of WWII.

Today, the history of the convent and, in particular, record of its use as a civilian internment camp during the war, is kept by one of the resident nuns, Sister Maureen Lamarche. I am deeply indebted to Sister Maureen for her contribution to this story, for her advice on usage of the Japanese language, and particularly for the translation of Chief of Police Nakao Masatake's address to the prisoners on their arrival in the camp.

MEMORIES

In the hills of Fukushima in the heart of Nippon's isle

There's a convent calm and peaceful, where the children used to smile,

And play and roam the gardens day by day, or linger for a while.

Where the convent sisters taught them all that they had to know

Of the world beyond the convent walls where the storms of life did blow.

But now alas the scene has changed; the gardens ring no more

With the sound of children's laughter as they did in days of yore

For with its devastating flame, the fiery tongues of war

Have reached out far across the seas and licked their native shore.

For Nippon with her lust for power has cast her hateful lot

With Hitler and his satellites in Europe's boiling pot;

And now that peaceful convent is a home for internees,

Men and women, children too, from lands across the seas

Who live and hope the day is near that they shall all be free

To return to their own homelands, lands of love and Liberty.

David Millar

Circa 1973

APPENDIX 1

Personal thoughts of Madeline Charnaud subsequent to release from Fukushima Internment Camp in September 1945

'The story of my experiences is not exceptional. I suffered mental torment and bodily indignity, but not more than many others. They were hard years, and there is not much that is good to be said about them. I do not believe that they improved my character. I know that they did not improve my constitution, and the mirror assures me that they did not improve my face! But they have taught me how individuals react in time of misfortune. I learnt never to think of the future, and never dare anticipate tomorrow. I lived for the present, the future was dark, not only because there was no hint of approaching victory, but it was dark as a primitive chaos, due to the volcanically uncertain temper of our captors. Whilst I was still in captivity I believed that my character had changed, that I felt cold, unable to be hurt, unable to hurt myself, but now that I am back to normal again, I feel just as vulnerable. I hope that the hard manual tasks that we learned to perform under Jap surveillance from now on will have no place in my life. People say there is a great joy, working with your hands which may be true, but a forced pointless labour on a starvation diet is very different. I also hope that there will be no occasion in my future life to steal or barter food. Those 38 months equipped me for just one thing, "prison". But before I go to prison again I will die, for captivity has taught me the value of freedom. In my life before, I had existed as a free woman and had come to expect freedom as a matter of course, and it was not until I had lost it that I really understood its value. Freedom means this to me: the right to be with, to love and to touch my husband and children; the right to look about me without fear of seeing people struck or beaten or punished; the right to hear a man's footsteps and know that it is not a guard. The right to work for oneself and one's people. The possession of a door and a key with which to lock it. Moments of silence, and a place to weep and be private with no one else to see you. The freedom of my eyes to admire the face of this earth, the mountains, trees, the fields, the sea, without barbed wire and a high wall stretched across my vision. The strength to walk with the wind in my face and no sentry to stop me. The ability to look at the new moon without seeing it as a symbol of passing time, and saying to myself "how many more times must it rise on my captivity?" These are things that make the freedom which I hope never to give up again. Knowing the utter desolation that was to face one, day after day, week after week, month after month, as our captivity continued and one felt one's moral courage weakening or ebbing away. Then one's optimism would be faltering, knowing the virtual dissolution of body and soul, which with certain conditions of living, even more than dying, bring about, and the constant ordeal to keep alive and not to give in, because your own child's life depended on it.

'Now that one is back amongst free people again, you feel a wide gap between yourself and them. It is an emotional gap due to the life that one has lived, and the things that one has seen, and the thoughts that one has thought. The remedy is not pills, though, because it is only people who have been through a similar experience who fully understand you, as they are on the same side of the gap with you. They alone may help you cross it one day, to help you join the rest of the world as it moves on. Each individual in the camp had a floor space of 6ft x 4ft in which to sleep, eat, live, or die without privacy and quietness. The mothers with children were the hardest hit of all, with the constant strain of lack of food and hunger, and the worry of how long the meagre rations would continue to be doled out to us. There were fourteen mothers in all, and we washed, shouted, hated, fought, laughed and wept together, and without exception all helped each other. Life was grim and we lived not far above the level of animals who feed, fight for, nurture, and love and protect their young. I use the terms "Prisoner" and "Prison Camp" instead of "Internment" because that is how the Japs conducted their war rules. At irregular intervals, usually if someone had been "naughty" by breaking one of the 150 odd rules, we would be summoned together and lectured and told that we had insulted "His Majesty the Emperor", who was practically regarded as a living presence with us. We would be reminded again of our status and told the rules for conduct of Prisoners of War. A guard was always right, and a prisoner always wrong, and so we were always victims of his inferiority complex which took the form of imaginary slights, and so in consequence we were often deliberately accused and punished for things that we never did. It was humiliating to be ruled, bullied, by ignorant, uncouth, uneducated peasant boys all under 25 who would make obscene remarks and gestures or shout and brandish their swords on the least provocation. In our women's camp all we had to complain of was starvation, weakness, occasional blows, constant regimentation, and work with no strength at all carried out on a ration of 15 ozs of daily bread and the loneliness of one's soul away from one's family. However, no women could have been kinder if one was sick, if one was being punished, or if your ration was cut. Not even your nearest and dearest could have given you the sympathy or done more than they did for you in those dark days of adversity. Because what one gives spiritually or materially in captivity is worth ten times more than in the normal everyday world. But the human body is tough and, with friendship, can survive sickness and starvation. My boy's life depended on me, and his only chance of health and growth and his whole future attitude to life and his character revolved around me. It was a great responsibility for me all alone.

'On the evening of our first day of Peace I sat down and tried to write. I wanted inspired, spectacular words. Words to express to the world just what freedom meant; but I could not find them. I wanted some way of expressing to others what had happened to us that day. I wanted to shout and tell them all what it was like to be a captive in Japan, and now what it was like to be once again free. Just what it meant to go through an ordeal like that for over three years, and to walk in the nightmarish company of death, with sadistic gaolers in the melancholy of imprisonment in a faraway land. I finally left the story to be told by more able pens than mine.

'On 11 September at 1½ hours' notice we were told to get ready to leave. I packed our bags, put on that frock that I had saved for 3½ years and, amidst tears, gave a silent prayer and thanks to that Unseen Force, or Power for Goodness, or God, call it what you will, Who had watched over us miraculously all these years. We departed still thinking it was yet another dream. To have remained undefeated in spirit amid all the circumstances of defeat is a man's most signal triumph, and my son and I had done it together, and we had both finally got through!

'A great many of us now in the aftermath may be a little surly, a little indolent, sometimes strangely irritable. But we are beings who fought for our pride, and saved it whole – a little bit of Britain in our minds, in a long, unchronicled, private war. A war in which no decorations can ever be given, but to have come out of it with the whole spirit intact is the highest honour one could ever wish to achieve, far more so even than mere survival. It was our spirit that in the end even procured for us the deepest respect of the Japanese themselves. I came away from that camp with nothing more than a greater tolerance and understanding of human nature, a greater sense of values, and a greater love for ordinary everyday people in their triumph over adversity.' **Madeline Charnaud**

APPENDIX 2

FUKUSHIMA CAMP RULES

Roll Call (*Tenko*)

1. Must not get up before the first bell.

2. Must be fully dressed for roll call.

3. May wear an overcoat but not a dressing gown.

4. Bedding must be folded up before roll call.

5. Must not cough, sneeze or blow nose etc. when lining up for roll call.

6. Must not wear towel round neck at roll call.

7. Must not smile or look sarcastic at roll call.

8. Must remain in line after *keireiing* (saluting).

9. Must not talk or chew when in line for roll call.

10. Must number in Nipponese.

Washing and Bathing

11. Must not strip naked for washing in washrooms.

12. Must not pour jugs of water over oneself in washrooms.

13. Bottom half of washroom windows must be closed.

14. Must use wooden clogs provided in washrooms.

15. Must dry soles of feet before leaving washrooms.

16. Must shave only during bathing hours.

17. Must not get into bath.

18. No clothes may be washed on Sundays.

19. Must not use hot water for washing clothes.

20. Must not wash after roll call at night.

21. Must not waste water.

22. Must not go out to clothes line except at stated times.

23. Must get into long bath five persons at one time on hot bath days and save water. (Cancels No.17)

24. The long bath may not be used for washing clothes.

25. From July to September internees may take cold baths between 11 and 12 o'clock in the morning and between 4 and 5 o'clock in the afternoon in the bathroom only.

26. Only one bucket of water may be used for a cold bath and the bucketful must be taken all at once.

Meals

27. Must not take more than 15 minutes for each meal.

28. Must not take whole rations of bread upstairs.

29. Must not eat in passageways.

30. Must not keep cutlery or cups upstairs.

31. Must not lock inner windows of dining rooms.

32. Must not enter kitchen.

33. Must not talk to kitchen staff on duty.

34. Must not wear headgear during meals.

35. If anyone breaks a cup or plate, he loses his food for one day.

36. Must not shut inner dining room windows if guard has opened them.

Smoking

37. May not smoke in corridors.

38. May smoke out of doors only near tin provided.

39. Must not smoke in bed.

40. Must not throw cigarette ends on asphalt playground.

41. Must not draw cigarette ration if a non-smoker.

42. Must not put ashtrays on sleeping mats.

43. Must not smoke after roll call at night or before roll call in the morning.

44. May use as ashtrays only those receptacles which have been approved and numbered as such.

45. Ten minutes before roll call at night, ashtrays must be emptied and placed outside the door of rooms beside the notice recording how many ashtrays pertain to the room.

Garden

46. Must go out when ordered, unless sick.

47. Must not come in without permission of the guard, even for lavatory.

48. Must not lie and sleep out of doors.

49. Must not look over the walls.

50. Must not walk beyond the limits of the asphalt playground or paths up to the door of the shoe-room (exit) and up to the S.E. corner of the building.

51. Must not spit on the asphalt.

52. Must not pick flowers, fruit or vegetables.

53. Must not take blanket out of doors.

54. Must not urinate out of doors.

55. Must wash feet outside before coming in, if not wearing shoes.

56. Must not sit on grass on north side of the playground.

57. Must not sit on back veranda.

58. Must not take books to read out into the garden.

Women Internees

59. Men must not wave or smile at the women and vice versa.

60. Men must not communicate in any way with the women except through the office and vice versa.

61. Unattached men may send mending to the women through the office.

62. Letters between men and women internees may be sent through the office only. (introduced June 1944)

Windows

63. Must not bow, wave or smile from the windows at passers-by.

64. Must turn back on passers-by seen from the window.

65. Must not stand naked to waist near windows.

66. Must not hang clothing out of the windows.

67. Must not lean out of the windows.

68. Must not look at women internees out of the windows.

69. Must not throw anything out of the windows.

70. Must not spit out of the windows but must use spittoons.

71. Must not eat at windows when visible from outside.

72. Must not keep windows more than "two fists" open at the bottom.

Footwear

73.   Must take off outdoor shoes immediately on entering the building.

74.   Shoe room must be left tidy.

75.   May only wear slippers without backs indoors.

76.   Must not wear slippers with leather heels indoors.

77.   Must not wear slippers when walking on sleeping-mats.

78.   Must not wear indoor slippers out of doors.

79.   Must not bring outdoor shoes upstairs.

80.   Must wipe feet on mat provided when coming indoors.

81.   Must not put shoes in the lockers in shoe room but only on the shelves.

Bedding

82.   Bedding must be kept folded, piled in one corner of the room and covered with a blanket during the day.

83.   Must not wrap blanket round body above the waist line in daytime.

84.   Must not sit on bedding during the daytime.

85.   Must not use quilt to lie on at night.

86.   Must not put up mosquito nets or make up beds before roll call at night.

87.   Must not use blankets at all during the daytime (while heating is on).

88.   Bedding must be folded in the regulation manner.

89.   The blanket issued by the Nippon Government must not be used to sit on in preference to Red Cross blankets and must not be wrapped around the feet.

90.   Sheets must be used to sleep on because they can be washed.

91.   Mosquito nets must not be hung in the sunshine to air but only in the shade.

Music

92.   Must not sing so loud as to be heard outside.

93.   Must not play any musical instrument except with permission.

94.   Must not whistle in corridors after dark.

95.   Must not sing or whistle when passing a guard.

96.   May only play classical or religious music on accordion.

97.   Piano may be played softly on Sunday afternoons in the assembly hall.

98.	Harmonicas may only be played on Sundays between 9.00 a.m. and 7.30 p.m. (introduced May 1944)

99.	Must not sing martial airs.

Official

100.	Must not try to be friendly with the guards.

101.	Must always do anything a guard orders at any time.

102.	Must bow to every guard on meeting.

103.	Must not bow with hands in the pockets.

104.	Must remove headgear when bowing.

105.	A bow must last about five seconds.

106.	Must bow when entering and leaving the office.

107.	Must not wear dressing-gown into the office.

108.	Must not wear headgear into the office.

109.	Must refer to a guard as "*tai yin*", to a sergeant as "*bucho*" and to the Japanese people as "*Nipponjin*".

110.	"*Bucho*" must not be referred to as "*bucho*".

111.	Must not *keirei* to any stranger in the camp unless he has been introduced as an official.

Church

112.	Must not come late to church.

113.	Must look straight ahead in church.

114.	Must not take hymn books out of church.

115.	Must not loiter outside church during service.

116.	Must not peer into church through windows during service.

117.	Must not wear blanket to church.

118.	Must not stand to watch the women going to church unless going oneself.

119.	Must not cross knees, put hands in pockets or fidget in church.

Sickness

120.	Must not go sick without previous permission.

121.	Must report on recovering from sickness.

122.	Must not take more than one aspirin without permission.

123.	Eyewash issued must be kept and used over and over again.

Lavatories

124.   Must finish going to the lavatories before 9.30 a.m.

125.   Toilet paper must not be used as writing paper.

126.   Must not put newspapers or solids down the lavatories.

127.   Must not use certain lavatories.

Indoors Miscellaneous

128.   May only use the back staircase.

129.   Must not run in the passages.

130.   Must not appear outside the rooms naked to the waist.

131.   Must not sleep during the day.

132.   Must not walk up or down the corridors after 6.00 p.m.

133.   Must always have the corridors swept clean.

134.   Must not do wood carving indoors.

135.   Must not slam doors.

136.   Must not enter other internee's rooms if they are occupied.

137.   Must not put chairs on the sleeping mats.

138.   Must not remove electric light bulbs from corridors or lavatories.

139.   Must not look over banister into the main hallway.

140.   Must not wet the floor.

141.   Must not dry clothes on the radiators.

142.   Must not read or play games between the hours of 9.00 a.m. and 11.30 a.m. and between 1.00 p.m. and 4.00 p.m. and between 7.00 p.m. and 8.30 p.m. except during inclement weather.

143.   No one may cut hair without permission, only one camp barber appointed.

144.   No one may go to the landings for prayers or any other purpose (later relaxed for those praying).

145.   Brooms must be hung up or stood on the handles and not kept resting on their business ends.

146.   Empty tins from Red Cross parcels must not be put in the rubbish bin, to be thrown out, but must be put into special receptacles.

Demeanour and Conduct

147.   Must not speak to or greet tradespeople delivering food.

148.   Must not be too happy.

149. Must not wear a contemptuous smile.

150. Must not behave in a suspicious manner.

151. Must not call other internees abusive words or names except through the two captains.

152. Must not fight.

153. Must not gamble.

154. Must not be unreasonable and ask for more and more.

155. Crowds must not collect in corridors or rooms.

156. Group leaders may not hold meetings without permission.

157. Must not do anything harmful to the Imperial Nipponese Government.

158. Requests to the Commandant may only be made through Captain Stratford.

159. Must always wear official number ticket.

160. Must not use articles issued by the Imperial Nipponese Government for any purpose other than that intended.

161. Must not alter in any way articles issued by the Imperial Nipponese Government.

162. Must not chew gum at Roll Call or when appearing in the office.

Air Raid Precautions (A.R.P.)

163. Must not sit on A.R.P. water-tubs.

164. Must not place anything on top of A.R.P. water-tubs.

165. Must not interfere with any A.R.P. equipment.

166. When going down to the basement for shelter must leave hands and arms free and must not carry any packages or blankets when the weather is warm.

Outside World

167. May not communicate with the outside world.

168. May not receive news or any other communication from outside the camp.

169. May not buy anything except through the Commandant.

170. Letters may not be written to the Commandant or higher authorities without previous permission.

171. May write 100 typescript words in letter about health once a month only. (Introduced 1st March 1944.)

172. May send cable only in reply to a communication from outside

173. May only send one cable a year.

APPENDIX 3

THE FUKUSHIMA PRISONERS OF WAR

Name	d.o.b.	Nationality	Occupation
Abdu *Keed*	1.1.1917	British–Arabian	Merchant Navy
Amilstakis *Nikolaos*	29.5.1900	Greek	Merchant Navy Boatswain
Amin *Hassan bin*	11.12.1911	British–Malay	Aircraft Fitter
Baergen *Gerhard*	30.8.1916	British–Canadian	Missionary
Bailey *Thomas G*	6.3.1921	British	Merchant Navy Seaman
Balonyon *Yalnip*	15.4.1901	Turkish	Merchant Navy Fireman
Bihos *Emanuel*	28.10.1920	Greek	Merchant Navy Engineer
Biswas *Subasini*	31.12.1894	British–Indian	Schoolteacher
Bok *Rosalind*	13.3.1919	British–Chinese	Housewife
Bok *Susan Ann*	18.8.1942	British–Chinese	Infant (born in camp)
Bok *Sye Foo*	10.5.1918	British–Chinese	British airline Clerk
Boyall *Charles S*	1.9.1893	Australian	Minister of Religion
Cashidonis *Beleklis*	27.12.1907	Greek	Cook
Charnaud *Madeline*	13.2.1897	British	Housewife
Charnaud *Michael*	31.3.1931	British	Child
Chin *Poon Chia*	18.5.1918	British–Chinese	Rigger
Con *Peet Fong*	Not Known	British–Chinese	Stenographer
Cook *Audrey*	16.10.1911	British	Bank Sub-accountant
Cook *David*	1.11.1941	British	Infant
Cook *Herbert J M*	2.5.1903	British	Bank Officer
Cook *Sally Louise*	19.7.1940	British	Infant
Corna *Felmin*	7.7.1915	Portuguese	Merchant Navy Fireman
Crocker *Herbert J*	30.12.1923	British	Merchant Navy Apprentice
Daniels *Arthur P*	2.4.1899	British	Bank Manager
Dimitrakopouloy *Schiriyanous*	2.10.1902	Greek	Merchant Navy Radio Operator
Dimitrakopouloy *Caroline*	Not Known	Dutch	Merchant Navy Stewardess
Drennen *Carl*	10.6.1909	British–Canadian	Merchant Navy Engineer
Edwards *Thomas E D*	1.6.1910	British	Bank Sub-accountant
Eleades *Ilias*	5.5.1888	Greek	Merchant Navy Chief Engineer
Elsey *David*	17.5.1917	Australian	Merchant Navy Purser
Erasmus *John A*	28.8.1910	British–S.African	Merchant Navy Seaman
Erskine *Neil B*	2.6.1898	British	Sergeant Royal Artillery
Ezmanmiel *Ari*	1.1.1898	British–Arabian	Merchant Navy
Fernandes *Jaqueline*	21.4.1941	British	Infant
Fernandes *Leopoldo*	19.12.1908	British	Company Secretary
Fernandes *Miguel*	3.5.1937	British	Child

Fernandes *Valerie*	28.8.1938	British	Infant
Fernandes *Rosalind*	1.7.1918	British	Housewife
Fleming *James Peter*	1.7.1922	British	Merchant Navy Apprentice
Foster *Vera*	21.6.1922	British	Not Known
Fox *Francis W*	24.3.1914	British	Merchant Navy Engineer
Furey *Charles W*	8.7.1895	British	Customs Officer
Golsworthy *Charles R*	12.11.1911	British	Missionary
Golsworthy *Joyce E*	7.4.1913	British	Schoolteacher
Garner *Fredrick F*	9.7.1910	British	British Consular Service
Garner *Muriel*	17.10.1907	British	Housewife
Gleeson *Elizabeth*	11.6.1901	British	Merchant Navy Stewardess
Gray *Evelyn E*	24.3.1891	British	Housewife
Gray *Colin G*	3.12.1892	British	Tea Planter
Gunstone *Howard*	21.7.1935	British	Child (son of Helen Guy)
Guy *Helen*	11.2.1909	British	Housewife
Hamid *Ali bin*	2.12.1914	British–Malay	Aircraft Fitter
Hannah *Malcolm R*	3.12.1905	British	Bank Sub-accountant
Hemy *Vincent M*	1.1.1887	British	Merchant Navy Engineer
Hercombe *Phyllis*	8.7.1907	British	Housewife
Ichiga *Hassan*	1.2.1896	British–Arabian	Merchant Navy
Jack *James M*	30.11.1906	British	Bank Sub-accountant
Jeffery *Audrey L*	4.4.1913	British	Missionary
Johnson *Ben*	Not Known	British–African	Merchant Navy Fireman
Kalalis *Antonios*	30.1.1903	Greek	Merchant Navy Oiler
Lambrinos *Lambros D*	16.7.1891	Greek	Merchant Navy Deck Officer
Lang *Wilfred McD*	31.1.1913	British	Chief Radio Operator
Larsson *Alfred E*	5.11.1904	British	Merchant Navy Boatswain
Law *Annie*	13.1.1888	British	Missionary
Lee *So Ye*	6.6.1906	British–Chinese	Children's Nurse
Lee *Siang Poo (James)*	14.4.1918	British–Chinese	Stores Clerk
Lee *Monica*	8.4.1922	British–Chinese	Housewife
Ligadis *Lebelios*	26.10.1906	Greek	Merchant Navy Seaman
Lyon *Gabrielle A J*	5.1.1914	British	Housewife
Lyon *Clive*	1.11.1941	British	Infant
Mack *Mona*	21.12.1921	British	Not Known
Manges *Vachibrigos*	1.1.1913	Greek	Merchant Navy Seaman
Mannering *Edward*	1.12.1913	British–African	Merchant Navy Fireman
Manusos *Nikolaos*	1.10.1891	Greek	Merchant Navy Engineer
Massquoi *Walker*	12.7.1905	British–African	Merchant Navy Fireman
McIntyre *Nichol*	26.10.1877	British	Merchant Navy Chief Steward
Melia *Thomas*	6.6.1925	British	Merchant Navy Galley Boy
Millar *David*	24.10.1911	British	Merchant Navy Officer
Miller *Joseph*	16.4.1900	British	Bank Sub-accountant
Mok *Ah Fong*	24.11.1911	British–Chinese	Fitter

Mok *Maria*	24.2.1918	British–Chinese	Housewife
Mok *Margaret S K*	26.6.1939	British–Chinese	Infant
Mok *Simon*	16.11.1940	British–Chinese	Infant
Mok *Joseph Koek On*	12.5.1942	British–Chinese	Infant – born on KMS *Thor*
Molphy *Michael*	10.10.1909	British–African	Merchant Navy Fireman
Murray *Daniel*	12.11.1905	British	Bank Sub-accountant
Murray *Barbara F*	21.12.1906	British	Housewife
Neymonitis *Leonidus*	26.8.1881	Greek	Merchant Navy
O'Halloran *John W*	4.9.1915	British	Merchant Navy Seaman
Ogovanis *Steffus*	1.12.1902	Greek	Merchant Navy Seaman
Olsen *Olaf*	18.1.1914	British	Merchant Navy Officer
Oon *Tom*	15.9.1919	British–Chinese	Clerk
Osborne *Henry*	16.10.1917	British	Missionary
Owsten *John Francis*	14.1.1919	British	Merchant Navy Seaman
Papis *Dimitorous*	12.02.1919	Greek	Merchant Navy Officer
Patrick *Daniel*	21.4.1921	British	Merchant Navy Radio Officer
Pederson *Jenney*	29.11.1912	British	Missionary
Phillips *Philip W*	Not known	British–African	Merchant Navy Cook
Phillips *Alice*	1.2.1900	British	Housewife
Phillips *Edmund C*	21.8.1904	British	Bank Assistant Accountant
Phillips *Glyn*	26.3.1916	British	Merchant Navy Officer
Phillips *John H*	21.2.1941	British	Infant
Piangos *John*	3.6.1911	Greek	Merchant Navy Captain
Piscopos *Panagyotes*	13.2.1910	Greek	Merchant Navy Seaman
Plagantes *Demtorius*	15.10.1902	Greek	Merchant Navy Steward
Plasumulis *Likolugoos*	21.6.1912	Greek	Merchant Navy Fireman
Platanishotes *Stefanos*	24.9.1903	Greek	Merchant Navy Fireman
Powel *Sydney*	4.12.1900	British	Merchant Navy Steward
Radford *Rosemary Patricia*	22.10.1923	British	Manageress
Rixon *Arthur H*	2.3.1925	British	Merchant Navy Seaman
Robertson *Walter H*	26.4.1925	British	Merchant Navy Mess Boy
Robson *Cuthbert S*	15.11.1919	British	Merchant Navy Seaman
Round *Alfred C*	6.10.1922	British	Merchant Navy Seaman
Salef *Ali*	1.1.1884	British–Arabian	Not known
Saunders *Cecil*	30.3.1899	British	Manager Anglo Iranian Oil
Scott *Malcolm E*	26.1.1906	British	Merchant Navy Radio Operator
Scott *Douglas*	12.6.1908	British	Banker
Scott *Elizabeth*	18.8.1913	British	Housewife & Registered Nurse
Seah *Hong Kiang*	11.2.1919	British–Chinese	British Airline Caterer
Shewan *John*	13.6.1906	British	Bank Sub-accountant
Skyshites *Aganitos*	1.6.1889	Greek	Merchant Navy Seaman
Sparke *Marion*	3.1.1912	British	Housewife
Sparke *Graham*	5.2.1932	British	Child
Stewart *Arthur C G*	7.1.1887	British	Customs Officer

Stewart *James Little*	24.9.1892	British	Customs Officer
Stewart *Gerald P*	3.5.1906	British	Indian Civil Service
Stratford *Harold C G*	2.3.1890	Australian	Captain of the Nankin
Temlet *Charles D*	11.5.1903	British	Customs Officer
Thoms *Alexander K*	3.7.1903	British	Jute Mill Assistant Manager
Thoms *Florence P*	28.3.1902	British	Housewife
Walker *Cyril H*	15.8.1913	British	Electrical Engineer (Exide)
Webster *William*	24.3.1924	British	Merchant Navy Seaman
Wee *Sian Leok*	24.3.1906	British–Chinese	Storekeeper
Wee *You Lian*	20.4.1913	British–Chinese	Housewife
Wee *Edwin*	25.3.1941	British–Chinese	Infant
Westly *Edward Dean*	28.2.1923	British	Merchant Navy Seaman
White *Vernon S*	14.7.1909	British	Merchant Navy Fireman
White *Andrew*	3.11.1927	British	Merchant Navy Seaman
Wichers *John H*	6.12.1908	British	Bank Sub-accountant
Xavier *Albert*	22.7.1920	British	Clerk
Yates *Arthur C*	30.4.1884	British	Tea Planter
Yates *Susan C*	28.10.1888	British	Housewife
Yates *Lavender C*	30.7.1918	British	Daughter of above
Youssef *Akmed*	Not Known	British–Arabian	Not known

ENDNOTE

The impact of Germany's Armed Merchant Raiders, in the context of the war as a whole, was very minor. Of the ten raiders that Germany produced, eight were either sunk by Allied forces or rendered inoperable due to other causes. The last operational raider was Günther Gumprich's *Michel*, sunk on 17 October 1943 by the USS *Tarpon* – German armed raiders played no further part in the war.

Between them, the ten raiders sank or captured 129 Allied merchant ships having a total tonnage of 796,612 Gross Registered Tons. *Thor* herself accounted for 21 of these ships. Impressive though the figures may seem, they pale into insignificance in terms of overall war losses. In total, and from all causes, Britain lost a staggering 4786 merchant ships amounting to just over 21 million tons. 29,994 British merchant sailors were killed bringing essential food and war supplies to a beleaguered Britain in ships that were slow, cumbersome and very poorly armed.

However, it was not the number of Allied ships sunk that formed the raiders' greatest contribution to the German war effort – it was the fact that they existed at all. By applying the principle of disproportionate response, Germany was able to force Britain to commit valuable warships, desperately needed elsewhere, to hunting them down. Further, no ship was safe in any ocean of the world unless in convoy and with an adequate escort force, putting further strain on scarce Allied resources.

The purpose of the raiders was to create confusion and uncertainty – in this they were largely successful.

The days of the raider are now over. Air and satellite surveillance now make it impossible for such ships to operate undetected.

GLOSSARY

abaft—behind.

aft/after—the back or rear part of a ship.

aimer—the member of a gun's crew responsible for the direction the gun is pointing.

all hands—everyone on board a ship, excluding officers.

anti-flash gear—cotton gloves and head mask impregnated with asbestos and worn to protect the wearer from flash burns.

beam on—a ship is said to be 'beam on' when it is lying at 90 degrees to the wind and weather.

boatswain's chair—a simple chair constructed of rope and canvas, used to transfer people at sea from ship to ship or ship to boat.

boot-topping—the painted band, four or more feet wide along a ship's waterline – normally a different colour to the paint used on the ship's side or bottom.

bulkhead—the nautical term for a wall.

cable—a nautical unit of length, being one-tenth of a nautical mile or roughly 200 yards or 180 metres.

classified—Information and/or equipment is said to be 'classified' when knowledge of its existence may be beneficial to a potential enemy.

davit span— a steel wire rope joining the two davits

davits—the steel brackets that hold a ship's lifeboats and allow the boat to be swung out over the ship's side and lowered into the sea.

dead-reckoning—the position of a ship calculated by projecting its course and speed from the last known position. It does not take account of variations due to wind, current or weather,

deck log—the formal record of a ship's position, course speed and all significant events happening onboard.

distance run—the distance travelled by a ship in the 24-hour period noon to noon.

dog watches—at sea, time is divided into seven 'watch periods' as follows:

2000 – 2359 – first watch

0000 – 0400 – middle watch

0400 – 0800 – morning watch

0800 – 1200 – forenoon watch

1200 – 1600 – afternoon watch

1600 – 1800 – first dog watch

1800 – 2000 – last dog watch

The 'dog' watches are normally split between 1600 and 2000 to allow all hands to have their evening meal.

falls—the pulley system of ropes used to lower and raise a lifeboat.

fix/fixing—any calculation or observation used to determine a ship's position is known as a 'fix'.

flying-bridge—an extension protruding from a ship's bridge from where the Captain or Pilot is able to see better to manoeuvre the ship in restricted waters.

focsle—literally, 'forecastle' – the raised deck at the very forward part of a ship.

glass—colloquial term for a barometer

hull-up—a ship is said to be 'hull up' when its hull is visible to the observer. Due to the curvature of the earth a ship's masts may be visible while the hull is still below the horizon. The hull normally becomes visible at a range of about 10 nautical miles.

Jerry—colloquial term for a German.

jumping-ladder—a rough ladder constructed from wood and rope to allow a person (often a pilot) to embark or disembark from a ship while stopped at sea.

ki—a hot chocolate or cocoa drink.

knot—nautical unit of speed, being 1 nautical mile per hour.

kumpit—A kumpit is a small, motorised, Malay wooden trading vessel.

lascar—an Indian seaman.

layer—the member of a gun's crew responsible for the elevation of a gun and hence, range.

leeward—down wind or away from the direction of the wind.

line astern—each ship following directly behind the other in a line.

lifelines—the ropes, normally manila, attached to the davit span, that the occupants of the lifeboat use to steady the boat as it is lowered into the water.

married quarter—a house or other accommodation provided to a uniformed or civilian member of the Royal Navy.

mile—where distances are expressed in 'miles' it refers to 'nautical miles' which is the distance subtended by 1 minute of arc of the earth's circumference or roughly 2000 yards/1800 metres.

merpass—short for 'Meridian passage' which is the time the sun crosses the meridian of the observer and reaches its maximum altitude on any given day.

met.—short for meteorological.

mizzen—the mast or sail nearest to the stern of a ship.

'oppo'—short for 'opposite number' – a man having the same station or duties as your own.

poop deck—the raised deck, normally at the stern of a ship,

quarters officer—the senior person stationed on a gun or weapon system, with overall responsibility for its operation.

samson-post—a short, strengthened mast-like structure, used to support a crane or derrick for working a ship's cargo.

scrambling-nets—rope nets hung over a ship's side to allow people to 'scramble' on board from lifeboats etc;

scuppers—the guttering where a ship's deck meets the side, allowing water to flow overboard.

sea-anchor—a 'sea-anchor' is any device, usually made of canvas, used to prevent drift and keep a ship 'head to wind'.

spider-web—the metal sight fitted on many guns – it looks just like a spider-web.

spring—a particular berthing line used when manoeuvring alongside a wharf or pier or to point a ship in a particular direction

stern sheets—that portion of a boats seating, nearest to the stern.

swain—short for boatswain or bosun – the senior non-certificated sailor on a merchant ship.

tannoy—a ship's internal broadcast system.

telemotor—a ship's hydraulic steering system.

track-angle—the angle between the projected course of a target and the track taken by a torpedo to achieve a hit; the closer the track-angle is to 90 degrees, the greater the chance of success.

tween-deck—the tween-decks on a merchant ship are the internal, auxiliary cargo decks fitted in each hold. In effect, they divide a ship's hold vertically and provide separation and ease of access for cargos of varying types. They are generally accessed via the main cargo hatch. The space below the tween-deck is known as the 'lower hold' or 'deep hold'.

upper-deck—a ship's uppermost, external deck ie that deck exposed to the elements.

well-deck—'well-decks' are the lowest open decks on a merchant ship. There is normally one forward of the bridge and one aft (behind the bridge). They are known as the 'forward' well-deck and the 'after' well-deck.

BIBLIOGRAPHY

The author gratefully acknowledges the use of source and background material from the following publications and papers:

Books

Hague, Arnold, *The Allied Convoy System 1939–1945*, Naval Institute Press, Annapolis, 2000

HMSO, *British Vessels Lost at Sea 1914–18 & 1939–45*, Patrick Stephens Ltd, London, 1988

HMSO, *The Admiralty Weather Manual – 1938,* HMSO, London, 1938

Jordan, Roger W, *The World's Merchant Fleets, 1939*, Chatham Publishing, London, 1999

Lloyd's of London, *Lloyd's War Losses: the Second World War, 3 September 1939–14 August 1945, Volume I,* Lloyd's of London Press, London,1991

Muggenthaler, August Karl, *German Raiders of World War II,* Robert Hale, London, 1978

Roskill, Captain S.W, *The War at Sea, 1939–45 Volumes I & II,* HMSO, London, 1954 & 1956

Slader, John, *The Red Duster at War,* William Kimber, London, 1988

Woodward, David, *The Secret Raiders,* William Kimber, London, 1955

Documents and other literature:

Best, Christine, 'Sinking of the SS Kirkpool and Ultimate Rescue at the End of the War', e-mail to author from daughter of Malcolm Scott, Internee, 2004

Blomfield, Jim, 'Account of the loss of the Nankin and as a POW in Kawasaki Camp No.1', Handwritten account provided to the author by Michael Charnaud, 2007

Charnaud, Michael, 'A Child's War', Internet at 'http://www.bbc.co.uk/ww2peopleswar/categories/c55186/', 2007

Derby, Mark 'Last Voyage of the Nankin', personal notes by Mark Derby provided to the author, 2004

Derby, Mark, *SS Nankin 1942*, Internet at *'http://www*.warsailors.com/ raidervictims/thor.html*', 2004*

Gunstone, Howard, *'The Story of Howard Gunstone up to Eleven Years Old'*, Personal notes provided to the author by Howard Gunstone, 2004

ICRC, *'Fukushima Prefectural Civil Internment Camp – First Red Cross Report'*, 1945

Knudsen, David Faye, *'The Capture of Aust, Life on Thor and Regensburg'*, Internet at 'warsailors.com/raidervictims/thor.html', undated

Konno, Shigeru, *'The Hidden Prison'*, Sakura No Seibo Junior College No. 20, 1966

Mackenzie, J Gregory, *'Blockade Runner Ramses'*, Internet at 'ahoy.tk-jk.net/macslog/BlockadeRunner.html', 2004

Mackenzie, J Gregory, *'Marauders of the Sea; Armed Merchant Ships During World War 2'*, Internet at 'ahoy.tk-jk.net/macslog/MaraudersoftheSea2GermanA.html', 2002

Murphy, R G, *'Fukushima Civil Internment Camp, 1942-1945'* dissertation submitted to the School of Asian Studies, University of Sheffield, 2006

Norwegian Victims of Thor – Norwegian Merchant Fleet 1939-1945, Internet at 'warsailors.com/raidervictims/thor.html', undated

Round, Alfred, *'Personal Notes and Diaries'*, provided to the author, 2004

Saunders, Cecil, *'Experiences as a German and Japanese Civilian Prisoner of War from 10 May 1942 to 14 September 1945'*, Internet at 'http://www.bbc.co.uk/ ww2peopleswar/categories/A2021013'

Scott, Malcolm Ingleby, *'Fukushima Civilian Internment Camp'*, personal notes, 1945

Stratford, Captain H C G et al, *'Fukushima Committee Report on the Civil Internment Camp at Fukushima, Japan from 11 July 1942 to 16 August 1945'*, 1945

Stratford, Captain H C G, *'Report on the Capture of SS Nankin by a German Raider'*, 15 September 1945 (report to the Managing Agents)

Wilson, David, *'Merchant Naval Seaman David Wilson'*, Second World War Experience Centre, Internet at 'http://www.warsailors.com/raidervictims/thor.html', undated.